THE JOURNAL OF
WILLIAM SCHELLINKS'
TRAVELS IN ENGLAND
1661–1663

THE JOURNAL OF WILLIAM SCHELLINKS' TRAVELS IN ENGLAND 1661–1663

Translated from the Dutch, and edited

by

MAURICE EXWOOD

and

H. L. LEHMANN

CAMDEN FIFTH SERIES
Volume 1

LONDON
OFFICES OF THE ROYAL HISTORICAL SOCIETY
UNIVERSITY COLLEGE LONDON, GOWER STREET, WC1E 6BT
1993

British Library Cataloguing in Publication Data

Schellinks, William
    Journal of William Schellinks' Travels
    in England, 1661–63.—(Camden Fifth
    Series; Vol. 1)
    I. Title   II. Exwood, Maurice
    III. Lehmann, H. L.   IV. Series
    914.204

ISBN 0–86193–135–1

Printed and bound in Great Britain by
Butler & Tanner Ltd, Frome and London

CONTENTS

ACKNOWLEDGEMENTS

We thank the Director of Det Kongeliche Bibliothek, Copenhagen and the Keeper of Western Manuscripts, Bodleian Library, Oxford, for permission to use their MSS for our publication.

Our annotations are aimed to confirm and expand on information in the Journal. We are conscious that this background research is limited in depth particularly in some areas. We have enjoyed help from many Local History and Record sources and have acknowledged these in relevant footnotes. We apologise for any failure to acknowledge which may have slipped our memory.

We have been greatly helped and encouraged by Dr K. Bostoen, Lecturer at the Faculty of Letters, University of Leiden, who at first agreed to help us with problems of seventeenth-century Dutch but generously gave us of his time and great knowledge of the period, with advice on a broad basis. We thank Dr Bernard Aikema, Nymegen University for information on Italian documentation; Prof. H. Roseveare, King's College London, for suggestions on the translation and notes thereto; Dr John Stoye, Magdalen College, Oxford, for advice on History; Miss Joan Holman for reading and correcting our English text and Professor Michael Jones, Literary Director, Royal Historical Society, for his help and suggestions on presentation.

April 1992   Maurice Exwood
                                                    H. L. Lehmann

Sadly Dr Lehmann died in April 1992. He and I had become firm friends over the years that we worked together on Schellinks' Journal. He generously shared with me his great experience on research and saw the completion of our work, all but the editing of the Introduction, before he died.

Ewell
April 1993   Maurice Exwood

ABBREVIATIONS

BoE	Sir Nikolaus Pevsner et al., *The Buildings of England*, Original series and revised volumes, London 1951–continuing
DNB	Sir Leslie Stephen and Sir Sidney Lee et al., *Dictionary of National Biography*, London 1885–continuing
EB	*Encyclopaedia Britannica*
Evelyn	*The Diary of John Evelyn*, ed. William Bray, with a prefatory note by George W. E. Russell, London: Everyman's Library 2 vols. 1907
EoL	William Kent, *An Encyclopaedia of London*, London, revised edn. 1951
Pepys	*The Diary of Samuel Pepys*, ed. Robert C. Latham and William Matthews, London 11 vols. 1970–83
VCH	*Victoria County History*

JOURNAL AND GAZETEER OF THE JOURNEY MADE BY MR JAQ. THIERRY JUNIOR AND WILLEM SCHELLINKS

through

1. England	2. France
3. Italy	4. Sicily
5. Malta	6. Germany
7. Switzerland	8. Holland

etc

Containing

besides their Experiences, clear and
accurate notes, of all that has been seen and heard
by them
in the Kingdoms, Republics, States and Regions
Between the 14 July 1661,
and the 24 August 1665.

[Translation of original title page of MSS]

INTRODUCTION

i. William Schellinks: Painter, Draughtsman, Etcher and Poet

William Schellinks, the author[1] of the *Journal* edited below, was born in Amsterdam in 1623[2] and died there in 1678. As a visual artist he flourished from c. 1642 to his death. So he lived and worked in the golden age of Dutch painting: the third quarter of the seventeenth century, a period notable for such renowned artists as Rembrandt, Frans Hals, Vermeer and Jan Steen. This could be one reason why he is not well known, another may be that much of his best output, drawings in ink, crayon and wash, was locked away in the Van der Hem *Atlas* (see **ii** below) and hardly seen by anyone.

In 1646 he travelled in France with a fellow artist Lambert Doomer and made many drawings there. He apparently kept a diary even then, which enabled him to write a journal of the trip some twenty years later (see **iv** below). In July 1661 he set out, in some style, with the merchant shipowner Jaques Thierry and the latter's young son, also Jaques or Jacobi, then thirteen years old, from Amsterdam for England. This was the start of a Grand Tour for Thierry junior, also covering France, Italy, Sicily, Malta, Germany and Switzerland, accompanied throughout by Schellinks, who again made many drawings, mostly of a topographical nature. The two returned to Holland in August 1665. Two years after his return to Amsterdam, Schellinks married the well-to-do widow of another fellow artist Dancker Danckerts.

Works by Schellinks are widely spread in museums and collections. The British Museum has 16 of his drawings,[3] but by far the largest number is in the Van der Hem *Atlas*. The English drawings in the *Atlas* were studied by Hulton for the Walpole Society,[4] those made in southern Italy, Sicily and Malta, by Aikema.[5] Both give much biographical material on the artist. No catalogue of his work seems to exist, but a good idea of the value and variety of his oeuvre can be obtained from the *Annual Art Index* and *Art Review*.

Two of his better known subjects of oil-paintings, which show his

---

1 The frontispiece of the *Journal* gives the name 'Jaq. Thierry junior' before that of Schellinks, but we have found no evidence that Thierry was a co-author.

2 Most artists' dictionaries give Schellinks's birthdate as 1627, following A.D. de Vries, *Willem Schellinks-Teekenaar-Etser-Dichter*, in *Oud Holland* I, 1883. Dudok van Heel of the Amsterdam City Archives confirmed his baptism as 2 February 1623.

3 Edward Croft Murray and Paul Hulton, *Catalogue of British Drawings in the British Museum* (cited as ECM) Vol I, 1960.

4 Paul H. Hulton, *Drawings of England in the Seventeenth Century by William Schellinks, Jacob Esselens and Lambert Doomer* in *Walpole Society* 35, 1959.

5 Bernard Aikema and others, *Viaggio al Sud, 1664–1665 Willem Schellinks*, Rome 1983.

talent and incidentally the change in relations between England and Holland after the Restoration, are worth mentioning. The first is of the embarkation of Charles II at Scheveningen for England in 1660, a large canvas 83 × 116cm, painted on commission for Jonas Witsen, a member of an influential Amsterdam family; it demonstrates the contemporary enthusiasm in Holland for the Stuarts. The original is said to be in the collection of Count Wachmeister.[6] An engraving was later made of this picture. The second shows the scene in 1667, when England and Holland were at war and the Dutch fleet entered the Medway and burnt most of the English fleet. Schellinks had made several drawings of the area (see Appendix I) when he was there in 1661. From these he produced several oil-paintings, four of which are in Amsterdam[7] and several versions in pen, wash, and crayon; two of these (c. 50 × 150cm) are in the *Atlas*. There are three more in the British Museum, one of them a rough sketch. There are also engravings by Romeyn de Hooghe and Stoopendaal, reproduced in several works.[8]

Like many of his fellow artists at the time, Schellinks, in his youth, indulged in writing poetry. Some of this, including much of Schellinks's was collected and published. De Vries[9] quotes eight such collections of the years 1654/5, when Schellinks was in his early twenties, some under the title 'De koddige olipodrigo' [the droll hotchpotch].[10] Some of these are illustrated with Schellinks's engravings. The poems themselves are not highly regarded.

The earliest known mention of Schellinks's *Journal* is in Houbraken's *Groote Schouburgh* (1718), a collection of biographies of Dutch painters.[11] This tells us very little about Schellinks the artist, but fortunately Houbraken saw and was fascinated by the *Journal*, then in the possession of a collector, Arnold van Halen (see **iv** below). He gives an extract of what he judged to be of interest to his readers: for England he picks three places in London and one college each in Oxford and Cambridge. He does not mention the *Atlas* and probably did not know about it.

De Vries, in 1883, provided a useful biography of Schellinks; he knew about the *Atlas* in Vienna, and about the *Journal*, but he did not know where this was, expressing the hope that it would be rediscovered one day.

6 U. Thieme and F. Becker, *Allgemeines Lexicon der bildenden Künstler*. Vol 30. Leipzig 1930. Another version was sold in New York in 1935.

7 See Laurence J. Bol, *Die Holländische Marinemalerei des 17. Jahrhunderts*, Brunswick, 1973, 297–9. Information from Gregory Rubinstein.

8 e.g. Gerard Brandt, '*Michiel de Ruiter*' (1687).

9 de Vries, p. 157–9.

10 From Spanish 'Olla Podrida', a kind of stew.

11 Arnold Houbraken (1661–1721), *De Groote Schouburgh der Nederlandsche Konstchilders en Schilderessen*, Amsterdam 1718/21. Reprint ed. P.T.A. Swillens, Maastricht 1943. It is a continuation of Karel van Mander's *Schilder-boeck*, 1604.

Schellinks arrived in England just a year after the Restoration, a momentous event, enthusiastically welcomed in the Dutch Republic, where it was hoped that the good relations which had resulted from the dynastic link between the Houses of Stuart and Orange, by the marriage of Mary Stuart and William II of Orange in 1641 (see Appendix II) would be fully restored. These good relations had suffered during the Commonwealth, when England challenged the rapidly growing domination of trade and shipping by Dutch merchants, resulting in the first Dutch war.[12]

Schellinks had that war very much in mind when he arrived seven years after its end and referred to it many times in his *Journal*. He recorded the captured Dutch ships he saw, now incorporated in the English navy, noting their original names, where they were captured and sometimes the captain at the time.[13] He referred to the then ruinous palace at Greenwich, where Dutch prisoners of war were kept, many of whom he says died there as a result of deprivation.[14] But all this and other bad things he noted such as the neglected buildings, the damage to church ornaments and other structures, are blamed on Cromwell.[15] He expresses no anti-English feelings: now that the King had been restored all that was in the past. But Schellinks carefully recorded the fortifications, armaments, strength and weakness, access, condition etc. of the fortresses he visited and the new and old warships which he saw. Many of the drawings which he made concerned harbours, shipping, naval bases and fortifications. Three years after Schellinks left England the two nations were again at war, and de Ruyter entered the Medway and burned all shipping there and the guns of the battle were clearly heard in London.

Schellinks's travels in England cover a period of notable events and great change: the marriage of the King to Catharine of Braganza, the re-establishment of the Episcopal Church, the Act of Uniformity, the revival of public entertainment (the Lord Mayor's Show, the theatre with the restoration comedies, bear baiting and wrestling), and also the trials and public executions of the regicides and of other 'traitors', and real or imagined uprisings against the throne. All of these Schellinks described accurately in his *Journal*, as comparison with the diaries of Pepys and Evelyn and other contemporary sources shows, and in a

---

12 The first Anglo-Dutch war, 1652–1654, with several sea battles in one of which the Dutch Admiral Tromp was killed; the blockade of the Dover Straits greatly damaged Dutch Trade. The Treaty of Westminster, signed April 1654, was considered lenient to the Dutch.

13 See *Journal* 21 July 1661, 18 September 1662.

14 See *Journal* 14 August 1661 and text-note 21.

15 See *Journal* e.g. Colchester 18 July, Canterbury 12 August, Greenwich 14 August, Charing Cross 17 August 1661, etc.

lively manner, especially where they are his own personal experiences. He was obviously very interested in pageantry, witnessing the Lord Mayor's Show in 1661 (when he and his companions travelled specially from Kent to see it), and again in 1662; in his description of these ceremonies he added to his own observations extracts from the proceedings of the event, printed at the time.[16]

When he related the history of a town or building, he must have used sources such as Stowe's *Survey of London*. We have noted these sources if found, but in some cases we have not been successful. Hulton says that the descriptions of Salisbury Cathedral and Falmouth harbour 'echo Camden',[17] we find that Schellinks says more than Camden about Falmouth, and Camden more than Schellinks about Salisbury. Schellinks and Camden both have the information about the number of windows, pillars and gates in Salisbury Cathedral (4 September 1662) and the number of ships which can be accommodated in Falmouth harbour (21 August 1662), both from Latin rhymes current at the time mentioned by Camden.

Schellinks describes some of the industries he saw in England: the fishing and processing of pilchards and the mining and smelting of tin (14 August 1662), the culture of oysters (19 October 1662), and the minting of coinage (28 March 1663). His description of the processes are confirmed as accurate by contemporary sources quoted in the notes to the translation.

Most seventeenth-century visitors to England did not travel much further than London, Oxford and Cambridge, perhaps Stonehenge, and if on the way, Canterbury; Schellinks and Thierry went further, to Land's End and King's Lynn. This brings us to the purpose of the journey, which has been suggested as twofold: to make topographical drawings on commission for Van der Hem, and for the education of young Jacobi Thierry. As to the first suggestion, we doubt whether he was instructed by Van der Hem (see below **ii**). The *Journal* makes it clear that Jaques Thierry senior, a substantial merchant, organised the journey and probably financed it. He wanted to introduce his young son Jacobi to his family in England and to his business associates there, and to start him off on a 'grand tour' accompanied by a person with some experience of foreign travel. So he crossed over with them in July 1661 and stayed for two months. In that period he saw his son accepted into the family of his friend, Sir Arnold Braems, who lived in great style on his country estate at Bridge (near Canterbury),[18] travelled with

16 See *Journal* 8 November 1661 and 7–8 November 1662, text-notes 59 and 220.
17 Hulton, p. xvii.
18 See text-note 16. For a history of Bridge Place see Malcolm Pinham, *Lesser Known Buildings, Bridge Place, Kent*, in *Blackmanbury*, August–October 1968.

him to London to meet his brother and other relatives, attended to his business there and in Dover, before returning to Holland via Ostend, leaving Schellinks and his son with the Braems family, with whom they stayed for three months.

Whilst Thierry senior was in England, Schellinks seems to act as his secretary, faithfully recording his master's movements, even when he did not accompany him, and he had time to do a number of drawings around Dover (see Appendix I). The great interest shown by Schellinks in fortifications and military installations, to which the two Dutchmen obtained access with surprising ease in spite of the recent war and increasing rivalry between the two nations, has led to the suggestion that he was working for Dutch military intelligence. This possibility cannot be ignored: the *Journal* often bears witness to this interest in military affairs, describing in some detail the strength and weaknesses of fortresses, their armaments and garrisons (e.g. Plymouth, 11–14 August 1662).

We do not believe however that spying was his object; as Hulton points out, Schellinks's drawings of the Medway cannot have been of great value in planning the Dutch raid in 1667. We think it more likely that Schellinks's easy access everywhere shows the respect in which Jaques Thierry senior was held: English by birth, a merchant of substance, with widespread contacts. In choosing what to describe in England Schellinks seems to have in mind the interest of his master.

ii. Schellinks and the Van der Hem *Atlas*[19]

Some 120 of Schellinks's drawings are incorporated in the famous Van der Hem *Atlas*, now one of the most prized possessions of the National Library in Vienna. This monumental work of fifty volumes, each c. 56 × 38cm, was put together by Laurens Van der Hem (1621–78), a member of a distinguished Amsterdam family.[20] His father Ysbrant was a prosperous merchant there, who married the daughter of a then well-known Dutch poet Hendrick Laurensz Spiegel. Laurens's uncle married

19 Since completion of this section an exhibition devoted to the Van der Hem *Atlas* was staged in the summer of 1992 in the Royal Palace, Amsterdam, where two volumes and 23 drawings from the original Atlas in Vienna were displayed, augmented with much contemporary material: *Een Wereldreizer op papier, De Atlas van Laurens Van der Hem 1621–1678* (Stichting Koninklijk Paleis, Amsterdam, 1992), with an historical introduction by Roelof van Gelder.

20 Most information on Van der Hem and his *Atlas* is extracted from Hulton 1959; Karl Ausseren, 'Der Atlas Blaeu der Wiener National Bibliothek', *Beitrage zur Historischen Geographie* ... , Vienna 1929; Gustaf Solar, *Jan Hackaert: die Schweiser Ansichten 1652–56*, Zürich 1981, and Aikema 1983. See also Roelof van Gelder 1992.

into a German noble family, which had served the court of King Ferdinand II and was knighted by him, when 'van der' was added to the simple surname Hem.[21] Laurens had two older brothers: Herman, a topographical draughtsman, who spent much of his short life around Bordeaux, making many drawings there (now in volume V of the *Atlas*), and Hendrick, a member of a Hague art circle and art collector like his brother.

Laurens travelled in Europe, part of North Africa, and the Near East, before he settled in Amsterdam as a lawyer and married there in 1650.[22] The family, of Catholic faith, was excluded from government posts, but that does not seem to have affected his ability to amass great wealth,[23] so that Laurens was able to assemble a great collection of art books and curios. Cosimo de Medici, of the illustrious Florentine family, who visited Amsterdam in December 1667, had his secretary record that he saw in the home of lawyer Van der Hem a 'cabinet' with a large collection of drawings of various towns, coasts and harbours of the Indies, excellent miniatures and exquisite detailed hand-made maps.[24] In 1671 Charles Patin, numismatist and Doctor of Medicine of Paris, reported seeing many curiosities in Amsterdam. He mentions four 'cabinets', the best that of Mr. Witsen, 'whose house is less suitable for habitation than for pleasure of the eyes'.[25] He also praised the 'cabinets' of lawyer Van der Hem, and Occo.

Whether either saw much of the *Atlas* is doubtful, because that must have been far from complete,[26] but many of the maps and drawings they saw must later have been incorporated into it. But by no means all: when the library was sold in 1684 in Amsterdam, after Van der Hem's death, the sale catalogue ran to 96 pages, detailing books on a variety of subjects, maps, drawings, and etchings, including those of the best Italian, German and Dutch masters.[27]

Patin continues that he saw 'in another place charts of extraordinary importance, which disclose all the secrets of navigation'. This suggests

21 Ausseren, pp. 5–6.

22 van Gelder, p. 10.

23 Aikema states that in 1676 he was assessed for tax on a wealth of 211,000 Guilders (*c.* £21,000), a large sum at the time: Aikema, 1983, p. 16.

24 G.J. Hoogewerff, *De Twee Reizen van Cosimo de' Medici', door ... de Nederlanden 1663–1669*, in *Historisch Genootschap Utrecht*, Amsterdam 1919, 3, 41.

25 Charles Patin, *Relations historique et curieuse de voyages en Allemagne, Angleterre ... etc.*, Rouen 1676, p. 161.

26 This is born out by Roelof van Gelder (note 19 above), who established that binding did not commence until the early 1670s (it was not completed at Van der Hem's death in 1678). Material dated up to 1677 was incorporated in the Atlas: Roelof van Gelder 1992, p.16.

27 *Bibliotheca Hemmiana* (Sale catalogue, Amsterdam 1684), British Library microfilm B 619/107. The printed copy in the British Library is the only one known to have survived.

that he paid a visit to the establishment of Joan Blaeu (1598–1673).[28] Blaeu had followed in his father's footsteps as official map maker to the Dutch East India Company, and with him had established a substantial printing and map-making business in Amsterdam: it had 15 presses, 6 of these for copperplate printing. The firm made atlases with maps including descriptions, gradually covering the whole known world, so that by 1662 an eleven-volume *Atlas Maior* was available with 600 maps and 3,000 pages of text. Purchasers would have their copy bound to varying degrees of luxury, and sometimes employed their own illuminator to embellish maps and script in colour and gold leaf.

Laurens Van der Hem, a friend of Joan Blaeu, acquired a copy of the *Atlas Maior* and set about augmenting Blaeu's maps and descriptions, with material collected relative to the geographical area as appropriate such as drawings of buildings, monuments, landscapes and seascapes, castles, national costumes, ceremonial processions, native animals and plants; also maps, charts and townplans, some engraved, but many hand-drawn with handwritten legends and descriptions in his own hand. So much material was added that the number of volumes increased from 11 of the *Atlas Maior* to 50, including four supplements.[29] The engraved and hand-drawn maps are embellished with colouring and goldleaf for which Van der Hem employed a well-known illuminator, D.J. van Santen,[30] who worked for years at his house. Most volumes are bound in parchment which is embossed in goldleaf, the pages are gilt-edged. Of the fifty volumes, thirty-eight including the supplements cover Europe (four for Britain and Ireland), three Africa, four the Dutch East Indies, the rest Asia, China and America..[31] It is clear that this was Van der Hem's lifework, which he left uncompleted at his death in 1678, when thirteen volumes were still unbound; probably he was still planning to add more material to these.[32]

---

28 Amsterdam became the major mapmaking centre of Europe in the seventeenth century; Jodocus Hondius took over Mercator's Antwerp business and with it his unique plates, and settled in Amsterdam. Hondius was succeeded by his son Henry, and he in turn by Jan Jansson, who married into the Hondius family. In 1671, when Patin was in Amsterdam, Jansson had died, but the business continued to publish some maps. Patin's comment on navigational maps indicates that it was Blaeu's business he saw. Blaeu's printing works were destroyed by fire in 1672. See R.V. Tooley, *Maps and Mapmakers*, (1978). For Blaeu and his family see Cornelis Koeman, *Joan Blaeu and his Grand Atlas*, London/Amsterdam 1970.

29 In 1847 twenty-eight large drawings, mostly by Schellinks, were removed from their original places and kept in a separate box in the director's room (Ausseren, 37).

30 Ausseren, 10, 11.

31 Ausseren, 12.

32 The auction catalogue (see note 27 above) of Van der Hem's library includes 24 pages 'illuminatarum' headed 'A large quantity of unusual and rare illustrative material, bound books of drawings of the best Italian, French, German, and Dutch artists … collected with great effort and expense … illuminated most beautifully by D.J. van

In 1711 Conrad von Uffenbach[33] visited 'Jungfer Van der Hem' in Amsterdam. This was Agatha, Laurens's eldest daughter, who had inherited the *Atlas*, and who, so Uffenbach reports, had refused 20,000 guilders for it, putting its value at 50,000 guilders. He gives a good description of its content and richness of decoration, and says that the most important volumes, on which most effort and money were spent, are those on the Indies, which the governors of the two companies (i.e. the Dutch East India Company, the powerful rival of the English East India Company, and the Dutch West India Company) were keen to buy, but Agatha refused to break up the *Atlas*. Uffenbach goes on to say that Van der Hem during his lifetime never showed the East Indies part to anyone, 'to avoid jealousy and bringing harm and mishap to the contributors'. The real reason was perhaps that Van der Hem was not supposed to have copies of the navigational maps of the Dutch East Indies Archipelago. The Dutch trading company jealously tried to protect its monopoly of the trade with the East Indies and would not want anyone unauthorised to see maps surveyed at their expense.

Uffenbach says that Schellinks was supposed to have travelled at Van der Hem's expense and infers that Agatha told him that. His is the only known source of this information, and for various reasons we doubt its accuracy. First Schellinks, in his *Journal* (which Uffenbach did not know about) never mentions Van der Hem, or anything related to him. As mentioned above Thierry is the leading figure in the early part of the work. Secondly, when Van der Hem's library was sold there were many drawings by several named artists, but none by Schellinks.[34] If he was commissioned by Van der Hem we could expect some of his work, which Van der Hem decided not to use for his *Atlas* to be in his collection. Thirdly, if Van der Hem commissioned him he got poor value for money: there are 120 drawings by Schellinks in the *Atlas*, forty-one of these in England, where Schellinks spent ninety-one weeks, nearly half in London, but there are no drawings of London by Schellinks, and only six by Esselens, another Dutch artist. Analysing Schellinks's English drawings in the *Atlas*, one does not get the impression that he followed any particular programme or instructions; it seems that he drew when he felt like it, and often he did not bother.

So we question whether Van der Hem influenced in a significant way the journey and the *Journal*. That is not to say that he may not

Santen ...' Clearly when Van der Hem died in 1678, there was still a large amount of material similar to that incorporated in the *Atlas*, which was probably intended for that purpose. We did not find any drawings by Schellinks in this catalogue, which seems to indicate that Van der Hem used all the drawings he bought, in the atlas.

33 Zacharias Conrad von Uffenbach, *Merkwürdige Reisen durch Niedersachsen, Holland und Engelland*, Ulm/Hemmingen 1753/56.

34 See note 32.

have recommended Schellinks to Thierry and offered to pay part of the cost. Laurens would have known Schellinks from his previous work, i.e. his travels in France in 1646, and, no doubt, he also knew Thierry. Probably when Schellinks returned to Holland and started his drawings from sketches made en route, he showed Van der Hem his work, who bought some and rejected others.

After the deaths of Agatha and her sister, the *Atlas* was sold at auction in 1730 by the bookseller Adrian Moetjens of the Hague for 22,000 florins.[35] The catalogue described the contents in detail and had an introduction by a well-known geographer of the time, Bruson-le-Mastinière.[36] The purchaser was Prince Eugene of Savoy.[37] After his death in 1736 and that of his heir a year later, the *Atlas* became the property of the Hofbibliothek, Vienna, now known as the National Library of Vienna, where it remains. Schellinks was the major but by no means only artist whose drawings were used in the *Atlas*. Ausseren mentions sixteen artists, many Dutch, amongst the signed drawings, as well as some 150 draughtsmen and engravers.

iii. The Thierry Family[38]

In **i.** above we have explained why we consider Jaques Thierry Senior to be the key figure, who brought about Schellinks's journey in 1661 and probably his *Journal*. This Thierry family came to England from Tournai (now in Belgium), towards the end of the sixteenth century: they were Huguenots, mostly French Protestants, many of whom left France and the Low Countries to escape religious persecution. Tournai in what became the Spanish Netherlands, was in the area where, after the revolt against Spain, Spanish forces ruthlessly and cruelly re-established Spanish rule and the Catholic religion. The town was taken by Spanish troops in 1582, causing a great exodus of Protestants.

Tournai was a town of silk weavers, many of whom came to England, where they were usually allowed to practise their craft; some (the

---

35 Ausseren, p.9; J. Van Gelder suggests 20,000 guilders, but draws attention in his note 30 to the controversy over the price paid.

36 Adrian Moetjens, *Atlas Geographique et Hydrographique de Laurens Van der Hem*, The Hague 1730.

37 Ausseren p. 9. Prince Eugene of Savoy (1663–1736), after a successful career as commander of the armies of three successive Austrian emperors, became a great collector and amassed a fine library.

38 The name Thierry appears to be common amongst Huguenots, spelled variously, Thiery, Therry, Thery, Tyere etc. In his *Journal* Schellinks consistently spells the name as Thierrij, (unusually for him: he is very inconsistent in spelling names, often different versions of a name are found in one sentence), but for simplicity's sake we have followed Elias, who uses Thierry.

Thierry family amongst them) settled in Spitalfields, which became a centre of weavers producing more refined products by their 'new drapery'. From records available in England, mainly in publications of the Huguenot Society,[39] and in Elias,[40] it is possible to construct a genealogy of some of the Thierry family (see Table I).

There were at least three brothers of the family, who left Tournai; it is with the next two generations that we are concerned. Four Thierrys were in London in mid-summer 1661, who are mentioned in the *Journal*, all with Christian names beginning with the letter J, so it is sometimes difficult to be sure to which 'Mr. J. Thierry' Schellinks is referring. The eldest of the four was Jan or Jean (6 in Table I), born in London, who was already in his sixties at the time. He lived in London with his wife Elizabeth, who was born, most likely in another Huguenot family from Haarlem, where they married. He was probably a weaver like his father, who, in his will, was stated to be a 'Citizen and Weaver of London' and left money to the Weavers' Company.[41] We have found no evidence that this Jean was involved with his brother's shipping business. Schellinks records that on 31 August 1661 Mr. J. Thierry arranged a great banquet at the Ship Tavern, Bishopsgate. This seems to be Jan (6), entertaining his brother Jaques (8). He later gave a dinner at the Wheatsheaf on 20 January 1662, joined Schellinks and Jacobi (20) on 30 June 1662 to buy horses at Smithfield and was present at the farewell party, which Schellinks and Jacobi gave on 12 April 1663, when the list of guests is headed by 'Mr. Jan Thierry, Englishman'.

His younger brother Jaques or James (8), the main personality of our story, was also born in London, but lived in Amsterdam, where he married Maria van Rijn, the daughter of a well-to-do silk merchant.[42] He set up in business there as a merchant and marine-insurer.[43] He owned several ships, and had some well-connected partners, one of whom was his wife's brother Pieter van Rijn. He came over to England

39 *Publications of the Huguenot Society of London*, especially Volume IX, Lymington 1896.

40 J. Elias, *De Vroedschap van Amsterdam* (The City Fathers of Amsterdam), 1903/1905. We understand that there is a large amount of archive material in Amsterdam, which we have not been able to consult.

41 Will of John Thiere, PRO, Prob 11/130 60L-60R, 1617.

42 Jaques Thierry was born in the Parish of St. Stephen, Coleman Street about 1604, according to submissions to the Admiralty Court HCA3–49 fol. 232, and baptized in the French Church, Threadneedle Street. He married Maria van Rijn, whose mother, on her death in 1629, left to her children 192,000 fl. Elias 270.

43 In 1666 his partners were Hendrick Reael, who operated a regular shipping service to Portugal, and Pieter van Rijn, his wife's brother, who later became an auctioneer, dealing in ships and shipping companies. Elias 270, 273, 572. Herman Watjen, *Die Niederlander im Mittelmeergebiet zur zeit ihrer Höchsten Macht Stellung*, Berlin 1909, records reports of several Dutch ships, plundered by the French c.1650, which were insured by 'Jacques Thiry'.

with his son and Schellinks in July 1661 and stayed for eight weeks. During that time he made contact with two of his ships off Dover, arrested a pirate ship there which had captured one of his, was received and entertained by the Controller of the English navy[44] on board his flagship, met his friend Sir Arnold Braems and other business associates and members of his own family,[45] and made representations and depositions at the Admiralty Court with his nephew Jan (15).[45] (All this whilst he was suffering from a sprained ankle and could not walk, according to Schellinks: see 18 July 1661). When he travelled from London to Dover to return home via Ostend, several persons accompanied him all the way to see him off. He was clearly a man of means, who had many business associates and other contacts in England, especially in the West Country and at Dover, several of whom were of Flemish or Dutch descent. When Schellinks and Jacobi visited St. Michael's Mount, John St. Aubyn, the owner of the castle, impressed on them the need to remind Mr. Jaques (8) of a business deal they had discussed.[46] His depositions at the Admiralty Court (see below) give a good insight into his method of trading.

Also in London was Jan (15), son of Jan (6), born in London in 1634. He too settled in Amsterdam as a merchant, trading with Italy and the Levant. He married Maria Eschwiller in Amsterdam in February 1662.[47] Schellinks first mentioned him on 29 August 1661, when 'Jan Thierry left for Holland', after they had paid another visit to the Admiralty Court. The only other mention of him is on 31 January 1662, when Schellinks reported going to Artillery Gardens for the hanging of the sign-board showing the Amsterdam Bourse,[48] which 'Mr. Jan Thierry had sent over for the Ward'.

The fourth in London was Mr. Jacobi (20) the 13 years old son of Jaques (8), Schellinks's companion throughout the Grand Tour. He was born in Amsterdam in 1648 and died there in 1709. Whether he followed his father in his business we do not know. The only information the Amsterdam City Archives has provided, apart from confirming his baptism and burial, is that he was a governor of the Old Men's and Old Women's Hospices in Amsterdam from 1682–90.[49] As Jacobi was born in Amsterdam he did not have English nationality; his father therefore instructed Schellinks to stay in London for the winter of

44 See text-note 18 of *Journal*.
45 See text-note 16 of *Journal*.
46 See *Journal* 19 August 1662 and text-note 145.
47 Elias 571.
48 The Amsterdam Bourse was built 1608/11 after the architect Hendrik de Keyser had visited London to see the Royal Exchange there. Schellinks (16 August 1661) remarks on the similarity of the two buildings.
49 Private Communication 10.5. 1990, Dr. W. Chr. Pieterse, Amsterdam City Archives.

1662/3 to await the reassembly of Parliament to organise Jacobi's naturalisation (see *Journal* 21 October 1662 and text note 215).

Other members of the family mentioned in the English *Journal* are: Margaret (17), Jacobi's elder sister, who joined in the farewell party on her father's and brother's leaving for England;[50] she was accompanied by Mr. van Streyen (18), her first husband, a Solicitor of the City of Amsterdam, at the Court in the Hague,[51] and 'Cousin Dentier'.[52] Mathieu Dentier (14) married to Judith Thierry (13), a cousin of Jaques (8). Later in the *Journal*, on arrival in Rome in April 1664, Schellinks reports visiting the Dutch Church there and seeing the entry in the burial record of Sr. Steffano Thierry who died in Rome in 1647. This would be Steven (11) brother of Jean (6) and Jaques (8). On his return to Rome in March 1665 he writes about an epitaph for the grave.[53]

The *Journal* mentions three visits to the Admiralty Court in August 1661, when both Jaques (8) and his nephew Jean (15) were in London; on the 23rd 'to see Sir Edward Walter', on the 26th and again on the 29th. Schellinks does not indicate what the visits were about, but a search through Admiralty Court records proved very illuminating.[54] The High Court of Admiralty dealt, amongst other things, with all cases of piracy anywhere in the world, provided the owner of the ship bringing the case was of English nationality. This was probably one reason why Jacobi's father wanted him to be naturalised.

On 22 November 1660 a request was recorded on behalf of 'James Therry' for a safe conduct for four ships laden with goods from Barbados to England. He was represented by Mr. Smith, who made quite sure that it was recorded that 'James Therry is an Englishman

---

50 *Journal* 15 July 1661.

51 Elias 639. She re-married Nicolaas Opmeer, five times Burgomaster of Amsterdam between 1681 and 1694. Elias 571.

52 Schellinks mentions him (without giving his christian name) on 24 March 1663, and in the list of guests on 12 April 1663, when he describes him as a Fleming.

53 The 'Dutch' Church in Rome, Santa Maria dell'Anima, now the German church there, was founded by a Dutch couple in the fourteenth century (see A.G. Luff, *A Christian's guide to Rome* (1990), p. 171–2). On 14 March 1665, Copenhagen MS p. 1093, soon after Schellinks's return to Rome, he records that he wrote to Holland 'about the grave of Sig. Steffano Thierry to have an epitaph erected on this by Mons J. Th. on which it was planned to carve ... in marble, after the titles:

> London saw my Spring life
> Oxford gave us the Wisdom
> Naples wealth; Rome the grave,
> On which nephew gave this citation'.

Steffano Thierry's death, as recorded in the parochial burial register, is given in G.J. Hoogewerff: *Nederlandsche Kunstenaars te Rome (1600–1723)*, The Hague, 1942, p. 200. Foster's *Alumni Oxoniensis* does not record a Thierry matriculating at the time.

54 The daily business of the Court is recorded in its Acts (PRO, HCA3, 1524–1749, 290 vols). The dates are in Old Style. Schellink's *Journal* uses New Style dating (at that time N.S. date was O.S. date + 10).

and Freeman of London'.[55] On 14 January 1660/61 a submission was recorded on behalf of 'Johannes Therry and Antonius ffarry' in respect of two ships, the *St. Peter* and the *Blessing*.[56]

Two complaints brought to the Admiralty Court were probably one reason why Jaques and his nephew came to London. The first was submitted on 17 August 1661 by 'Jacob Therrij and Bernard Sparke' about their ship the *Dolphin* which carried £6,000 worth of sugar and other goods from Barbados and was captured in June 1659 by the *Robin*, whose owner was then living in Dunkirk (a notorious pirate haven). The owner and captain of the *Robin* were summoned to come to court on 4 September to be examined.[57] We found no record on that date that they complied!

The second complaint on 20 August 1662[58] concerned the *Golden Dolphin*, 280 tons, which set out in 1657 for the coast of Guinea, where she loaded 138 negroes and set course for Barbados; she ran into foul weather and lost her rudder near the island of St. Thomas, then, as now, a Portuguese possession. At first the Governor was friendly and allowed 'the provisions, victuals and negroes to be taken off and put into warehouses'. After two weeks the ship's crew and cargo were forcibly seized and the negroes sold. The master and crew were imprisoned and 'used barbarously'. The complainant was reliably informed that the master and his son were still held prisoners. He stated that the value of the slaves was £4,200, the ship's £1,600, his consequential damage £1,500 and that of his crew £2,000, a total of £9,300. He declared that he, the deponent, was born in the parish of St. Stephen Coleman Street and 'was and is free of the right worshipfull Company of Weavers, London'. The deposition was signed by 'James Therry' on 20 August 1661. The minutes of the Weavers' Company record on 30 September 1661 that 'Mr. James Therrij did accept to be of the livery paid 05.00.00, and the said Mr. Therrij did freely give 05.00.00'.[59]

It is clear that Jacques Thierry was in business in a big way, owning quite a large fleet and trading profitably. Hermann Watjen[60] lists him as eleventh in a list of importers from the Mediterranean in 1646/7, bringing in nearly 48,000 florins' worth of goods, compared with the largest, Jeremias van Ceulen's 152,000 fl. Most of his business was

55 HCA3–49 fol. 85. The ships are given as: *Golden Fleece, Seaven Starres, Dergaudammer Kirke* and *Blashelf*. Edward Smith, Englishman is listed as one of the guests on 12 April 1663. He was apparently the Thierrys' legal adviser in London.

56 HCA3–49 fol. 112.

57 HCA3–49 fol. 230v, 231.

58 HCA3–49 fol. 231, 231v, 232.

59 Weavers Company, Minute Book MS4655/3, 30 September 1661.

60 See above note 43.

TABLE 1
THE THIERRY FAMILY

Jean (John) Thierry (1)
bur. 7 July 1617
m. Jane (Jenne) du Bo (2)

Robert Thierry (3)
m. Katherine des Planques (4)

another
(d. before 1617)
m. Sara (5) . . .

Jacob Thierry (12)

Judith Thierry (13)
m. Mathieu Dantierre (14)

Jean Thierry (6)
b. London 1601
m. Elis Sabé (7)
b. Haarlem 1602

Jaques Thierry (8)
b. London 1604
d. Amsterdam 1677
m. Maria v.Rijn (9)
b. 1609

Catheline Thierry (10)
b. London 1605

Stephen Thierry (11)
b. London 1608
d. Rome 1647

Jean Thierry (15)
b. London 1634
d. Amsterdam 1707
m. Maria v. Eschwiller (16)
b. Amsterdam 1640
d. Amsterdam 1692

Margaretha Thierry (17)
b. Amsterdam 1633
d. Amsterdam 1684
m.(1) Jacob v. Strijen (18)
m.(2) Nicholaes Opmeer (19)

Jacobus Thierry (20)
b. Amsterdam 1648
d. Amsterdam 1709

1   Frenchman, Weaver, Burial Register St. Stephen Coleman Street 1617. Will of John Thierie, PROB 11/130, 60L-60R.

2   Baptism Register French Church, Threadneedle Street, H.S. IX 44 etc. Remarried with Jacques Lamy pre 1626, Elias 572.

3   Mentioned in the Will of 1 above. Letters of denization, H.S. XVIII p. 19, 1611 'born in the City of Tourney'.

4   Baptism Register as above H.S. IX 97, mentioned in Will of 1 above. Will of Catherine Terry, PROB, 11/220 p.250, 1651. Died in St. Mary's Parish Whitechapel.

5   Mentioned in the Will of 1.

6   Baptism Register H.S. IX 44, Elias 571 says b. London 1601.

7   Elias 571.

8   Baptism Register H.S. IX 50, Elias 572 says b. London 1604.

9   Elias 572.

10   Baptism Register H.S. IX 59.

11   Baptism Register H.S. IX 70. Mentioned in Will of 1.

12   Mentioned in Will of 1.

13   Mentioned in Will of 1.

14   Bapt. of daughter Catherine Dentier H.S. IX 121.

15   Elias 571.

16   Elias 571.

17   Elias 572 and note 51.

18   Elias 639.

19   Elias 571.

20   b. Amsterdam 3 May 1648 – bur. Amsterdam 27 March 1709. Priv. Com. Amsterdam City Archive, 10 May 1990.

H.S.:   *Huguenot Society Publications*
Elias: *De Vroedschap van Amsterdam*

probably with the West Indies: buying slaves at the African coast, to sell in the English colony of Barbados and loading sugar to sell in London or Amsterdam was a profitable business. He was a wealthy man,[61] who had no difficulty in financing a 'Grand Tour' for his son and his companion lasting more than four years, and incidentally having his son's portrait painted en route by eminent portraitists: by Vaillant in Paris in April 1663 and by Voet in Rome in April 1665.[62]

iv. The Manuscripts of Schellinks's *Journal*

Two versions of the manuscript are known: one now in the Royal Library, Copenhagen,[63] the other in the Bodleian Library, Oxford.[64] The Copenhagen version has a total of 1,466 quarto pages (152 × 190 mm), written in the same hand, average 30 lines to the page, divided into three volumes. The first volume includes 95 separately numbered pages covering Schellinks's journey with his fellow artist Lambert Doomer to France in the summer of 1646. This part was transcribed and studied by Herma Van den Berg in 1943.[65]

The Journey from 1661–5 is covered in 1,371 consecutively numbered pages. The departure from Amsterdam in July 1661 and the travels in England up to arrival in France in April 1663 (270 pages), is in Volume I, which also includes twenty-nine pages of Schellinks's notes on London, 'written for my amusement and to refresh the memory', and a place index of the following French journey. The second volume (pp. 318–791) covers the journey through France and Italy, up to his departure from Rome for Naples. The third volume (pp. 794–1371) covers the rest of Italy, Sicily and Malta, the return to Rome and through Italy, Switzerland and Germany to Holland in 1665. Some of the numbered pages, mainly between chapters, are blank. Detailed work has been limited to the journey of 1661–3 in Volume I, which has been transcribed in full and translated into English.

Aikema[66] has established that the handwriting throughout this MS is that of Schellinks himself, made from diaries he kept en route, after his return to Amsterdam; he left the writing-up of his earlier travels in

61 See note 23 above.

62 Wallerand Vaillant (1623–1677) in Paris 1659–65, where he painted several members of the Royal Family. Jacob Ferdinand Voet (c.1639-c.1700) portrait painter at the Papal Court in Rome.

63 Ny. Kgl. Saml. 370, I–III.

64 MS d'Orville 558, 559, 560.

65 Herma van den Berg, *Willem Schellinks and Albert Doomer in Frankrijk*, in *Oudheidkundig Jaarboek*, series IV, deel 11, 1943.

66 See above note 5.

1646 until that time, as remarks in his journal make clear (see Van den Berg, pp. 7 and 12). There is no doubt that this manuscript is original, confirmed by the following:

1) Bound in with Volume I is the 'laissez passer' on his departure for France (see text-notes 239 and 240).
2) In Volume II a printed inventory of 1659 to the royal Tombs in St. Denis, as well as several other little guides, then recently printed and detailed by Kernkamp[67] are bound in.
3) On three pages in Volume I there are some small sketches to illustrate the adjacent text, clearly from Schellinks's hand: of the running game seen on 21 July 1661 (see text-note 10), an entrance gate to a house in Lincoln's Inn Fields on 19 August 1661 (text-note 43), and part of the lettering in the stone parapet at Audley End on 3 October 1662 (text-note 191). There are more small sketches in later parts of the manuscript.
4) There are a number of 'afterthoughts'; we noted in Volume I writing between the lines, in the margin, or the insertion of unnumbered pages.
5) In many cases a date, name, distance or translation of an English text is left blank, presumably with the intention of filling in later.

The Copenhagen MS was part of the Royal Library before 1831[68] when the Ny. Kgl. Saml. [New Royal Collection] was founded.

The Bodleian MS is also bound in three volumes, written on folio paper (230 × 360 mm), about 45 lines to the page, MS d'Orville 558 covers the journey through England and France, up to the entry into Italy, covering 298 folios. MS d'Orville 559 has 407 folios of which only three are part of the *Journal*: a trip outside Rome in April 1665 also covered in the Copenhagen MS (in correct chronology). The major part of 559 is a description of palaces, gardens and over 400 churches in Rome. This would appear to be a MS transcript of a printed source, which however (like some in France) is not bound in the Copenhagen MS and remains to be identified. MS d'Orville 560, 289 folios, continues the journal from the end of 558, i.e. departure from Rome for Naples, up to the return to Amsterdam in 1665. The folios in each of the three volumes are numbered separately in pencil.

The Bodleian Library acquired the d'Orville MSS in 1804 from the grandson of Jacques Philippe d'Orville (1696–1751), Professor of History

---

67 G.W. Kernkamp, *Verslag van een onderzoek in Zweden, Noorwegen en Denemarken, naar Archivalia* ... , The Hague 1903.
68 Private communication Erik Petersen, Research Librarian, Royal Library, Copenhagen.

at the Atheneum Illustre, in Amsterdam 1730–42.[69] The 1646 journey, the notes on London, and the index in Volume I of the Copenhagen MS do not appear in the Bodleian MS.

On comparing the two MSS, we noted some interesting differences, e.g.

a) Whilst the Copenhagen MS is throughout by the same hand, there are several changes in handwriting in the Bodleian MS, e.g. at Volume I, 65/66 and at Volume III, 259/60.

b) The Copenhagen MS has in the first pages substantially more information on personalities and places, which is not in the Bodleian MS (see text-note 2).

c) In the Copenhagen MS Schellinks sometimes uses the singular 'I', where the Bodleian MS uses 'we'.

d) Often there is a difference in syntax between the two MSS: the Bodleian paraphrasing the Copenhagen MS.

e) There are differences in spelling: the Copenhagen MS uses a later spelling, the Bodleian MS uses mostly an older type of spelling already considered conservative in the seventeenth century.[70]

f) There are a few instances in which the Bodleian MS gives more information than Copenhagen: e.g. the Bodleian MS, on 16 July 1661 mentions that Owen Spann the innkeeper at Harwich is the postmaster, a fact not given in the Copenhagen MS. Also, on describing the customs on St. Valentine's day, the Bodleian MS correctly makes it clear that they apply to married as well as to unmarried people, as would be concluded from the Copenhagen MS (see text-note 73).

It is therefore clear that at least for the early part of the *Journal* the Bodleian MS is not a slavish copy of the Copenhagen original by a clerk. Either the scribe of the Bodleian MS knew what was described because he was there, or he had access to the original notes. As to the first alternative, the only person who was there throughout with Schellinks was young Jacobi Thierry; he may well have been the writer of some of the Bodleian MS; the additional information in the Copenhagen MS referred to in b) above is mostly the names of Jacobi Thierry's relations and friends who see the travellers off. Jacobi may have thought it immodest or unnecessary to include these; another scribe would appear rude in omitting them. As the other alternative, the copyist had access to and used Schellinks's original notes. This too is possible. There may be more to be found out.

69 Falconer Madan, *A Summary Catalogue of Western Manuscripts in the Bodleian Library*, (1895–1953), IV, p. xxii, and Private Communication, Dr K. Bostoen, Leiden University.
70 Private communication, Dr. K. Bostoen.

Towards the end of the part of the *Journal* describing England, the first copyist seems to give up: there are two blank pages in the MS, which then continues in a different, more easily readable handwriting, possibly that of a professional scribe (see text-note 238). We then see for the first time an indication that the Bodleian MS, at least from that point, with its new copyist, was intended for publication: on fol. 67 there is, above the heading 'Rey' [Rye], a blank space with a pencilled instruction (in Dutch): 'Note. Here should be a print of the town'. On 67v, after the heading 'France, of which now follows all that we found in our journey in the Kingdom remarkable to have seen', there is also nearly half a page blank, with another pencilled note: 'Note. Here should be a print of Dieppe or a map of France'. Both these notes are in a different handwriting, which seems similar to that of the Copenhagen MS, so that it looks as if Schellinks himself kept an eye on the copying. The new copyist continues in the old-fashioned spelling referred to above. All the 'afterthoughts' in the Copenhagen MS are copied without editing.

Aikema draws attention to a statement between pages 685 and 686 of the Copenhagen MS which translates as: 'These descriptions of Rome should be written separately', which he sees as an instruction to the copyist who had to prepare the manuscript for publication. We believe that this may be the instruction to the copyist, which resulted in the Bodleian MS 559: the description of the Rome Palaces etc., the largest volume of the three. Aikema also established that the description of Malta in the Bodleian MS (560, 162–180) is copied from Olfert Dapper's *Naukeurige Beschrijvinge der Afrikaensche Gewesten*, of which the first edition was published in 1668, thereby proving that this part of the Bodleian MS was written after that. In the Copenhagen MS (pp. 964–1004), the description of Malta was either copied from other sources or written from Schellinks's own observations, a matter which remains to be settled.

So we can reasonably assume that Schellinks's autograph was written after his return to Amsterdam in June 1665 and at least for 80% completed before 1668 and that the Bodleian copy was probably started by Jacobi Thierry and completed by various copyists after 1668.

The Copenhagen MS was acquired by Arnaud Van Halen[71] who built up a collection of portraits of Dutch literary people and would have been interested in Schellinks the poet. He may have acquired it after Jacobi's death in 1709 and before 1718 when Houbraken reports in his *Groote Schouburgh* having seen it and 'leaved through it'. Probably

---

71 Arnaud Van Halen (d. 1732) was also a poet and engraver, excelling in grisaille work. *Nieuw Nederlandsch Biographisch Woordenboek* VI, 684. He produced *Panpoeticon Batavum*, a collection of portraits of Dutch poets.

after Van Halen's death in 1732, it became part of the collection of the Danish Crown, where it was before 1831. De Vries, who wrote about Schellinks in 1883, did not know where the MS Journal was and expressed the hope that the three volumes might be re-discovered sometime. When Kernkamp visited Copenhagen in 1900, searching in Scandinavian archives for material of value to Dutch Historians on behalf of the Dutch Government he found the MS there in the handwritten catalogue of the Royal Library (housed in a primitive building but manned by co-operative staff). He went through it and gave sufficient detail in his report, published in 1903 to confirm that he saw the original autograph. This report was apparently not well known for neither Karl Ausseren in his 1929 study of the Van der Hem *Atlas*, nor A.M. Hind in his 1931 *Catalogue of Drawings*[72] seem to be aware of the *Journal*'s existence.

In or before 1933[73] Mary Ethel Seaton visited the Royal Library, Copenhagen, where she found the MS of Schellinks's Journal, probably after consulting Kernkamp's report (which includes many of the MSS related to her subject). Although Schellinks's journal is not Scandinavian, she went through at least part of it to supplement her scant material on plays, to extract from nearly 200 diary pages in Dutch, covering a period of some fifteen months, all but one of the plays mentioned by Schellinks, which she added as an appendix to her book, *Literary Relations of England and Scandinavia in the seventeenth century*, based on her 1920 London University MA thesis and published in 1935. Seaton worked at St. Hugh's College, Oxford, and used the Bodleian Library extensively, but she was apparently not aware at the time of the copy of Schellinks's Journal manuscript there, although it was in the printed catalogue in 1897. Seaton's work may have started the subsequent chain of events for in 1937 the MS was lent by the Danish Royal Library to the Dutch Royal Library at The Hague. This was in response to a letter from 'the conservator' at The Hague to the Director of the Copenhagen Library dated 10 August 1937 on behalf of 'Herr W. Pieterse, who needed this for some research'. On 24 August the three large folios were in The Hague, where they remained until 5 May 1938.[74] We have not discovered who Mr. Pieterse was, nor is there any record of him having published anything about it. Whilst the documents were in The Hague, the whole of the work was photographed; this

---

72 A.M. Hind, *Catalogue of Drawings by Dutch and Flemish Artists preserved in the British Museum*, Vol. IV, 1931.

73 The year 1933 is established by her acknowledgement by name of the Librarians in Copenhagen.

74 Private communication, Mrs H.F. Peeters, Royal Library, The Hague, Oct–Nov. 1990.

(negative) copy is now kept in the RKD,[75] at The Hague; it is unfortunately now incomplete. We have only been shown part of Volume I of this copy.

While the MS was in The Hague it was seen by Mrs. I. Gerson-Nehrkorn, who made an extract of the English part. In her handwritten lecture notes she says: 'By chance this travel journal came into my hands, when someone else had arranged for the manuscript, three bulky quarto volumes, to come from Copenhagen to the KB' (i.e. The Royal Library, The Hague).[76]

At some time a transcript of the English part was made, which is also kept in RKD. This transcript is mentioned by Herma van den Berg. We were provided with a photocopy of this transcript, a typewritten document, which was a great help to us. Unfortunately this too is now not complete, and has several omissions, as we were able to ascertain when we obtained a complete photocopy of the Copenhagen MS: e.g. sometimes one or two lines are missed out in transcript, particularly towards the end. Herma van den Berg does not make it clear who made this transcript. From Hulton's remarks (see below) we could assume that it was made by Professor Horst Gerson, but in a letter to Lehmann dated 16 December 1973, Professor Gerson refers to a 'photostat' in RKD, not to a transcript. In further correspondence RKD declared that they do not know who made the transcript and for what purpose, but add that the transcript is not known as the 'Gerson transcript'.

Herma van den Berg used the material in RKD for her study.[77] In a footnote she states that 'Dr. H. Gerson and Mrs. I. Gerson-Nehhrkorn hope to publish this (Schellinks 1661–5) Journal'. This hope was not fulfilled, but it is clear that Horst Gerson used the Journal before completing his *Ausbreitung und Nachwirkung der Hollandischen Malerei des 17 Jahrhunderts* (Haarlem, 1942). This was based on his entry (in Dutch) to a competition set by the Teyler Foundation of Haarlem, submitted, just in time, in December 1937, of which publication was postponed at Gerson's request, who hoped to submit his final version by October 1939.[78]

Gerson also knew of the Bodleian version and saw it in Oxford (before 1940). He probably became aware of it from S. Stelling-Michaud's work on 17th century drawings of Swiss Landscapes, published in 1937[79]: his is the earliest mention of the Bodleian version we

75 Rijksbureau voor Kunsthistorische Documentatie (Netherland Institute for Art History), The Hague.

76 Manuscript notes in RKD, seen October 1990.

77 See above note 65.

78 Private communication, Mr. Sieswerda, Teylers Museum, Haarlem, Aug. 1991.

79 S. Stelling-Michaud, *Unbekannte Schweizer Landschaften aus dem XVII Jahrhundert*, Zürich/Leipzig, 1937.

have found. (Although it was catalogued in 1897, it had slumbered in the Bodleian since the acquisition of d'Orville's collection of MSS in 1804.)[80] We do not know how Stelling-Michaud came to hear of it. His mention also alerted E.S. de Beer, who in a foreword to Hulton's 1959 work, for the Walpole Society, says that he learned of the existence of the Van der Hem *Atlas* from Stelling–Michaud. De Beer also told F.L. Clark (a local historian who was working on the History of Epsom Spa),[81] that there was a drawing of Epsom Wells in the Van der Hem *Atlas*. Clark's work was continued by Lehmann[82] who published his research in 1973 and in 1985 a translation of Schellinks's description of Epsom Wells.[83]

80 The collection of MSS acquired from d'Orville's grandson in 1804 has 578 items. His library of nearly 5500 items (but no MSS) was auctioned in Amsterdam in 1764 soon after his death. *Bibliotheca d'Orvilliana*, Auction Catalogue, 1764.

81 F.L. Clark, 'The History of Epsom Spa', *Surr. Arch. Coll.* 57 (1960), 1–41 (posthumously published).

82 H.L. Lehmann, 'The History of Epsom Spa', *Surr. Arch. Coll.* 69 (1973), 89–97.

83 H.L. Lehmann, 'A description of Epsom Wells 1662', *Surr. Arch. Coll.* 76 (1985), 77–79.

Appendix I – Schellinks's Drawings based on his travel in England known to us

Journal Date 1661	Place	Cat. No.	Schellinks's Subscript (translated)	Schellinks's remark in the Journal
20 July	Gravesend Greenhithe to Tilbury	Hem 8 ECM 9	Gravesend [The River of London]	Going through Gravesend up the Hill to the corn mill which stands there there is a wonderful view all round (20 July 1661)
22 July	Margate	Hem 7	Thus Margate shows itself seen from the North East	
22 July	Dover	Hem 2	Dover	
→	Dover	Hem 3	Dover	
→	Dover	Hem 4	The chalk hills of Dover	
→	Dover	Hem 5	In the suburb of Dover	
→	Dover	Hem 6	Dover	
to	Dover	ECM 11	[Distant view of Dover and the Castle from the south west]	
→	Dover	ECM 12	[Archcliff Fort, Dover, from the south west]	
→	Dover	ECM 13	[Chalk cliffs near Dover]	
8 Aug				
28 July	Deal	Hem 1	Deal or the roadsteads of Downs in England	

Journal Date 1661	Place	Cat. No.	Schellinks's Subscript (translated)	Schellinks's remark in the Journal
8 Aug to 4 Dec with two breaks	Bridge	Hem 20	The homestead of Sir Arnold Braems Knt.	
	Bridge	Hem 21 Witt 4207 Ryks	The village of Bridge	We went walking and drawing in the countryside and the villages as far as Canterbury. (Journ entry before 6 Oct 1661)
	Canterbury	Hem 22	[no subscript] Canterbury	
	Canterbury	Hem 23	View of the town of	
	Canterbury	Hem 24	Canterbury if one comes from Dover, Kent, or the south east side	
14 Aug and 8 Sept and	Rochester & Chatham	Hem 11	The town and river of Rochester and Chatham	
	Chatham/Medway	Hem 14	Chatham	
	Rochester/Medway	Hem 15	Rochester	
	Rochester/Medway	Hem 17	The entrance of the river of Rochester	
	Rochester/Medway	Hem 18	Rochester, Castle of Rochester	
	Rochester/Medway	Hem 19	Rochester	
7 Nov and	Rochester-Sheerness	ECM 8	[The Dutch fleet in the Medway] Sketch with instructions by Schellinks (to an engraver?)	

14 Nov →	Medway Rochester/Medway	ECM 10 ECM 14	[The Dutch attack on the Medway] Thus the town Rochester shows itself opposite Chatham from Upnor Castle behind the roadstead	
14 Aug and 25 Oct 62	Greenwich	Hem 9	Greenwich	
1662 23 April	Windsor Windsor	Ryks 1905/19 Hem 30	Windsor The town of Windsor and the Castle in Berkshire	
	Hampton Court	Hem 29	Hampton Court	
5 June	Epsom	Hem 27	Epsom 10 miles from London where one drinks well water	I have added hereto my drawing of the said place (5 June 1662)
13 July	Bristol	Hem 55	Bristow alias Bristol	
19 July to	Bath	Hem 25	Bath in Somerset where the warm baths are	I went to make a drawing of the town from the height (21 July 1662)
21 July	Bath	Hem 26	The King's bath in the town of Bath	
25 July to 4 Aug	Exeter	Hem 42	Exeter from the land side in Latin Exonia	
and 26 to 31 Aug	Exeter Exeter	Hem 43 Hem 44	Exeter from the river side The bridge of Exeter	

Journal Date 1662	Place	Cat. No.	Schellinks's Subscript (translated)	Schellinks's remark in the Journal
5 Aug and 6 Aug	Dartmouth Dartmouth	Hem 40 Hem 41	Dartmouth seen from the sea Dartmouth seen from the land	After having thoroughly looked at Dartmouth and made a drawing of it . . . (6 Aug 1662)
11 Aug | and | 24 Aug	Fowey Fowey Fowey	Hem 51 Hem 52 ECM 3	Fowey in Cornwall The entrance of the river of Fowey in Cornwall Fowey a sea harbour in Cornwall	Whilst there I drew in haste a prospect of the town and harbour (24 Aug 1662)
17 Aug	St. Michael's Mount St. Michael's Mount St. Michael's Mount St. Michael's Mount St. Michael's Mount	Hem 53 Hem 54 ECM 1 ECM 2 ECM 2v	St. Michael's Mount in Cornwall The Mount St. Michael in Cornwall The Mount or St. Michael's Mount in Cornwall drawn ad vivum anno 1662 The Mount St. Michael in Cornwall The Mount St. Michael in Cornwall	
21 Aug and	Falmouth	Hem 49	The famous large sea harbour of Falmouth in Cornwall	I again made in a hurry a rough drawing of Penrhyn,

Date	Place	Catalogue	Description	Note
22 Aug	Falmouth	Hem 50	The entrance of the harbour of Falmouth with the castles on either side	Falmouth and the castle (22 Aug 1662)
24 Aug	The Cheesewring The Cheesewring	ECM 4 ECM 5	[on reverse a description of the Cheesewring]	
6 Sept	Stonehenge	ECM 6		
7 Sept	Stonehenge	ECM 7	Thus Stonehenge shows itself, near Salisbury on the plains	
7 Sept	Salisbury	Hem 36	Salisbury	Towards evening I went quickly to make a sketch of the town (7 Sept 1662)
9 Sept	Winchester	Hem 35	The town of Winchester	Walked round and through the town and drew the view front the hill as a memorial. (9 Sept 1662)
12 Sept	Isle of Wight	Hem 45	A part of the Isle of Wight as it shows itself when one comes from Southampton	
4 Oct	Cambridge	Hem 28	Cambridge from the north west	
12 Oct	Norwich	Sotheby	drawn ad vivum outside Norwich in England, verso; See the other side	In the afternoon we climbed up Monastery Hill (12 Oct 1662)

Journal Date 1663	Place	Cat. No.	Schellinks's Subscript (translated)	Schellinks's remark in the Journal
15 Apr	Rye	Hem 39	Rye in England seen from the north side to the west	

Notes

This schedule is arranged, with few exceptions, in chronological order of Schellinks's travel.

'Catalogue' abbreviations:

Hem   The Van der Hem *Atlas* in Vienna.

No   The number in the catalogue when known. For Van der Hem *Atlas* the original number i.e. the original number of the drawing in vol. XIX/XX of the *Atlas*. (Many of the listed drawings were transferred to a separate box in 1847, kept in the director's room according to Ausseren, p. 37).

ECM   Edward Croft-Murray and Paul Hulton *Catalogue of British Drawings in the British Museum*, vol. I, (1960), 572–3.

Witt   Witt Collection, Courtauld Institute.

Ryks   *Dutch Drawings of the 17th century in the Rijksmuseum Print Room* (Amsterdam 1987).

Sotheby   Auction Catalogue Sotheby, Amsterdam 25 April 1983, lot 36.

Subscripts in [ ] are notes on the field of the drawing. There are many more 'fieldnotes' than given here.

APPENDIX II – THE DYNASTIC LINK

The House of Orange

The House of Stuart

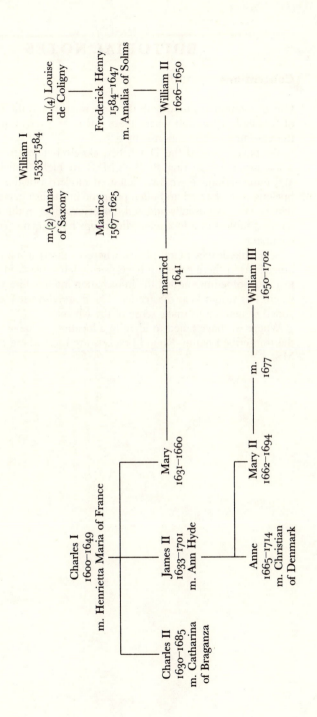

EDITORIAL NOTES

Conventions

Our translation has used both the Copenhagen and the Bodleian MSS of Schellinks's Journal; where these differ the version giving more, or more accurate information is used.

We have followed the Dutch text closely but felt free to make the whole into readable English. Both MSS are highly deficient in capitals and punctuation, so we have followed modern practice to aid clarity. Spelling is haphazard and often phonetic in English personal and place names. We have usually adopted modern spelling in the text unless the name is subject to a footnote. Minor slips have been corrected without comment.

Schellinks leaves many blanks where to insert a name, distance or other fact; in these cases we have usually left a blank in the translated text, but sometimes added the information intended in square brackets where this would help the reader. These are also used where we have added something to make sense of the whole.

Where we have failed to identify a location we have added (?) after the transcribed name. Round brackets are used where they are in the MS.

Anno 1661

On the 14th July at 7 o'clock in the morning I went by boat with Monsr Jaques Thierry and Madame his wife and Mr. Jacobi his son from Amsterdam to Haarlem, and came at 10 o'clock to the pleasant homestead of Mr. Rombouts called Westerhout. Having refreshed ourselves we walked from there with Mr. Rombouts, Mr. Grotius, Monsr Jacob van Rijn, and Monsr R. Block to the Leiden canal, where we found Mr. Rombouts's very elegant pleasure yacht ready, with silken flags flying from mast and stern, and well provided with all kinds of special delicacies and drinks, fruit and other things in plenty. The draught horse was harnessed, and we started off through Leiden, and went with Mr. Rombouts and some of the party to his country house at Zoeterwoude. There we refreshed ourselves and then went by waggon to the canal, where the yacht with the rest of the company awaited us. We sailed on to 's Gravenhage, arrived there at 10 o'clock in the evening, and stayed the night with Mr. van Streijen.

On the 15th we went in the same yacht together with Mr. van Streijen, Miss Margaret Thierry and others to Delft and on to Maaslandsluijs, where we again, as we had done all the time on the yacht, merrily refreshed ourselves and drank the foy.

From there Mr. Rombouts returned home in his yacht, and we crossed the Maas at 4 o'clock in a large 'damlooper'[1] to den Briel, and rode from there the same evening in three waggons to Hellevoetsluijs, where we arrived at night and took our night's rest.[2]

The 16th at half past one in the afternoon we boarded the packetboat, master Thomas Langley, with many other travellers and acquaintances, being ferried in a sailing boat to the ship, which lay up stream waiting for the mail and the passengers; having taken these on board we set sail and, the wind being from north north west, drifted with the ebb tide past Goeree to sea; at 10 or 11 o'clock in the night the wind turned east with a dead calm, the weather being very fine. On the 17th it remained calm until 1 or two o'clock in the afternoon, then the wind, which had turned to north east, blew up bravely and we got up a good speed. At about that time we got sight of a privateer flying the French flag who hailed us; we called to him from where he came, he answered,

---

1 *Damlooper*, a flat bottomed boat, suitable for dragging over a dam.

2 Up to this point the two MSS differ greatly, the Copenhagen MS giving more personal information, which is included here.

from Calais; we asked: where to?, he called, to Rotterdam. That was clearly not true, as shown by his course. He came upon on us, sailing down wind, and our sailors became suspicious; one of them climbed up to the yard and saw all his crew lying down on his deck. He shouted to us from where we came, and our master shouted back: from Whitehall, whereupon he turned away from us, hauled his flag down, and sailed towards a ship which was to the north of us and chased it. We lost him from view and soon after that sighted land, Aldeburgh, and a little later the point of Orford Ness; we sailed along close to the land, the coast was low and flat. There was a large fire beacon standing on the beach, and above that was a smith's workshop. A man in a small boat came alongside, who had been at sea since 4 o'clock in the morning waiting for the packetboat, to warn us that the customs-men had gone to sea at 11 o'clock the night before in a small boat with two rowers to search us before we came on shore, as they suspected that we had some goods on board which might be smuggled or not declared, which was not far from the truth. When they heard this some of our countrymen rushed down and hid everything away and stuffed it down their trouser fronts.

In the evening we sighted this boat, which, with great difficulty, came alongside, expecting that we would throw them a rope, but with our great speed we gave them the slip and left them behind, merrily jeering at them. We held our course along the coast with good speed and arrived at 11 o'clock at night up the river in the roads of Harwich, where we were rowed ashore in a small rowing boat, and went to stay in the Golden Angel, with one Owen Spann, postmaster, who had come over with us. We were entertained there in the English manner, which we and some others, who had not been to England before, found not a little strange, as in this small seaside place accommodation, food and drink were rather quaint and funny.

Having slept there the night and having had breakfast we went to look at the small town and the countryside around. As to Harwich, it is a reasonable market town in the county of Essex, lying at the mouth of a river, which, coming from a town called Ipswich, flows there into the sea. From there various boats and other craft sail to London, Newcastle, and elsewhere. Across the river on the other side lies the county of Suffolk, very pleasant and fertile.

On the 18th we left Harwich for Gravesend at about 11 o'clock in the morning in a coach drawn by four miserable nags, who, in spite of their miserably putrid and ulcerated legs, showed an astonishing courage and strength. Monsr le commandant or the coachmaster, a funny so-and-so, on shanks's pony, went as a guide on the road in front or beside us, providing entertainment; he was called Mr. Francis Dagger alias Poniard. His servant Thomas drove the four poor creatures, caressing them mercilessly with a whip, for which they in their turn upset the coach head over heels upside down. Upon this arose a great argument with horrible cursing and swearing between my Lord Dagger and the unbelieving Thomas, who could not or would not accept that he was to blame for the accident. Old Dagger's little footboy, a dwarf some 25 years of age called frog or kickvors, whose seat was below or between the coachdriver's legs, got some of the blows in the beating which followed, and cried his eyes out with laughter.

Travelling from Harwich on a pleasant road we came after 2 English miles to a village called Caveriad (?), then after 2 miles to Ramsey, a village delightfully situated on a hill; in the valley below was a wooden bridge over a river and some marshy ground, good meadow and arable land with many oaks but only a few fruit trees.

NB. After driving a while our coach overturned, fortunately without anybody being hurt, but after the coach was righted and we were ready to get in again, Mr. Jaques Thierry twisted his foot and sprained his ankle, so that he could not stand on it for seven or eight weeks and had to be carried everywhere, and whatever masters' methods and remedies were used, it did not respond to warmth and bathing, but needed the help of surgeons. This unfortunate accident upset us not a little and did greatly affect our journey and our pleasure.

Continuing our journey we came to a great river and drove along this for 2 or 3 miles with beautiful views, 4 miles to Thabelett (?), 3 miles to Manningtree, a small market town lying on the river, 3 miles to Ardleigh, a pleasant road throughout; 4 miles to Colchester, which we reached at 3 o'clock in the afternoon and went to stay at the King's Head, an excellent inn, where we were extremely well treated. We had our midday meal there, and then went to look at the town, which is quite large, but not very neat, the churches, houses and the castle were badly damaged in the war between the king and parliament. Colonel Goring was then in command of the town, which, after a three months' siege, was forced by hunger to surrender, having survived by eating cats, dogs, rats, and mice. Sir Charles Lucas,[3] an ardent royalist, was executed, having been condemned by a court-martial in the very room in which we had our meal, a big place decorated in the English style.

Colchester has a big trade in baize and woollen goods which are much in demand, and which is widely exported.

NB. On coming into the town we saw in passing a very old man chained to a post in the street, with heavy iron rings round his neck

---

3 Goring: Earl of Norwich (1608–57), and Sir Charles Lucas (1613–48), served in the Royalist army in the Civil War. On the surrender of Colchester in 1648 they were both taken; Lucas was court martialled and shot in Colchester Castle, Lord Norwich was tried by his peers, condemned, but later pardoned (DNB).

and feet, his feet locked together and with a chain fixed to his neck, asking passers-by for alms to keep himself from starving, else he would die from hunger and thirst. We asked him what crime he had committed, and he answered he was only suspected of having stolen a pig.

On the 19th at 4 o'clock in the morning we rode on, and after 2 miles came to Lexden, a village, 3 miles to Stanway, then to Feering, a large market town; on our left was a large wood and many cultivated fields. We had nice views to Witham, also a large market village, to Achim (?), a village, on to Boreham. A quarter of an hour from there, on the right hand side, lies New Hall,[4] an estate of Lord Buckingham with a very beautiful palace.

On through Springfield, a village, to Chelmsford, a large market town with a beautiful church and a lot of fine shops, lying on a river which is crossed by a stone bridge. We stopped at the Golden Lion for our midday meal, and rode on from there at 1 o'clock in fine weather; to Shenfield, through good farmland, with nice views; to Stock, a village, to Billericay, a large market village, on a hill, with a wide street with fine houses and shops. It happened to be market day, and there was a large concourse of neatly dressed women on horseback, buying and selling, mostly without their menfolk. We went on, the road became bad and troublesome, and our coach broke down, and we all got off, except Mr. J. Thierry, who could not stand nor walk because of his sprained ankle. After our coach was repaired we came with a great effort and much difficulty to a steep hill, which we climbed on foot; from the top we had a beautiful view over the finest landscape we had so far seen in England, towards the county of Kent just across the river Thames, and the county of Essex on this side, a memorable sight. We descended from this hill into a fertile valley full of wooded groves; I went by myself on foot until the village of Laindenhill, which lies on a low hill, where we refreshed ourselves, and went on from there in the coach downhill to West Tilbury, a village at the bottom of the valley. In the descent we saw the river Thames straight in front of us, with many English and Dutch ships lying up stream, and some drifting on the ebb tide down the river to the sea. On the opposite side of the river lay Gravesend, a nice sight, and on this side, directly opposite Gravesend, in the county of Essex, was a castle or blockhouse, built there by order of Queen Elizabeth. We reached this fort at 8 o'clock in the evening, and parted from the comical coachmaster, his servant and footboy, and the guide whom we had taken on at Horndon on the Hill. We crossed the river to Gravesend in a 'prevoor',[5] and went to

---

4 New Hall, Elizabethan mansion (on the site of a Tudor house of Henry VIII) near Boreham, now a school. (Pevsner, *BoE, Essex*).

5 *Prevoor, parvoor, paravoor*, a small rowing boat with two oarsmen, frequently referred to by Schellinks and defined later. See text-note 40.

the White Swan Inn to one Arthur White, where we were tolerably well accommodated and regaled; as however the English fleas were very aggressive and I did not want to have anything to do with that hungry and bloodthirsty mob, I took my night's rest on a hard bench.

On the 20th we looked at Gravesend. It is a fine market town with a decent street going up from the river, with shops, but mainly with inns for arriving and departing travellers. Going through Gravesend up the hill to the corn mill which stands there, there is a wonderful view all round, upstream towards London, and downstream towards the sea, and behind over the county of Kent.[6]

As Mr. Thierry had to go to Dover for business reasons, and because of his injured leg did not think it advisable to travel by road, we decided to go there by boat, down the river and along the coast to Downs and Dover; this should have been a very pleasant journey, but the sea and the weather decided otherwise.

So on the 21st Mr. Thierry hired a post boat (a lighthorseman in English) manned by four men and a boy, the master skipper or helmsman called John Klery. This boat was about the size of a small Maerse or Breuckelse ferry,[7] narrow and fast rowing, with a sunshade of blue cloth, as it was then fine, hot weather. We went aboard this boat at 6 o'clock in the morning in fine weather, taking some provisions with us, and went before the wind down the river, with the county of Kent on our right, and Essex on our left. There were several Dutch and English warships on the river, amongst them the *St. Mathias*, now called the *Love*, which had been taken in the English war when Keesie Louw of Amsterdam was her captain, also the *Lion* and *Anna* and some other ships ready to sail to the Downs to join the fleet which lay there at anchor waiting to go to Portugal to fetch the royal bride.[8] Leaving Gravesend we saw on the left, up on the hill, West Tilbury, then East Tilbury, where Queen Elizabeth reviewed her fleet in 1588. On the right, in Kent, was Schacxmill (?), 3 miles, and Cliffe, 7 miles from Gravesend. Drifting down the river in a dead calm we passed at 16 miles from Gravesend on our left the small town of Leigh in Essex. On the other side of the river near Rochester was West Swale, and, running before us to sea, a convoy of merchant ships bound for Holland, commanded by Captain Hendrick Adriaensen. We passed Cobury (?) and soon after Shoebury, both in Kent [sic], at the bend of

6 The drawing of this view is in the British Museum. Edward Croft-Murray and Paul Hulton, *Catalogue of British Drawings at the British Museum*, London 1960 (Referred to as ECM) i, 573.

7 Maarsen and Breukelen, two places near Utrecht on the river Vecht, a small river, so the ferryboats would be of modest size.

8 The royal bride Catherine of Braganza; she finally arrived in Portsmouth in May 1662, and at Hampton Court on 8 June 1662, see below.

the river near the sea, past the Isle of Grain and West Swale and the Isle of Sheppey on our right. 6 miles out at sea from Sheerness we had our meal from the provisions which we had brought, and in the afternoon we sailed past East Swale.

It is worth mentioning that 4, 5 or 6 miles from land small oysters are caught and subsequently cast or seeded into the water at the mouth of the river, where they grow very large and good; nobody is allowed to fish for them in the months of June and July.[9]

At 3 or 4 in the afternoon we came near the beach at Swale Cliffe and rowed along there, but could only make slow progress against the incoming tide, whereupon three of the crew jumped on land and towed us 2 or 3 miles towards Reculver.

I went on land with Mr. Thierry's servant and walked a little way towards a small hill, and on a large level field we came across some people, mostly dressed in white, running very fast against each other, watched by a large crowd of spectators. At first we could not make out what it was all about; from afar it looked as if it were riders exercising their horses, but coming nearer we saw that it was a kind of running contest called in English runne.[10] The rules for this are as follows: At the time of the annual contest a place, town, or village issues a challenge; in the afternoon of the appointed day the runners of that place, men and boys, assemble on a large level field to meet the contestants of all the neighbouring villages around, and a large crowd of people also come, and there are booths with refreshments and all kinds of trinkets. When they have all assembled they undress, most down to linen pants and barefoot. While they are getting ready some people on horseback and some on foot with sticks arrange the spectators round a large square; when the contestants are ready they each take a shilling in the mouth and stand hand in hand in a row, the two teams facing each other like the children in Holland playing the herring game. Then comes one who has been appointed for that purpose and checks their numbers, such as twenty in each team, and takes the shillings from the contestants, first from the challengers and then from their opponents, both teams remaining in their places. The money they consume together after the contest. Then the game starts: each party stands in one corner of the field, and one runner runs out from his corner, and is immediately pursued by one of the other party who tries

9 Schellinks describes the culture of oysters in Essex in detail on 19 Oct. 1662, see text-note 213.

10 The game they saw being played seems to be a form of Prisoner's Base, see e.g. Joseph Strutt, *The Sports and Pastimes of the People of England*. New edn. 1969, pp. 67–69 Iona and Peter Opie, *Childrens Games in Streets and Playgrounds*, 1969, pp. 143–6.

There is a sketch along the bottom of the relevant Copenhagen manuscript page, showing positions A and B and many running figures.

to tag him, and so others, running round the field back to their corner. When a runner is tagged his opponents and the spectators jeer and shout and laugh at him derisively. The party which first looses seven people are the loosers.

After watching this running game we walked along the beach to Reculver, a small seaside town with a church with two towers with spires, where we refreshed ourselves and then rejoined the boat.

At half past eight in the evening we sailed in very good and pleasant weather from the shore out to sea to go with the ebb tide round the point of Margate Bay and sail on to Deal and the Downs. The wind was from the east, and the shore low. At about half past ten dark clouds appeared and the wind rose and became very strong and developed into a terrible thunderstorm with torrential rain, thunder and lightning; the sea went frighteningly hollow, and our little boat went wildly up and down. Our terrified boatmen, who were more used to the river than to such a raging sea, had their hands full with rowing to keep the boat head-on to the waves and would greatly have liked to reach land, but could not do so in the dark because they were afraid of the sands and submerged rocks. We could not understand very well what they said, but our fear was much increased when they said that they did not know where we were, and they appeared just as frightened as we, and we had nothing in prospect but the danger of stranding or foundering. And still the weather became worse and worse, and they still continued rowing. At last, by great good fortune, we got, at twelve or one o'clock in the light of the continuous lightning sight of a fishingboat which lay there at anchor in the roads, and with great effort and in great danger of having our light boat dashed to pieces against this boat, rowed towards it and hailed it. Our people shouted as loud as they could, and after some time the astonished fisherman appeared with a lantern; after an exchange of words he threw us a rope to make our boat fast to his; this was still quite dangerous, as we could easily have been smashed to pieces against him the waves, and our boatmen had to keep us off him all the time with their oars, and to hold our boat straight to the sea. The fisherman told us where we were, and how far out from Margate, and then went back into his cabin.

There were here and there some large fires on the beach and we were told by our people that this was seaweed which was burned to obtain its ashes. Lying there tethered to the fisherman's boat we wished a thousand times that day would come. The weather did not improve, it rained steadily with terrible thunder and lightning, and we were wet through to the skin from the rain and the overlapping waves, and all lay down on some straw under the sunroof in the open boat, exhausted by anxiety. At long last day broke, and with the incoming tide our boatmen shed the tow and set course for Margate, where we got, God be praised, safely into harbour at about 6 o'clock in the morning of the 22nd.

We went to the King's Head to the postmaster to dry ourselves and all our wet luggage and clothes, and rinsed the sorrow from our hearts with cup of sack, had our meal, and paid off the sturdy watermen. We heard from them later that it took them two days to make their way back to Gravesend.

This storm did a lot of damage in this area to the corn as well as to all other fruit.

After having recovered from our ordeal we went to look at Margate, and then tried to get a coach to take us to Dover or to Sandwich, but there was none to be found, and we had to make do with a funny farm wagon drawn by four miserable horses.

NB. Margate lies on the Isle of Thanet in the county of Kent, which is one of the most fertile corn districts in the whole of England; it has a small harbour with a platform with cannon on one side.

We left Margate at 11 o'clock in the morning in good weather and passed after $\frac{1}{2}$ mile Schasten (?), a village or suburb. The ground was high and fertile, but we saw some very large cornfields which were completely flattened by the storm of the night before.

Flif (?) one mile on from Margate, then after 4 miles Manston. From the heights a little further on there was on our left the most beautiful view in the world, straight ahead appeared a large inlet, from the sea and on a headland Deal or Downs, where a large English fleet and some Dutch ships lay at anchor, all along the coast from the North Foreland to the Downs, and on our right the rich pastures of Kent. We descended from the heights with Sandwich straight ahead of us and drove along the beach next to the sea. There were some fertile fields with blue pebbles and boulders as far as one could see. Most of the English coasts are by nature protected against the raging seas with an unbreachable wall of these boulders.

At 2 o'clock in the afternoon we got to Sandwich and went to the Dolphin Inn to refresh ourselves with their excellent beer, which they served up in 4 wooden tankards at a time. Sandwich is a medium size town, lying on a river, but besides the church there is not much of interest to be seen. We left there at 4 o'clock in a peculiar waggon drawn by four mules with bells on their heads, harnessed in single file; our commander, called John Haenbrouck, was on foot, an extremely funny fellow (who would have made a good clown) and his servant or boy Josaphat alias hang-ear, who made the way appear short with his funny stories and grimaces. We passed Est (?) on our right, Eastry, Worth, Ham (a parish), Down, Narham(?), on the heights, with a fine view over the sea, then Ringwould, also on the heights; a little further the village of Charleton, a suburb of Dover, with the town of Dover far below, a wonderful view with the setting sun behind it.

We arrived at Dover, 9 miles from London,[11] at half past eight in the evening and went to the Hotel à L'Escu de France, to a Mr. Neufveu an excellent inn, with a large room at the back with a view over the harbour and the sea, where we were well accommodated.

On the 23rd we went to look at Dover, and in the afternoon we went to see the castle, which lies high on the chalk cliffs, which fall off horribly steeply into the sea. The castle is an ancient building, surrounded by three extremely thick and strong ring walls with very deep ditches carved out of the rock.

NB. The circumference of the castle is about as large as that of Naarden in the Gooij,[12] facing the sea it has four or five platforms well set with cannons; there is, amongst others, an uncommonly long serpent, 24 English or Dutch timber feet in length, which carries the arms of England and a picture of Libertas or Freedom, and the following inscription in old or bad Dutch:

> Breeck Schureet al, Muer ende Wal, ben ik geheeten
> Doer Bergh en Dal Boert Minen Bal van mijn Gesmeten.[13]

The approach to the castle gate is very steep and arduous. In front of the gate is a wooden bridge over a deep ditch; inside the gate there are sentry boxes on both sides, and all kinds of weaponry lying ready against the wall; two pieces of cannons stand in the inner court in front of the gate to guard the entrance; nobody, of whatever rank, is allowed inside carrying arms, these have to be handed over to the guard. Then one or two of the guard, carrying halberds, show one round and explain all the interesting things. Inside the innermost wall there is a royal palace with a number of large rooms or halls, not very well kept. Several stone stairs lead right to the top, which is a lead covered flat roof with a drain which leads the rainwater below into a large lead-lined cistern for emergency use.

NB. In the lead on the roof are scratched-in the footprints of some people inscribed with their names, amongst them those of King Charles II, which he had marked there when he landed at Dover on his restoration.[14]

11 There is no figure given in the Copenhagen MS; the distance is about 80 English miles. Schellinks generally uses English miles; he roughly defines a Dutch mile of the time on 21 Aug. 1662 as 4 to 5 Dutch miles to 12 English miles.

12 Naarden, ancient fortified town in the 'Gooi', east of Amsterdam.

13 The inscription copied by Schellinks differs slightly in spelling from that quoted in R.A. Brown's *Guidebook of Dover Castle*, 1966, for 'Queen Elizabeth's Pocket Pistol', where it is translated as: 'Breaker my name of rampart and wall,
Over hill and dale I throw my ball'.

14 Charles II landed at Dover from Holland on his Restoration, arriving on 25 May 1660 old style (o.s.).

Next one sees an ancient chapel, somewhat neglected, where a
service is held now and again. In a side chapel, separated by iron bars,
is the tomb of Henry Howard,[15] of white and black marble, very
graceful, his kneeling figure on top, and lower down four figures at the
four corners. On the wall of another chapel is the much damaged
tomb of another governor of the castle in white marble. Next we came
to a covered place in which is a deep well, hewn through the rock,
from which the water is drawn up in a barrel by means of a large
wheel. Nearby in the open is a similar well fearfully deep. Then we
climbed up on to the walls to get a view of the whole castle; there is a
large meadow and some cornfields within the walls. After having seen
all this, we went to refresh ourselves in a cave or grotto, cut into the
rock, where they keep at all times several pipes of a very good beer,
which for that reason is deliciously cool, and which they serve in the
English fashion in four wooden tankards. They also show there an
ancient curved copper horn, with which, so they say, the workers at
the building of the castle were called together, and many visitors drink
from this horn as a curiosity. Now in 1661, the governor of the castle
was Sir Francis Vinsen, Kt or Bnt, at the time of Protector Cromwell
it was Mr. Celsy.

On leaving the castle we saw through the bars of a door six Quakers
sitting in prison.

On the 24th we went to a French Church Service, which is held in
a room reserved for this purpose at the warehouses of Mr. Jacob
Braems,[16] which are situated on an island in the outer harbour.

On the 25th eleven or twelve Straits' ships passed by Dover, bound
for London.[17]

On the 26th at 2 o'clock in the night one of Mr. Thierry's ships, the

15 Henry Howard, earl of Northampton (1540–1614) was Warden of the Cinque Ports,
buried in the chapel of Dover Castle. The monument erected on his grave was removed
in 1696 to the chapel of the College of Greenwich (DNB).

16 Arnold Braems (1602–81), descendant of a Flemish refugee, Dover merchant active
in the development of Dover harbour, owner of wharves and warehouses, was a fervent
Royalist who joined Prince Rupert's fleet with his own ship. He was instrumental at the
Restoration in ensuring Lawson's fleet came over to the King.
In 1660 he was knighted by the King (who was on his way to London) at Canterbury,
and for a short time he was M.P. for Dover. He bought the manor of Blackmanbury at
Bridge near Canterbury and built there a mansion, described by Schellinks on 12 Sept.
1661. His son, Walter, mentioned by Schellinks, succeeded him at Bridge, which was sold
by his descendants in 1704. See Wm. Minet, 'Some unpublished plans of Dover harbour',
Archaeologia lxxii (1921–2), 185–224, a reference owed to Mrs P.M. Godfrey, Dover
Libraries. See also B.D. Henning, *The House of Commons, 1660–1690*, 3 vols. 1983, iii, 707
(with references to State papers) and *The Visitations of Kent in 1663–1668*, p. 24.

17 'Straits' ships traded with the Mediterranean countries through the Straits of
Gibraltar.

Hope, which had been lying in the Downs waiting for two months for Mr. Thierry's arrival, left, bound for Barbados.

On the 28th four of us rode on horseback to the Downs, keeping to the high land near the sea, a very pleasant road. During a hard gallop my horse stumbled and fell forwards to its knees, and I, being unprepared, was unseated and shot over the horse's head; it was a great miracle that I did not break my neck. We remounted and rode on and passed two forts on the right on the sea side. We got to Downs and went to the posthouse, the Greyhound, for our midday meal. After the meal we had ourselves taken in a small boat to a captured prize loaded with brandy, cork, wine, and prunes; this was a Schellinger galleon which had sailed from Nantes with the French fleet, and, expecting no danger, had left its protection near Brielle, and was boarded by a small privateer disguised as a pleasure yacht, under captain John Penny, which had a small cannon and a crew of 30 men.

NB. This was the same privateer which tried to come alongside us on our crossing to Harwich; he had afterwards captured a Schellinger hooker or fishing boat with a crew of 8 men, which he took with him for ten days and then let go. The crew of the captured galleon had been taken to Holland, leaving only the captain and the mate on board, to stay with their ship and its cargo.

Next we went to the admiral's flagship the *Henrietta*, 70 guns, and were there bid welcome by the lieutenant, who had long been in the service of the States and been present at the capture of many places. The admiral, Sir John Mennes,[18] an elderly man, was however not on board. We looked at the admiral's cabin, a splendid large and expensively furnished room, then, as we went up, seven trumpeters blew magnificently to welcome us. Going below deck we were sumptuously treated with claret, ale, and delicious beer, first by the lieutenant in his cabin, and then once more in the mate's, the English were indeed very hospitable. As we left the trumpeters blew once more as a farewell. We then went to the Dover to discuss with the admiral the matter of the privateer and the prize, but on coming on board were told that he was on board the *St. George*, so we went there and went on board. While we were looking over the ship the admiral came out of the cabin to return to his ship, so he took us with him in his sloop; as we approached his ship the trumpeters blew wonderfully. He received us politely in his cabin and entertained us well, and we learned from him that the commission of the privateer was not valid. While we were with him, a noble lady arrived on board with her companions, to pay a visit to the admiral; the admiral's wife, who had broken her arm when the carriage

18 Sir John Mennes, comptroller of the Navy Nov. 1661–71, frequently mentioned by Pepys.

in which she was travelling to Rochester overturned, was staying with her. We took our leave and went back to the privateer or prize, which was completely surrounded by English boats and sloops, which buzzed like bees round their hive, all filling their pitchers, cans, and tankards with aquavit brandy. Master John Penny, like a second St. Martin, let no one go short, as long he could help him and comfort him with refreshment, but this genial rogue vanished the same night with one of his fellows, to the great regret of the many good-for-nothings, and nobody ever found out, to where he had vanished and flown. We then returned to Downs, mounted our horses and rode back to Dover.

On the 30th two East India ships passed, and later in the day *The Seven Star* came into the harbour from Barbados with a cargo of sugar and cotton, and also had eight civet cats on board and two pigs. She had come in to meet Mr. J. Thierry, and her captain William Donston joined us for the evening meal, and we drank a rummer to celebrate his safe arrival.

On the 1st August Sir Arnold Braems paid us a visit.

On the 2nd we went up the hill about one hour from Dover to watch a running game between a party of young gentlemen and others from Dover against a mixed party of countrymen, who kept them on the run.

On the 3rd came a small ship, a privateer from Dunkerque, into Dover harbour and tied up next to the Barbados ship. This ship had sometime before under a Swedish commission captured the *Dolphin*, one of Mr. Jaques Thierry's ships which was returning with a rich cargo from Barbados. This fact had just been ascertained from one of the sailors of the *Seven Star* who had previously sailed in the *Dolphin*, and thereupon Mr. Jaques Thierry immediately impounded the privateer, but her captain, who had gone to an inn for a drink, escaped, in spite of all the efforts which were made to get hold of him.

On the 4th we visited Commander Sir Wadeward, keeper of the small fort at the foot of the hill below the castle, and were hospitably entertained by him with claret wine. While we were there, a gun in the castle above us, as well as one at the small castle on the other side of the town, was fired to salute his princely highness Count Maurits of Nassau,[19] who had travelled down from London to Dover to sail across to Calais.

19 Prince Johan (Jan) Maurits of Nassau-Siegen, in England as ambassador of the Elector of Brandenburg, to discuss the guardianship and education of the ten years old orphaned Prince William of Orange, the future King William III of England, whose mother Mary, a sister of King Charles II, had just died; the Elector of Brandenburg's wife was a sister of prince Willem's father (L. Bittner and L. Grosz, *Repertorium der diplomatischen Vertreter aller Länder*, Oldenburg/Berlin (1936), and *Rijks Geschiedkundige Publ. XXVIII*, letter of Constantine Huijgens to Sir Edward Nicholas, 1 April 1661).

At 5 o'clock in the morning of the 5th his Princely Highness Count Maurits went on board an English packet boat; a salvo was fired from the two castles and the little fort.

On the 6th we were merrily entertained by the younger Sir Arnold Braems with French wine and light refreshments.

On the 7th Mr. J. Thierry rode with his party to the seat of Monsr Nevu outside Dover and was, with other invited guests, well entertained.

In the afternoon of the 8th we had a farewell dinner in our lodgings with some friends and acquaintances and left Dover at 3 o'clock in a carriage, which Sir Arnold Braems had sent to take us to his delightful residence at Bridge, one hour's walk from Canterbury and 12 miles from Dover. Along a very pleasant road all the way, we passed Bethlem Church (?), Northfield (?) and saw Sandown Castle and the Downs below us on the right, and Whitfield on the left, passed through Waldershare and Womenswold, then past Barham up on the hill and through Kingston and Bishopsbourne in the valley, on to the estate of Sir Arnold Braems, also down in the valley. We arrived there at 8 o'clock in the evening to a friendly welcome and were magnificently entertained, and drank quite a few good healths with sack.

On the 9th we played on the bowling green on the hill near Sir Arnold Braems's place.

On the 10th we saw a hart shot with a crossbow in the deerpark of Sir Arnold Braems; everybody, especially the ladies, washed their hands in the warm blood, to get white hands. The hart was immediately gutted and cut up into quarters.

On the 11th a venison pie and other dishes of the hart were on the menu. After the meal I walked to Canterbury and explored the town.

On the 12th we rode in two carriages with Sir Arnold Braems and Mr. Adriaens of London and several ladies to Canterbury and went to the cathedral to hear the canons sing the prayers and looked at the sepulchres or gravestones of kings, bishops, and other notables, some very old and much ravaged by age and war. In the recent troubles between the king and parliament, Oliver Cromwell had here, as elsewhere throughout the country, everything which looked like popery, such as glass, statues, crosses and the like, in and on churches and other public buildings, torn down and broken to pieces.

Jan Maurits (1604–79), a nephew of Willem the Silent was a soldier and naval commander, governor of Brazil for the Dutch West Indies Company, etc., since 1647 also in Brandenburg diplomatic service. Founder of the Maurits House and art collection at the Hague.

Kent

This county was in olden times a kingdom called Cantium or Angelus, as being angular and lying in a corner of the large island of England. It is the foremost region of the whole of England because of its fertility and pleasantness, full of cornfields, pasturage, and orchards, especially of cherries and apples, planted in straight rows in square fields. It extends for 50 miles from east to west and 26 miles from north to south. Its middle part is considered the healthiest and most fertile. There are two bishoprics, Canterbury, the head of all, and Rochester. It is defended by 27 castles, has four royal palaces, 24 market towns and is densely populated and has good seaports and anchorages for ships, some outcrops of iron and marl, a kind of fat chalk or clay, which is used to fertilise the fields. Most of its soil is chalk shot through with flint, some describe it as one piece of chalk. It is also very rich in birds and fish of all kinds, and has plenty of woods and timber for hunting and for fuel. Canterbury is the primate and metropolitan archbishopric of England, its Latin name Durevernum, by the ancient Britons called Kaerkent, burgh of Kent, and later by the Saxons Canterbury. It has long streets and markets full of handsome shops. In the town one can still see the ruins of the fortified castle of the Kentish kings, now called Malady, the wooden palace.

Canterbury

is the capital town of the ancient and renowned county of Kent; there is a notable and beautiful cathedral or main church, standing in the middle of the town, well nigh as large as St. Paul's in London, now somewhat damaged. Between the nave of the church and the choir is a very high square tower, in which hangs a bell called Bell Harry, brought from France by King Henry. At the two ends of the west front are two towers, one called Dunstan and the other Arnold tower. In each of them is a number of bells, to ring the changes in the English manner.

In the church was a painted window in which the entire story of Christ from his birth to his passion and resurrection was skillfully depicted, which was so beautifully painted that a Spanish ambassador offered for it 100,000 guilders and more.

In the choir is the bronze tomb of Edward the Black Prince and many others. Below this church is the French church, a handsome place. Around the church the canons, deans and other clerics have very beautiful houses with great privileges.

The Archbishop of Canterbury is called Totius Angliæ Primate, without any addition.

There is also a public school called The King's School.

There are further the following churches in the town: St. George, St. Andrew, St. Mary, St. Peter, All Saints Westgate, St. Margaret, St. Mary Magdalene, St. Michael, St. Alphege Northgate, St. Mary Bredman, St. Paul, St. Martin, St. Mildred, besides those in the suburbs.

There was formerly an old castle, built by the Danes, now in ruins. The town has walls and ditches, all the walls are of flint. There are two weekly markets. The mayor and the aldermen walk in scarlet robes to hold their session or law court.

Our Journey to London

On the 13th August, Saturday morning at 5 o'clock, after having taken our leave from Sir Arnold Braems and all the ladies and the others, we went in Sir Arnold Braems's carriage to Canterbury and from there at 6 o'clock by coach through the suburb of St. Dunstan's, and past Harbledown, Boughton, Preston, Stone Norton, over some hills, Bapchild and others; there were some grand and pleasant views, and many fertile cornfields and large orchards, mostly cherry trees, although the harvest was bad that year. At 9 o'clock we got to Sittingbourne, a very large and long stretched out village, where we refreshed ourselves with new oysters and a cup of sack. Going on we passed Cranbrook, then on a hill Rainham, and at 12 o'clock came to Chatham, a kind of suburb of Rochester, a large town with busy market places, it took us almost an hour to get through.

Rochester

lies on the river Medway, not very far from where it flows into the sea. It is a famous and ancient town, renowned for its convenient situation as much as for the fact that it is the most beautiful, strongest and best arms depot or arsenal in the whole of England. Here lie afloat, as in an open bay, the largest ships, protected at all times from all storms and winds by the surrounding hills. On each ship is usually a watch of seven commissioned officers. At the foot of the hills, where a very fine bridge lies across the river, are two forts, one on each side, to guard the river, which is blocked there by chains slung across on boats, leaving only a narrow passage for ships to pass. This town has, by its situation, a very great advantage over all other places in the realm.

The meaning of the name Rochester is castrum in rupe, the castle on the cliff. Many place names in England end with chester, a reminder of the old Roman Castra or camps. Rochester is a bishop's seat and has four churches, 1. the Cathedral Church, 2. St. Nicholas, 3. St. Clement (ruined), 4. St. Margaret. At Chatham there is also a very large store house, built there by order of the Protector Cromwell, in which all kinds of naval equipment are stored while the ships are lying there in the harbour or on the river. There was also there a galleon recently taken from the Turks.

Continuing our journey from Rochester to Gravesend, we passed Strood, Gadshill, Chalk, Denton, with many fine views, especially on the left (*sic*) towards the Isle of Sheppey and the Thames and towards the sea. We arrived at Gravesend at 2 o'clock in the afternoon, and, as we had missed the tide, had to stay the night there, and stayed at the King's Head, where there were very fine and handsome rooms with a view over the river, and where we were well and very courteously served.

On the 14th, Sunday, we had intended to go by boat up the river to London.

NB. In the whole of England it is not permitted to travel on the Sabbath by water or on land in any vehicle, or to hire horses, carriages, or coaches. As we did not want to have to pay a fine of 10 shillings per head we applied to the Lord Mayor of Gravesend for a free pass, which we obtained by pretending that we had some dispatches or secret letters for their Excellencies the Dutch ambassadors.

So we left Gravesend at 10 o'clock in the morning in a prevoor or light boat similar to a northern yawl with two rowers and a small sail. The wind was from the north west and we therefore had to sail mostly into the wind, which in some reaches, with the river running a strong tide, made a lot of rough water.

Going up river, we passed first the village of Northfleet on our left, then Grays and St. Clement on the right in a bend of the river, then Greenhithe and Stone on the left,   miles from Gravesend. Two miles further we passed Purfleet at the foot of a hill on our right, and one mile on, on the left, the hamlet of Erith. Here the East Indiamen usually discharge some of their cargo to reduce their draught, to enable them to sail up the river to Woolwich and Blackwall, where they drop anchor. Then we passed on the right Barking, where many fishermen live, 4 or 5 miles from London by road. From this place the fisherman came, who threw us the rope in the night of the storm near Margate. Past Woolwich on the left, the river was full of large and small boats. Here many ships are built; the *Royal Sovereign*[20] was built there, and there lay a new East Indiaman of a beautiful and interesting design. Sailing on a bit further we passed Charlton, lying on a hill, and ahead on our right Blackwall, where the warehouse of the East India Company is, a large handsome building, and also their carpenters' yard. Many

20 The *Royal Sovereign*, built 1637, see Pepys ii, 15–16.

large capital ships were lying there, East Indiamen, Straits and Barbados ships, and a large number of other vessels.

Past this inlet or bight we came to famous Greenwich on our left, pleasantly situated on the river. The royal palace stands close to the water along the river, a very large, long building first begun by   .[21] It was damaged in the recent troubles and is at present in a badly ruined state; it was used by Oliver Cromwell as a prison during the war against the Dutch, of whom many died there of privation and disease. A little inland is the Queen's House or palace, a fine, stately building with many large and small rooms and nice stone spiral stairs with iron banisters leading up to the upper rooms and to the flat roof, which is lead-covered and railed in, from where one has beautiful views all round. This building too has suffered some damage in the recent war and is at present without furniture and pictures, but is now on the King's orders being repaired. There is a fairly large deerpark, sur- rounded by a wall, but the soldiers have killed all the game, which used to be there in large numbers. On a hill in this park are the ruins of a castle, which has been razed to the ground by the parliamentarians.

Greenwich is a fair sized market town with some nice streets and many fine houses. It is renowned for the Queen's House, the birthplace of Queen Elizabeth. Its name derives from the old English Green 'Creek' or 'Inlet' from the river.

Sailing a little further up river we passed Deptford, lying very pleasantly on the same side as Greenwich. Next followed a bend of the river to the left, which the English call Cuckoldshaven; a tall flagpole stands there, to which horns of all kinds and descriptions are fixed, in honour of all the English cuckolds or horn carriers[22] (of whom there are quite a few in London!), and the English have much fun and amusement with each other, as they pass by and doff their hats to each other and to all around.

Past this bend of the river, one comes within sight of the city of London, with its suburbs Redriff [Rotherhithe] on the left and Ratcliff on the right, extending for 3 miles along the river up to London Bridge. There was a great throng of all kinds of craft, amongst them some Dutch ships, which the English had captured in the recent war.[23] As

21 This refers to the Tudor Palace of Placentia, mainly of Henry VII's time. It was badly neglected during the Commonwealth and its demolition was about to start; Evelyn reports on 19 October 1661 o.s. being consulted on the siting of its replacement, and on 24 January 1662 says 'His Majesty entertained me with his intentions of building his Palace of Greenwich and quite demolishing the old one, on which I declared my thoughts.' See Pevsner-Cherry, *BoE.*, *London South* and note 216 below.

22 Horn Stairs and Cuckolds Point are still to be found in Rotherhithe. For the legend of Cuckolds Point and its flagpole see *The Diary of Henry Machin (from 1550 to 1563)*, Camden Society xlii (1848).

23 First Dutch war (1652–4); see *Introduction* note 12.

we sailed by, a foreman of the waterman came alongside in a rowing boat to challenge us, but when we showed him the permit from the Lord Mayor of Gravesend he let us pass. We went past the Tower and stepped on land at the Tower Wharf at midday at about half past twelve.

Having thus arrived at London we went to stay with a cloth merchant at the Three Mariners in Tower Street, where Mr. Willem de Peyster had booked two rooms for us.

I went for a walk with Mr. Jacob Thierry to the bridge and saw there all the heads on stakes, 19 or 20 in number, amongst them the head of Hugh Peters the preacher.[24] From there we went to the Tower, which we inspected from the outside, and to St. Katherine's, a little further along the river; in this neighbourhood live many Dutchmen, innkeepers and others.

On the 15th August we went to see the Tower from the inside; first we came to the Lion Tower, built by Edward IV to hold the three leopards which Emperor Frederic had presented to him. People of high rank used to be their keepers, who drew a remuneration from the Crown.[25] The lion cages, which are two feet high, have strong wooden bars. The lions are kept on the upper ones; first one sees two lions, then one lion with a dog as companion, then the King Charles Stuart lion, then the York's lion, and then the Duke of Gloucester's lion. After that a large beautiful leopard, then two eagles, then a lioness called Queen Mary, and finally a very young leopard.

From there we went down to the river and through the royal guard house, which is manned by a strong watch. There we asked for permission to go in, and they detailed a soldier to escort us and to show us round. As one passes through the gate, one sees behind one several pieces of cannon facing the large square to protect the gate. Four pieces are mounted on a platform in front of a watchhouse. At the time there was there a lot of large and small cannons, mortars, grenades and other war materials lying around. Next we walked round the inside of the walls, in circumference about as large as that of Flushing, well provided with cannon and guards, and protected almost all round by very wide water-filled ditches. There is, amongst others, a watergate, fitted with a very strong iron portcullis, through which criminals and traitors are generally brought in by water and kept in gatehouses and towers.

After we had seen the grounds and walls from the inside we went to

24 Hugh Peters (1598–1660), Commonwealth preacher, who, after the Restoration, was condemned for allegedly plotting with Cromwell for the execution of Charles I. Hanged at Charing Cross in October 1660 (DNB).

25 For the office of Lion Keeper see Strype's 1720 edition of Stow's *Survey of London*, p. 118, and Howel's *Londinopolis* (1657), p. 24.

look at the armoury;[26] first up some steps we were shown a large room full of new muskets, carbines, firelocks and pistols, heavy pistols or long tubes, copper muskets, some leather-covered lances, which of old the knights on horseback used to carry. Also a strange piece, six barrels mounted in wood, the height and shape of a small table, standing on small wheels, whose barrels can all be opened and closed together at the rear by means of a screw, and are all fired off together at the same time. Next there are several rooms full of old and new shooting gear. There is also the carbine, fowling piece and pistol of Henry VIII, which are very heavy and of a strange make, also an interesting small gun belonging to the present King Charles II, and another of the Duke of Gloucester, which they are said to have used to practise when young.

Then follow several rooms full of all kinds of strange, ancient arms, such as morning stars, evening stars, peculiar Polish and Danish fist-hammers and iron clubs, some with one, two, or 3 pistols in front between the steel spikes, some metal-clad right up to the end, strange javelins, spears, and pikes, also some ancient shields with pistols mounted through their centre; some old Spanish pikes covered with velvet and other tack for the accommodation of the shoulder, further a lot of other arms, most of them captured from the Spanish in several battles by the gallant and shrewd naval commander Sir Francis Drake and others. They also show here a peculiar relic, King Henry VIII's swansdown coverlet,[27] which he used to wear over his codpiece, into which the English girls and women as an obeisance stick a pin and remove it and take it with them as a titillating keepsake.

In the next room there are thousands of pieces of horsemen's armour and equipment, and also foot soldiers' gear, and lots of horse armour. Next follows a long room, in which behind a rail the body armour of several Kings and their horses' armour are lined up in a row, of very ancient and uncommon fashion, but all well looked after and kept polished. According to the keeper, there is the armour of Prince Henry, King Henry VIII, King Henry VII, Edward III, Charles I, Edward IV, Henry VI, the Duke of Gloucester,[28] Charles Brandon, Duke of

26 Mrs Sarah Barter-Bailey, librarian of the Royal Armories, has kindly compared Schellinks's description with contemporary inventories and thereby enabled us to identify some armour and locations described, and also several personalities, whose names are grossly misspelled in the MSS. The correct spelling is given where identified. It seems that Schellinks's tour started in the 'small gun office', where some curiosities were at the time included amongst new arms. He ends his tour in 'a room full of pikes'. These were kept at the time in 'the long storehouse', which was partly behind the chapel, which would explain the comment that he 'saw the chapel through a window'.

27 The Swansdown Coverlet covering the codpiece can be seen on some contemporary portraits of Henry VIII.

28 Schellinks says here 'Duke of Gloucester', but the contemporary inventories (note 26) prove this to be that of the Earl of Leicester.

Suffolk, and that of William the Conqueror. Then an enormously large cuirass and a long horseman's sword of John of Gaunt, Duke of Lancaster. Next to this is a cuirass of the jester or buffoon of Henry VII, the helmet with large iron ramshorns on the top and large iron spectacles on the nose, and the visor a grinning face. Nearby is a heavy iron ring with pointed iron spikes inside and out; at the time of the religious persecution of the Protestants this was put on their bare necks and shoulders to torture them.

Then follows a lot of war armour and weaponry captured from the French, and a very large lance of Henry VII, and the cuirass which he wore when he was only 7 years old, also the cuirass of Lord de Courcy, who was a prisoner and went over to France to fight a duel with the King, and won the sword which is shown here.[29] Further the lance of Charles Brandon, and a cuirass of King Edward. Then in a case with bars two suits of body armour, one a present from the Great Mogul to the present King, the other the cuirass which the King wore in his youth in the battles between his father Charles I and parliament. Next much other uncommon armour for men and horses.

In another room there are some very strange cannon with three and seven muzzles, flat, oblong, rectangular, and also some large cannons mounted on timber, which Henry VIII used in the war against the French. After all these and other curiosities one descends into the naval armoury, full of all kinds of warships' stores, large and small cannon, grenades, mortars, strange missiles, incendiary and others, bolts, hand grenades and the like, and a lot of horse harness for pulling cannons. There was also a room full of pikes, and through a window we looked into the Tower Chapel, in which a service is held every Sunday.

On the tops of the four pinnacles on the roof of the Tower, Oliver Cromwell had gilt balls fitted to replace the crosses and copper weather vanes, which carried the King's arms. Likewise were, on all towers and spires all over England, the crosses replaced by weather vanes, except in one place in London, which was not easily accessible. In the Tower is also the Royal Mint, which employs a large number of people, and which we saw working at a later date;[30] it consists of eight or ten workshops in a line like shops in a street.

Still on the same day we went to the Moorfield, which not so long ago was just a muddy bog, but is now firm and dry. Coming from the city through a gate built in 1641 one has on the left the Moorgate, on

29 'Lord' de Courcy, the conqueror of Ulster (d.c.1219), was at one time imprisoned in the Tower. His exploits and great strength were legendary (see e.g. Fuller's *Worthies of England, Somerset*). Fuller's tale differs substantially from the one hinted at by Schellinks. In the eighteenth century Lord de Courcy's armour was shown in the Tower armoury with 'the very sword he took from the Champion of France'. See DNB and note 26 above.

30 See Schellinks's description of his visit to the Royal Mint on 28 March 1663.

which many limbs of traitors or accomplices of Oliver Cromwell are displayed on stakes. The Moorfield is now divided by some fine avenues into three large squares, the one nearest to the town wall fenced in with wooden railings round its green fields and provided with comfortable seats; some steps at the side of the dividing wall lead up to the second square, and similarly to the highest level, where, on summer evenings, there is always wrestling and fencing with sticks and billhooks, watched by crowds of people, who stand around in a large circle.

The procedure for the wrestling is as follows: An old man who is called vinegar or umpire throws two leather belts to the ground; one of the countrymen steps into the ring, takes up one of the belts and chooses west or north; if nobody takes up the challenge, vinegar calls west out or north out. If there is a contest the fighters put the belts on above their waists, and they are not allowed to attack each other below the belt, but they are allowed to kick the legs from under their opponent.[31]

From Moorfields we went to a nearby music hall; this hall has a gallery like the Lutheran Church in Amsterdam and is divided into alcoves, and people go there to dine and listen to the music of an organ, dulcimers, bass violins etc. There was also a remarkable performance by a buffoon or jester, who played a drunk and danced with a tame monkey and two or three burning candles, and made his exit by turning somersaults. There is also an eagle on show and a flamingo, and some other birds, and some other animals outside.

On the 16th August we went to the Bourse or Royal Exchange, built in 1568 by Sir Thomas Gresham. The City sold for 478 pounds sterling all the buildings and dwellings standing on the site, which had cost more than 3532 pounds before, and an alderman, on behalf of the City, gave the possession of it to the said knight, who had several times been acting as agent of her Royal Majesty Queen Elizabeth, and he erected this magnificent building at his own expense. The foundation stone was laid by him on 7th June 1566, and in 1570 her Majesty, accompanied by her nobility, came from her house in the Strand, called Somerset House, to dine at Sir Thomas Gresham's residence in Bishopsgate Street, and afterwards rode to the new exchange and, having inspected every part of the new building, and especially the shops, so richly furnished with all sorts of fine and costly goods and rarities, it gave her Majesty cause to have proclaimed by an herald and trumpets, that in future this place should be called the Royal Exchange and not otherwise. This building is very similar in style to the Bourse at Amsterdam, but

31 Wrestling was apparently between contenders from Devon and Cornwall (the West) and Cumberland (the North). See Strutt *Sports and Pastimes*, pp. 69–73 Pepys ii, 127. The Vinegar was a fellow who made the ring and kept order (OED). Fencing and prize fighting using various weapons, often with bloody results, is mentioned by Pepys several times.

somewhat more square; it has a tower in Cornhill, on whose top, as well as on the four corners of its roof and above every arch, stands a gilt grasshopper. In niches all round stand the statues of 26 Kings and queens, each with an inscription of the date of his death and some other particulars, as shown in the following list and notes[32]

List of the Kings of England
as they stand in order at the London Exchange

		years	ms	dys
Edwardus Confessor rex obit 4 January	anno:1060			
Haroldus rex obit 14 October	anno:1066			
Guillielmus rex Conqueror obit 7 September	anno:1087			
reigned		20:	11:	23
Guillielmus Rufus rex obit 2 August	anno:1100	12:	11:	18
Henry primus rex obit 1 December	anno:1135	35:	4:	11
Stefanus rex obit 25 October	anno:1154	18:	11:	18
Henry II rex obit 6 July	anno:1189	35:	9:	1
Richard I rex obit 6 April	anno:1199	9:	9:	0

NB. he has a stag on his left side and a lion under his feet

Johannes rex obit 14 November	anno:1216	17:	7:	0
Henry III rex obit 16 November	anno:1272	56:	1:	9
Eduward I rex obit 7 July	anno:1307	34:	8:	6
Eduward II rex obit 21 September	anno:1327	19:	7:	5
Eduward III rex obit 21 July	anno:1377	51:	5:	7
Richard II rex obit 29 September	anno:1399	22:	3:	14

NB. he has two crowns on his sword

Henry IV rex obit 20	anno:1412	13:	6:	3
Henry V rex obit 13 August	anno:1422	9:	5:	24
Henry VI rex obit 21 May	anno: 1471	38:	6:	8
Edward IV rex obit 9 April	anno:1483	23:	1:	8
Edward V rex obit	anno:1483		2:	18

NB. He is very young and the crown is not on his head but only hangs there

Richard III rex obit 22 August	anno:1485	2:	2:	5

Note: he looks towards the young Edward

Henry VII rex obit 22 April	anno:1509	23:	10:	12
Henry VIII rex obit 28 January	anno:1547	37:	10:	2
Edward VI rex obit 6 July	anno:1553	6:	5:	19
Maria regina obit 17 November	anno:1558	5:	4:	22
Elizabeth regina obit 4 March	anno:1602	44:	4:	16
Jacobus rex obit 27 March	anno:1625	22:	0:	3

32 The building described burned down in the great fire of 1666. The list below is as in Copenhagen MS; the Bodlerian MS differs slightly. Like the following Latin, neither is entirely accurate.

NB. Carolus primus monarcharium magnæ Britaniæ secundus Franciæ
et Hiberniæ, martirad coelum missus per ultimo, Jannuario 1648.
[Charles I, second King of Great Britain, King of France and Ireland,
martyred on the last day of January 1648]. This was put there by his
son; on Oliver Cromwell's order the earlier statue had first its hands
knocked off and was then altogether thrown down and had inscribed
above it in golden letters 'Carolus primus tiranus est'. The present
statue has on the righthand side a scroll with the inscription 'mag.
car.', and the orb lying under his feet, and an additional inscription by
the present King that his father reigned for 23 years, 10 months, and
2 days. For the present King the following inscription was made:
Carolus secundus monarcharium mag. Britanniæ tertius, Franciæ et
Hiberniæ Rex Anno ætatis suæ trigesimo, regni duodecimo, restau-
rationis primo, Dom. 1660 [Charles II, third King of Great Britain, of
France and Ireland King, in the thirtieth year of his age, the twelfth of
his reign and the first of his restoration, A.D. 1660]. This statue too
has a scroll inscribed with the word 'Amnestia', with the royal seal
hanging on it. *NB*. There are spaces left for two more Kings.

We then went to look at Leadenhall Market, where Mondays,
Wednesdays, and Saturdays much meat of all kinds comes for sale from
inside and outside the town; on Tuesdays there is a leather market
there, and on Thursdays and Fridays a well stocked hide market. In
the afternoon we went to see the bear and bull baiting at a place at
the upper end of St. John Street; the performance at the bear garden
was well worth seeing.

On the way back we looked at St. Paul's Church, and also the
hospital or orphanage. There are now 995 children in their care, the
youngest still being nursed out, all dressed in coats of blue cloth and
the boys with a flat cap with a flap on their heads, and a strap or belt
round their waist.[33]

We also saw the four triumphal arches,[34] very large and high and of
a fine design, one in Cornhill, another in Cheapside, a third in
Leadenhall, and the last in Fleet Street.

On the 17th August we went to the New or British Exchange; this
stands on the site of the stables of Durham House, built by Bishop
Thomas Hatfield, which were pulled down by the Earl of Salisbury,
who had the new Exchange built on the site. The first stone was laid
on 10 June 1608, and the building was completed in the following
November. The earl entertained the King and the Queen at a sump-

33 Refers to Christ's Hospital, founded 1553 as a home for orphans and poor children.
The boys' school moved to Horsham in 1902, where they wear the uniform described
(*EoL*).

34 Erected for the coronation of Charles II, 23 April 1661 o.s. Some of these were
blown down in the storm on 28 February 1662 (see note 74 below).

tuous banquet, and the King named the building the British Exchange. There are excellent shops all round on two floors, in which all kinds of fine goods can be got.[35]

From there we went to Charing Cross, so called because of an ancient monument, a stone cross, which King Edward I had erected in honour of his wife, Queen Eleonora; she died at Harby not far from Lincoln, and as her body was brought from there to Westminster, the King ordered that at every place where the cortège rested a stone cross should be erected bearing a statue of her and her coat of arms. The places where such crosses stood were Grantham, Woburn, Northampton, Stony Stratford, Dunstable, St. Albans, Waltham, Westcheap, and Charing. In 1644 the crosses at Charing and Westcheap were thrown down by order of the House of Commons and, under blowing of trumpets, totally broken up, as they had to be repaired so many times, not so much because of natural decay due to their age as from wilful damage done to them by people at night.[36]

In this place, Charing Cross, which is now surrounded by a wooden fence, many people of standing have been executed.

From there we went to look at the King's palace in Whitehall, from the outside a very handsome building. It was built by Cardinal Wolsey, Archbishop of York, who, when he lost the King's favour, was summoned to court and died on the way, allegedly from poison, so it was with all his possessions forfeited to the King, who renamed it Whitehall; before that it was called York Place. We then went to St. James Park, where the King, the Duke of York, General Monck and others of the nobility were sitting in great splendour in the royal carriages, two in each, the King with Monck, the Duke of York with his wife. They were setting out to go to the chase in great state and flourish, with a large retinue of knights and other noblemen, escorted by a group of horsemen, and went through the gate of St. James Park into Hyde Park. We went on towards Westminster, which we viewed inside and out. It is a very ancient building, its statues and fabric much damaged by their age. This location was originally called Thorney[37] because it was overgrown with thorns and thistles. These were rooted out by King Lucius anno 186; a temple of Apollo is said to have stood on the site, which was destroyed by an earthquake. On the ruins Stebertus, King of the East Saxons, is said to have built again a temple

35 The New Exchange opened in 1609: a shopping arcade with sleeping accommodation above, near the Adelphi. Pepys went shopping there several times (see Pepys iv, 100 and vii, 70 etc.).

36 Charing Cross: Parliament ordered its destruction in 1643, the actual demolition took place in 1647 (*EoL*)

37 Much of what follows, describing the ancient history of Westminster Abbey and London Bridge, comes from Stow's *Survey of London*, first published 1598.

to serve God, and to have dedicated it to St. Peter in the year 610. This building was destroyed by the Danes and rebuilt in 960 by Bishop Dunstan, who turned it into a monastery for twelve monks, which he called St. Peter of Westminster, as it lies to the west of London, and there was a church called Eastminster on Tower Hill. This famous Church of St. Peter has been added to over the years by many builders, in 950 by King Edgar, in 960 by Bishop Dunstan, then by Edward the Confessor, and finally by Henry III; he pulled down King Edward's building and started rebuilding it in magnificent style in 1229. This rebuilding was completed within 50 or 60 years. A chapel was added at the east end by Henry VII, which, for its outstanding beauty of build and decoration, inside as well as outside, is counted amongst the wonders of the world. At the bank of the river close to this chapel once stood the famous Old Palace, which in the time of Edward the Confessor was destroyed by fire. In this church of St. Peter or Westminster are many interesting ancient monuments and tombs of Kings and Queens of England, and of dukes, earls, princes, bishops, and other learned people. Next to this church is a collegiate church and a high school. In St. Peter's Church the Kings of England are crowned; there is a stone chair which once was one of the perquisites of the Scottish Kings and was brought here by Edward I from Scone in Scotland in 1297. There are also some statues in royal garments to be seen in wooden cases.

After we had seen all this we went in a prevoor from Westminster through London Bridge back to Tower Wharf, passing on our left 1. Whitehall. 2. Northampton House, now belonging to the Earl of Northumberland.[38] 3. York House or Buckingham Palace,[39] now the residence of the ambassadors. 4. Durham House, owned by the Earl of Pembroke. 5. Salisbury or Worcester House. 6. Savoy House, where, in the church, they preach in French but follow the English book of Common Prayer. 7. Somerset House, then Strand Bridge. 8. Arundel House, then Milford Lane and a square building, eight storeys high, called the Waterhouse. 9. Essex House. 10. the Temple Stairs between the two Temples. 11. Lord Dorset's, White Friars, Bridewell, Puddle Wharf. 12. Baynards Castle, Paulus Wharf, Broken Wharf, Queen Hithe, Three Cranes, Steelyard, Coldharbour, Old Swan, London Bridge, Lion Quay, Billingsgate, Customs House, Tower Wharf. At many of these places are stairs or jetties with steps to allow one to board boats and to disembark, and on each jetty or ferry lie many light

---

38 Northampton House, later Northumberland House, completed in 1605, demolished to make way for Northumberland Avenue c. 1873 (*EoL*).

39 York House or Buckingham House: between Charing Cross and the river, let in 1661 to the Spanish ambassador, according to *EoL*. This and most of the buildings, wharves and streets mentioned can be found in *EoL*.

boats to ferry people across. There are about   such watermen and scullers between Gravesend and Kingston, about 30 miles from London, the scullers row a skiff alone, and the boats which are rowed by two men are called 'paravoors'.[40]

On the opposite side of the river is Lambeth and three or four royal boathouses and others of the nobility, some still being under construction. On a bend of the river stands a Dutch sawmill.

On the 18th August we had a look at the Bridge and went over it to Southwark. This stone bridge across the river is a very fine and handsome building of 19 arches, and one walks over it as if it was through a street with large shops on both sides. These get most of their light from the rear over the river, and join across above, so that one passes under them as through an arcade or gallery. Most consist of one long rectangular room with dwellings above; the buildings are divided into sections with some breaks between them to allow a view of the river, and an opening for the daylight to come in to light up the passage. The shopkeepers live mostly upstairs. The river is deep enough to allow large merchant ships to lie at anchor close to the bridge, and the water flows very fast under the bridge, with a great roar and a tidal change of 6 to 7 feet.

London Bridge

To begin with people were set over there in boats; there was a ferry or crossing, which was owned by a man and his wife as long as they lived; when they died this was continued by their daughter Mary, who from her inheritance and the income from the ferry built a nunnery on the east side across the river, which was later converted into a monastery. The monks built a wooden bridge across the river, which they kept in repair at great cost. This bridge stood there for many years and was standing in 994 when Gosweyn, King of Denmark, in the reign of King Ethelred, besieged London. In 1135, the first year of King Steven, the bridge burned down with a large part of the town and the cost of the rebuilding and its upkeep were paid from the rents of the lands belonging to the bridge, and from the bequests made by several people over 215 years, before the building of the stone bridge. In 1176 the bridge was first built in stone by a priest and chaplain called Peter of Colechurch, with contributions from the King and a cardinal legate, and the Archbishop of Canterbury gave 1000 marks for the foundation. The course of the river was temporarily diverted by the digging of a ditch from Rotherhithe in the east to Battersea in the west. The bridge

40 Schellinks here defines a type of craft, seen in contemporary illustrations, used on the Thames for passenger transport. He variously spells it as *prevoor*, *parvoor*, or *paravoor*.

with its arches and the chapel on it was 33 years in building, and was finally completed by three citizens, Serle Mercer, William Almaine, and Benedict Botewrite, Peter Colechurch having died four years before. Next there was a fire in Southwark in the night of 10 July 1212, which set the Borough alight as well as the Church of Our Lady, and thousands of people came from the town over the bridge [to look]; a south wind set the north end of the bridge on fire, so that nobody could go back, and a little later the south end caught fire as well, and the people on the bridge, with death before them whichever way they turned, pressed together; many boats and all kinds of craft came to the rescue, but, because of the great throng of the people, a large number of them fell from the bridge into the water, so that more than 3000 people were drowned, besides those who were burned to death.

In the great frost and heavy snow in the year 1282 five arches of the bridge fell in with all that stood on them. In 1289 the bridge was so weakened through lack of maintenance that the people did not dare to walk over it. In 1381, when John Britain was Custos of London, the clergy raised large funds for the maintenance of the bridge. On St. George's day 1381 [according to Stow 1395] a great tournament was held on the bridge by Lord Crawford of Scotland and Lord Wells of England, so that at that time not so many houses can have stood on the bridge. The tower on London Bridge at the north end of the drawbridge, which was operated there for a long time, was built in 1426, and in 1633 the north side of this was so badly damaged by fire that three quarters of it were wrecked and this part is not yet properly rebuilt, because of the recent war as well as for other impediments. Further descriptions of the bridge and other matters relating to it can be read in the book *The Survey of London or Londinopolis* by James Howel Stow.[41]

On the 19th August we went to see Smithfield, a well known old established market. In former times tournaments were held there, and many martyrs suffered there at the stake for their religion. Regular market days are Tuesday and Friday, and on Fridays many horses are sold there in the open market,[42] but the best horses are to be found in the large number of stables which are around there. Much hay too comes there for sale, and cattle and sheep, for which stalls and pens are provided. There is also a horse pond for the horses. In the middle of Smithfield is a large square fenced in with a railing where executions are carried out.

41 *Londinopolis*; Schellinks seems to have mixed up here Stow's *Survey* (see note 25) and James Howel's *Londinopolis, an Historical Discourse of the City of London*, 1657.

42 Schellinks and Thierry later bought horses here for their journey to the west country, see below, 30 June 1662.

From there we went to Lincoln's Fields, a large square lying behind Lincoln College, where law students are taught. Round this square are many fine palace-like houses, all with forecourts behind high walls; one can count there seventy entrances with stone pillars and double doors[43] and many of the nobility live there. The Protector Cromwell had a row of new houses built there and established a place of execution in the square.

We then went from there to a place called Convent's garden or Covent Garden, because a large convent or nunnery once stood there; there is a large piazza or market place with excellent residences resting on pillars, which form a large arcade to walk through.[44]

From there we went to the Temples and saw there the walks and the fine halls, and the views over the river. In both these Inns of Court are colleges for the students of English Law. On the west side of the church or temple one sees on a round walk some ancient tombs on the ground, surrounded by iron railings, with stone figures on them of grey marble, eleven in number, eight of them knights in armour. Five lie with their legs crossed, as is the custom in the Holy Land to distinguish them from Turks and Jews, and three lie stretched out straight. The other tombs have plain tombstones. The first who lies cross-legged is William Marshall, the old Earl of Pembroke, who died in 1219, then William, his son, who died 1231, and his brother Gilbert Marshall, slain in a tournament in 1241.[45] In the English histories these two colleges are called the Middle Temple and the Inner Temple, and each has its own hall and gardens.

On the 20th August we went by boat to Lambeth and on to Vauxhall to see the very large and most beautiful and interesting gardens, called the new Spring Gardens.[46] Lots of people come there to amuse and refresh themselves, as it is a very pleasant place. From there we went to Lambeth, past the house of the Marquis of Worcester, and then to the King's brigantine or pleasure yacht, which is very light and elegant and decorated with all kinds of fine, richly gilt carvings, carrying three lanterns on her rear, and three or four pieces of cannon, and rowed

43 There is a small sketch at the bottom corner of the Copenhagen MS page, where Lincoln's Inn is described, showing one of the entrance gates with stone pillars.

44 Inigo Jones's famous Piazza and St. Paul's Church, Covent Garden, were built in the 1630s.

45 The effigies in Purbeck marble in Temple Church were badly damaged in the last war, but have been restored. Pevsner-Cherry, *BoE. London I*, lists these. The idea that those with their legs crossed had been on a crusade to the Holy Land, and Schellinks's explanation that the custom arose to distinguish them from Turks and Jews, does not have any foundation in fact.

46 New Spring Gardens, later better known as Vauxhall Gardens, laid out after the restoration. Visited by Evelyn on 2 July 1661, and by Pepys, who went to both the Old and the New Spring Gardens in May 1662 (Pepys iii, 95).

by 24 men. When the King goes in her to parliament she is decked out with an extremely costly embroidered cover, and the King's standard is flown from her stern, and all his trumpeters blow lustily.

On the 21st August in the morning we went to the Dutch church for the service, and in the afternoon to Whitechapel and from there to a small village called Hackney. There, in a place called Bethnal Green, stands a fine house within a stone wall called the Blind Beggar's House;[47] this was built by a beggar who also was able to give his daughter a large sum of money as dowry when she married. At Hackney there are two or three finishing schools, in which young girls are taught and instructed in good manners and gentility; on some days they practise dancing there.

From there we went past Stepney and Poultney to Islington, a nice walk from London.

On the 22nd August we went to the Moorfields and watched the fencing with sticks.[31]

On the 23rd we went by coach to the Admiralty Court to Sir Edward Walter,[48] herald and secretary of the king, and on to Westminster and Chelsea, a small but very pleasant place by the river. There are several fine villas and palaces there, one belonging to my Lord Roberts,[49] but especially Buckingham House, which is beautiful and was at the time the residence of the French ambassador. On the opposite side of the river lies Battersea.

On the 24th August we went by coach to the French Church, and also changed our lodgings and went to stay with a Mr. Camby, opposite the gate of the Dutch Church and close to the Exchange.

On the 25th we went by coach to Westminster and saw there the great hall, which was built by King Edward II, others say by King Richard II. This is the largest hall in England, and all the timber in it is supposed to be Irish oak, which is rot-proof. Here is the High Court of Justice, the highest the King's Bench, Common Pleas, and the Chancery, also the two chambers of Parliament, the Star Chamber, the Exchequer, the Court of War,[50] and the Court of the Duchy. Then

47 Blind Beggar's House, also called Bednall House or Kirby's Castle, at Bethnal Green, an Elizabethan mansion. Shown on Rocque's map of 1760. Pepys admired the house, and dined there in June 1663 with Sir William Rider, and stored his valuables there during the fire of London. (Pepys iv, 200; vii, 272). For the legend and ballad of the 'Blind beggar of Bednall Green' see F.J. Child, *English and Scottish Ballads* iv (1857), 161.

48 Sir Edward Walker (1612–77), Garter King of Arms (DNB); Pepys i, 160, vii, 410 etc.

49 Sir John Robartes, Lord Privy Seal (1661–73), lived at Danvers House, Chelsea (DNB); Pepys ii, 149 etc.

50 The Bodleian MS reads 'Court of War'. Stow does not mention such an office in his description of Westminster Hall but includes all others referred to by Schellinks. The

we saw the chamber of the lower house, with cloth covered seats all round in tiers, and the chamber of the upper house, hung all round with splendid tapestries, magnificently depicting all the sea battles of the reign of Queen Elizabeth and Edward, and on the panelling very lifelike portraits of the naval commanders; the king's throne stands under a splendidly embroidered canopy, its back very precious with gold and silver, worked with the needle by Queen Mary[51] during her imprisonment, in its middle the picture of a woman representing Spring, very good design and fine workmanship. Before the throne lie four large sacks or bales stuffed with wool and covered with red serge, as a constant reminder of the importance of the wool trade of the realm. Around this are the seats of the bishops and other lords. From there we were led to the king's chamber, which is hung with very ancient tapestries, depicting strange old legends and sceneries, exquisitely worked in gold and silver, really remarkable. Then we were shown some more chambers, too many to describe.

After having seen all this we went by boat from Westminster to look at a recently designed bowling green on board a large barge, which lies in the river near Whitehall, moored front and back on two anchors. On coming on board we saw first a large room, its walls and seats covered in green cloth; in a second, the king's room, everything was clad in red cloth and there were windows and mirrors all round. Outside is a gallery all round, and at one end is a spiral stair to the bowling green which is on the top; this is covered with green cloth when the king comes there to play. It is level like a green in the open air, with wooden tubs all round planted with all kinds of flowering plants and trees, and was to be surrounded by a decorative fence. This was invented by a Scotsman and was almost ready to be sold to the king, when it happened that he shot and killed his wife, and the whole establishment became forfeited to the king, and is now called the Scot's Folly.

In the afternoon we went to a great dinner at Mr. Luces,[52] and after the meal to the Moorfields to watch the wrestling, and then for a walk.

On the 26th August we went to Whitehall and saw there many rooms and galleries full of outstanding paintings by old and new Italian,

---

Copenhagen MS does not include these words, ending at 'Chancery'. See John Stow, *The Survey of London*, 1603 (Everyman's Library edn. 1987, pp. 416–8).

51 Mary, Queen of Scots developed her passion for embroidery during her years of confinement in various castles. The piece Schellinks described has not been traced. See Antonia Fraser, *Mary Queen of Scots*, 1969, p. 412.

52 Probably Jacob Lucie, an important merchant of Flemish descent, Alderman, London 1683–7, Deputy Governor, Royal Africa Company, 1684–5. See Pepys, ii. 66; x. 236; J.R. Woodhead, *The Rulers of London, 1660–89* (London and Middlesex Arch. Soc., 1965).

Dutch, and other masters. We went into the King's Chapel for the service, with the organ being played between the singing and the prayers. From there we went to the king's dining room and heard the reciting of the grace before the king's meal, and saw the king eat in public with his brother and the duchess. Then we returned to our lodgings, and in the afternoon we went again to the Admiralty Court, and from there to the Steelyard, where we had jolly refreshment at an excellent wine lodge, whose landlord hailed from Cologne.

On the 27th we went for a walk through the town and looked at the shops, markets, and everything else.

On the 28th August we went by coach to the Savoy House and went to the French Church at the Strand, which used to be the residence of the Dutch ambassadors and which had recently been repaired. The English Book of Common Prayer is used there.[53] On the way back we saw the Lord Mayor coming out of St. Paul's Church magnificently attired, with a heavy golden chain hanging back and front over his tabard down to the ground, and mounting his horse, which was very preciously and elegantly decked out in the old fashion with gold, velvet, and jewels. The sword was carried before him, its scabbard richly beset with jewels of golden emblems. Behind him rode two sheriffs, richly dressed in tabards with golden chains over these, their horses also richly decked, to escort the Lord Mayor, as is the custom, to his residence. In the afternoon we went to the Dutch Church and then went for a walk.

On the 29th we went again to the Admiralty Court, and after that Mr. Jan Thierry left for Holland.[54] After we had seen him off we went to the Moorfields to watch the fencing with sticks and cudgels.

On the 30th we went for walk; on the way from the Exchange we were at midday the guests of Mr. Chapplin, and in the afternoon we went to see the king's catering department, bakery, slaughterhouse, etc., a very large establishment.

On the 31st to Covent Garden and on to Whitehall, visiting some artist friends on the way. In the afternoon we were at a great banquet arranged by Mr. J. Thierry at the Ship Tavern in Bishopsgate. After the meal I went round on the outside of the town to Wapping and nearly to Limehouse, and returned home by way of St. Katherine's.

On the 1st September we went out walking with some friends.

On the 2nd in the morning Mr. Thierry had his trunks packed and went for form's sake out of town to keep out of the way, as they wanted

53 The French Church had in that year moved into the chancel of the original Savoy Chapel. A translation of the Book of Common Prayer was used (see Pepys iii, 207).

54 Mr. Jan Thierry, cousin of young Jaques Thierry, Schellinks' companion. For the activities of the Thierrys at the High Court of Admiralty see *Introduction* iii.

to make him an alderman.[55] In the afternoon we went to Whitehall and Westminster and set over to Vauxhall and Lambeth and to the Marquis of Worcester's house to deliver a letter to Caspar Calthoff,[56] crossed back to Westminster and returned by way of Covent Garden, where evening prayers were read to the soldiers.

On the 3rd we visited the St. Bartholomew Fair, the great market or fair held at Smithfield, which was full of stalls and all kind of conjurers and gamblers.

The 4th we went to the Dutch Church; after the service holy communion was served. One of the Dutch ambassadors, Heer van Goch from Zeeland, was present. We then went to the Italian Church and on to St. Paul's, where we again saw the Lord Mayor. We went to a Dutch tavern kept by man called Coppys for our meal, and then went for a walk outside.

On the 5th we walked about a little and had our meal again in the tavern mentioned and then took Mr. Thierry's trunk to the Dutch boat. In the afternoon we went again to the Moorfields to see the fighting. *NB*. This was an executions day after the sessions. There were some fifty persons condemned to be hanged, but the king had given them the choice to hang or to be transported as slaves to Jamaica or Barbados, and they all had accepted this.

On the 6th we had our meal at a tavern,[57] the King's Head, and then went to the St. Bartholomew Fair and watched some performances, and saw there also a young lion, a camel, and other animals.

On the 7th we went in the morning in a prevoor down the river to Greenwich, which we looked over thoroughly. Two elegant gilded pleasure yachts lay close to the palace, one a Dutch present, and the other of English make. On the way back we bought from a fisherman a basket of fish, which we had cooked and ate at an inn at St. Katherine's called Vlissing and got off past the Spring Gardens at a place called John the Diskin,[58] where one can see in a large long room

55 Schellinks uses the English word 'Alderman', however no record has been found of any Thierry having been proposed or appointed an alderman of the City. According to the minutes book of the Weavers' Company James Therry paid on 30 September 1661 o.s. his subscription and a £5 donation on his admission to the livery.

56 Edward, second marquis of Worcester, had leased Vauxhall Manor (on the riverside, near Spring gardens) from the Crown, where he carried out his mechanical and hydraulical experiments, assisted by Caspar Kaltoff, a 'practical working engineer or machinist, stated to be a Dutchman' (H. Dircks, *The Life, Times, and Scientific Labours of the second Marquis of Worcester*, London 1865, and *Survey of London* xxiii (Lambeth, 1951), part 1, 418 and appendix G).

57 He uses the term 'ordinary', an eating house, where meals were provided at a fixed price.

58 John Tradescant (d.1638) and his son John (1608–62) amassed a large collection of naturalia and other curiosa at their home in Lambeth, which was accessible to the public on payment of an admission fee. These were inherited by Elias Ashmole and transferred

a collection of rare antique curiosities, costumes of various nations and strange weapons, also fishes, plants, horns, shells, and many other things.

Our Departure from London

Thursday, the 8th, we took our leave at our lodgings and went over the Bridge to the Bear Inn, where some of our friends came and we had a farewell meal with them and drank some merry rounds. This place is at the corner of the bridge and has at the back a very pleasant view over the river. A fine decked barque lay there ready with six or seven oarsmen. At half past two in the afternoon we went on board with a large company, and so went from London down the river to Gravesend, where 12 or 13 warships were lying in the roadstead. We arrived there at half past six and went to stay at the Hen and Chickens, where we made good cheer with our friends deep into the night.

The 9th at 8 o'clock in the morning some of our friends took their leave, and we went by coach, and some of our friends on horseback, to Rochester and from there to Sittingbourne, where we had our midday meal at the White Hart. We continued our journey to Canterbury and in the evening took our lodgings there in the Lily, where many friends and acquaintances of Mr. J. Thierry, his correspondents, came to see him. All were entertained with a great meal, and rounds of farewells and healths were drunk into the night. Meanwhile word was sent to Sir Arnold Braems to let him know that we had arrived.

On the 10th September Sir Arnold came to our lodgings to welcome Mr. J. Thierry, and we had our breakfast with Mr. du Bois, a relation of Braems. We went on to Bridge, where we were sumptuously entertained in his great hall by Sir Arnold Braems with a large company of friends, ladies and gentlemen, and spent the afternoon in making good cheer and other pastimes, and left in the evening at 6 o'clock by coach for Dover. When we got there we were again merrily entertained by Mr. Walter Braems, the son of Sir Arnold Braems. We waited there till midnight for the tide to turn, when Mr. Thierry and his servant boarded the packet boat for Ostend, with the brother of Thomas Hill and the son of Voster, the postmaster of Dover. They had a strong favourable wind and arrived at Ostend early the next morning.

The 11th ditto, Sunday, the weather was bad and rainy all day. We went to the French Church, and at 5 o'clock in the afternoon Mr.

---

by him to Oxford, where they formed the foundation of the Ashmolean Museum. The tomb of John Ashmole the Elder is at St Mary's Church, Lambeth (see '*Ark to Ashmolean*', Ashmolean Museum and Tradescant Trust).

Thomas Hill and Mr. W. de Peyster left for London, having come all the way to see Mr. J. Thierry off.

On the 12th Mr. Jan Bollen, who had so far travelled with Mr. Jacques Thierry, rode at 11 o'clock in the morning to Rye, 30 miles from Dover, so we too left in the afternoon for Bridge, and safely arrived in the evening to a friendly welcome. Sir Arnold Braems gave us a room where we both could stay as long as we remained there, in fact we stayed for three months.

This estate of Sir Arnold Braems lies in a valley of outstanding beauty; it contains, in addition to his own fine residence, a large number of rooms, chambers, halls, and other good apartments; there is also a large deerpark with many deer and does, woods, a rabbit warren in the hills, and very beautiful, well kept pleasure grounds with fruit trees, well watered by a fast flowing, fresh sparkling stream of wonderfully clear sweet water. This splits up into several branches and rivulets, also some fishponds, in which a certain kind of fish called trout is bred, which is very similar to a large carp, and, prepared in the English manner, tastes very delicious. There are also some vineyards round the house and gardens, producing yearly two to three hogshead of wine. There is a dovecot like a chapel, in which are at all times so many young pigeons that throughout the whole summer and longer 12 to 14 dozen can be taken out every week to put into pies or prepared otherwise. His people go out hunting every day and catch a lot of partridges and pheasants, which we had every day on the table, besides a choice of other delicate food, all with the most delicious English sauces; there is an ample supply of drinks, different kinds of wine and perry, which is made from pears. He also has his own brewery, bakery, wine press, hop garden, barns, stables, oxen, cows, sheep, pigs, geese, ducks, corn and fruit, everything that one can desire in such an establishment. And because he is, with all this, so kind and hospitable, and keeps such a princely table, he has so many visits from noblemen, gentlemen and ladies, so that his table is always surrounded by his own people and outside guests. The church stands not far from his house, and he has the right to nominate a minister of his choice for it. He has planted a fine avenue of lime trees from his house to the church, under which one is protected from rain and sun. His lands and his annual income, which amounts to a considerable sum, had suffered much damage in the war between the king and parliament, but is now all restored to him. As we now had the freedom of the place we went walking and drawing every day in the countryside and in the villages in the neighbourhood as far as Canterbury. Sir Arnold Braems and his lady and others often went out hunting or driving in a carriage to visit friends in the neighbourhood, and Mr. Jacobi Thierry often went with them for his pleasure.

On the 6th October a general muster of seven or eight companies of the militia was held on the hill above Bishopsbourne, which lies at the bottom of the valley, each company 200 men strong. They were brought on and off, skirmishing in one or two groups, firing spiritedly at each other, commanded by numerous officers on horseback and on foot. They started in the morning, but had to stop it all towards evening because of strong winds and oncoming rain. All the men get a drink allowance to refresh themselves. This muster usually takes place about once a year. Every parish and household has to supply and arm as many men as it is able.

*Our Journey from Bridge to London
to see the election and show of the
New Lord Mayor*

Monday, the 7th November, at half past five in the morning we went in Sir Arnold Braems's coach from Bridge to Canterbury, and at 7 o'clock by the ordinary coach from there to Gravesend; we got to Sittingbourne at 1 o'clock and had our midday meal and refreshed ourselves. At 5 o'clock in the afternoon we passed through Rochester and arrived at half past six at Gravesend, where we found that almost all boats, barges, tiltboats, and lighthorsemen had gone taking people to London. We just managed to get the same waterman who had taken us to Margate and to London before, and went to the King's Head to refresh ourselves with mulled wine. We left at 8 o'clock in a prevoor, in bright moonshine and a favourable wind and tide, but soon the weather turned dirty and it started to rain. We arrived at London at 1 o'clock in the night, landed at Billingsgate and stayed at the Swan. The next day, the 8th November, we went at 7 o'clock in the morning to Mr. de Peyster and then to Sir Arnold Braems, whom we found still in bed, and then to Mr. Thomas Hill, who went with us to the river, and from there by boat to Paul's Wharf to a house with a view over the river, from where we could see all the elegant barges and everything which went on on the river. To get a still better view we took a rowing boat and had ourselves rowed through the crowd of all kinds of large and small craft up and down towards Westminster, and back again to Paul's Wharf; there was heavy rain in the morning, but the weather cleared up by 9 o'clock.

The London Show of the new Lord Mayor
proceeded like this[59]

On Tuesday the 29th October or the 8th November new style at 8
o'clock in the morning the new Lord Mayor was joined by the Master
Wardens or Sergeants of his Company in their tabards trimmed with
[foyns[60]], with their caps or hoods, the livery men in their gowns
trimmed with [budge] and their hoods, then 50 gentlemen ushers or
other magistrates in their plush coats, each with a golden chain about
his shoulder and round his body, and a white staff in his hand, twelve
other gentlemen carrying twelve banners, namely those of His Majesty,
the Duke of York, St. George's, the Lord Mayor's, the Duke of
Albemarle's or Monck's, Sir Thomas Foot's, Sir Thomas Allen's, Sir
William Wilde's, Recorder of the City, the Grocer's Company's, and
four more; then came 36 trumpeters, 14 drummers, and 3 pipers, then
various officers and officials, and 45 pensioners, all in their uniforms
and order according to the ancient rules and customs.

When the new Lord Mayor and all this company were assembled at
the Grocer's Hall, they were put in order by the marshall and in this
order went from there down the Old Jewry. The procession started
with the pensioners or gentlemen ushers, until they came to the Lord
Mayor's door. There all the aldermen and two sheriffs waited in their
scarlet fur-trimmed gowns with their gold chains round their necks,
and after a little while, mounted with the new Lord Mayor their
elaborately decked horses and rode with all this state to the Guildhall,
where the old Lord Mayor received the new Lord Mayor and rode
with him down St. Lawrence Lane and Soper Lane to the Three
Cranes Wharf; on the west end of this wharf the Lord Mayor, aldermen
and their attendants boarded his barge, and so also all the 24 guilds
according to ancient use and custom.

All these Companies' and other barges or long light rowing sloops
were most elegantly decorated, gilded and painted with all kinds of
devices, and with covers with their coats of arms draped over them,
with banners, vanes, pennants, flags, standards etc. fluttering all round,
below and above, also front and rear full of musicians competing with
each other in playing their bass-viols, cornets, crumhorns, shawms,
trombones etc. The barges were rowed by 12, 16, 18, even 20 men,

59 The Lord Mayor installed in 1661 was Sir John Frederick. See John Tatham,
London's Tryumphs ... in honour of ... Sr. John Frederick, London: Thomas Mabb 1662, which
describes the ceremonies of 1661. J. Flesher, *The order of my Lord Mayor, the aldermen and the
sheriffs...*, 1656, laid down procedures for formal occasions. Schellinks may have used
these sources for his accurate description, cf. note 220.

60 The MSS leave a blank here. The description is completed by reference to the
sources quoted in note 59. *Foyns* = beech marten. *Budge* = lambskin dressed with the
wool outside.

and many of these oarsmen were very neatly dressed, those of the Lord Mayor's with leopards' skins, etc.

Many other barges, which did not belong to any particular Company or Guild, were also on the water, and were vying with the others in their finery. Many yachts and other craft fired salvoes as the barques of the Lord Mayor and the Companies passed, and from across the river opposite Westminster three rounds were fired from 30 cannons as these most elaborately and beautifully decorated Companies' barges passed. The liverymen of each guild, dressed in their tabards, sat in their barges, which could be recognised by their Companies' banners.

When they had all gone on board they hastened up the river rowing to Westminster. Near the temple the Lord Mayor was rowed close to a rigged and manned ship. On its forepart was placed Galatea, a sea nymph, riding in a chariot drawn by two dolphins, with two nymphs sitting on their backs playing on harps, behind them two sea-lions riding on the surface of the water, and on their backs sat two tritons.[61] As the Lord Mayor drew near, the boatswain gave orders to the crew to perform some boat drill. After this the captain of the ship addressed the Lord Mayor with an eulogy, and in this manner the barges came, under the firing of cannons, to Westminster.

There the Lord Mayor, aldermen, and companies disembarked, proceeded through a passage cleared for them to the hall and there performed several ceremonies, duties, and obligations, as the oath to be true in his government, and the sealing of writs to the upholding of this court. This done he took his leave of the Lord Chancellor, the Barons of the Treasury and having given some alms to the poor, all returned to their several barges and went down the river to Baynard's Castle,[62] where the burghers stood to on the walls, firing off cannons and muskets.

The Lord Mayor and the Companies landed at St. Paul's, where they were received by a line of the bachelors and gentlemen ushers, who had not been to Westminster. As they neared St. Paul's the Lord Mayor was met near the school by another display representing the Temple of Janus, with a gryphon in front and behind, and persons in antique dress on them, each carrying a banner in one hand and a shield in the other. As the Lord Mayor came up to Janus he was addressed by him with an eulogy. This done, the display was conveyed to the wide street Cheapside and there set up between a display of a graceful large merchant ship and another of two sea-lions on which sat

61 This barge can clearly be seen in the 'Aqua Triumphalis' print, showing the arrival of the King and Queen at Whitehall on 23 August 1662.

62 Baynard's Castle, a medieval castle, last rebuilt by Humphrey, duke of Gloucester, which stood near the present City of London School. Leased to the Earl of Pembroke at the time (Pepys i, 178 and *EoL*).

some figures nicely dressed and of fine stature. The procession moved on into Foster Lane, where another display awaited the Lord Mayor: Galatea, Polyphemus, and Acis, with a fountain running with wine and milk. Here the speech was addressed to the Lord Mayor, His Majesty, and the nobility. The speech over, the Lord Mayor and his entire procession moved on and were met at St. Lawrence Lane by another display, Justice and Mercy: Justice, with a wreath of stars, does homage to Mercy, dressed in white, with a lamb emblem on her breast. Justice addressed the Lord Mayor with an oration, and after that the Lord Mayor went to the Guildhall for the banquet.

In the afternoon he was met at Foster Lane by a display of Americans trading with the Christians. First appeared some Europeans, in the dress and fashions of various nations. Their leader was sitting on a camel and addressed the Lord Mayor with a speech about the increase and growth of the trade, and, after some more expressions of respect and a dialogue between Justice and Mercy, the Lord Mayor passed several other displays, amongst them one full of clowns, who performed all kinds of drolleries and pranks, playing on viols, dulcimers, clapbones, castanets, bladders on a stick strung with strings, and the like. In this manner the Lord Mayor is escorted to his house, and there the Companies, who had accompanied him, departed in order and at ease, each going to their own particular hall with their vanes, banners, standards, and pennants of silk, richly decorated with golden and silver devices and jewels, carried by the watermen in front of their companies. These are kept at their guildhalls for the annual [Lord Mayor's] show and great Silkworkers' show, and were taken there from the Grocers' Hall. This guild has twice in a short time borne with great honour the costs of such a large and splendid show.

Nota: This show was held in the presence of His Royal Majesty, of his Highness the Duke of York, the Lords or Privy Councillors, and other great noblemen and courtiers, and an incredibly large crowd of sightseers, from the country all round as well as townspeople and strangers to London.

Nota: On this day the old Lord Mayor rides alone from his house to the Guildhall, without aldermen or attendants, except a gentleman usher, bareheaded, his huntsman and Water bailiff, and his personal servant etc., and after he arrives with the new Lord Mayor at the palace of Westminster, they put on their robes and go up to the [Exchequer] where the new Lord Mayor takes the oath. After that they return to the King's Bench and the Commons, take off their robes and go to the royal tombs at Westminster Abbey, and go back by water, and after they have disembarked ride to the Guildhall to the banquet.

Having seen the Lord Mayor's show we left London with Sir Arnold Braems on 14th November at seven o'clock in the evening for

Gravesend, where we arrived at twelve o'clock and stayed at the Posthorn, and rode the next morning by coach to Canterbury.

On 19 November went again to Canterbury.

On 1 December we sent our luggage in advance to London.

On Sunday, 4 December after the evening meal, we took, with our thanks, our leave from Sir Arnold Braems and Madame his wife and all the ladies.

Our Departure from Bridge

As we had bid adieu to Sir Arnold Braems and Madame in their bed chamber, we went early in the morning of the 5th with Mr. Pamer, the brother of Madame, and the falconer, who was to take back our horses, before daybreak from Bridge to Canterbury, where we arrived at 7 o'clock and had our breakfast at our old inn, the Lily. We went on from there by coach and got to Sittingbourne, the normal posting station, at 8 o'clock, but did not stop there because of the shortness of the day, rode to Rochester, and arrived at Gravesend at 5 o'clock in fine weather, and stayed, as before, in the Posthorn, where we found company, an acquaintance of Sir Arnold Braems and Mr. Pamer, Sir Anthonester and another knight with his lady and other friends.

On 6 December at 8 o'clock in the morning we went 18 strong in a lighthorseman, a large boat with a helmsman and five oarsmen, which Sir Anthonester had hired. Setting out we headed straight into the wind, which was blowing up strongly and it stormed so badly that our foremast snapped while we were under sail, and in the end we had to strike our main sail and take it in, because our gunwale was continuously dipping under water, and the ladies groaned loudly and the gentlemen swore and threatened the waterman mightily and wanted to cut the sheet, as he insisted to sail some reaches, because they could not use the oars properly, as the tide was running against the raging wind, and the river ran so hollow, and the boat kept shipping water, so that in the end several guzzlers of our company presented the morning offering to the river god, indeed were so generous as to throw to the fishes (as if they had cost no money), all kinds of English fancy sustenance such as sack, Spanish wine, buttered eels, spirits, brandy, small and strong beer, cakes, pudding, and other delicacies more, for the crabs to scramble for their share of the treat. The zeal of several to play piquet was soon extinguished by the spray. Some became so pale round their beak as if they were indisposed, and they were not the only ones. In the end it was much the same, except that it was not night, as our experience in the lighthorseman near Margate in the stormy night at sea. Now, thanks to the efforts of our oarsmen, we got at long last past Cockleshaven, landed at 3 o'clock in the afternoon at Tower Wharf, and went to our lodgings at Messrs Abraham and Thomas Hill in Lime Street. This was to be our winter quarters for the next two months, and we were there well boarded and lodged.

It was very unsafe to travel by night on the river because of the river pirates, who attack the boats going up and down river and beat up the passengers, demanding their money; the Lord Mayor's waterman was sitting with some others in gaol for such an offence.

On the 7th December a weaver called John James was hanged and quartered at Tyburn for having preached against the King at a certain house in Whitechapel; his head was put up on a stake as a warning for others.

On the 9th we went with Mr. Hill by coach to the King's playhouse and saw there the play 'Love the First'. The annual rent of this playhouse is 3000 guilders; the King has presented to it his richly embroidered tabard, which had cost 15000 guilders, in which he rode to his coronation at Westminster.

Anno 1662

On 11th January we went to Lincoln's College and saw there the triumph of the 'Prince de la Grange'.[63]

Nota. At the beginning of a King's reign one of the students is chosen by the professors of the college whose turn it is, to act as a prince, who has to keep open court for his college for 13 days from Christmas until Twelfth Night; during this time the professors and governors have nothing to say, while he holds court like a king, appoints all kinds of high and low officers, and has an expensively dressed retinue. The prince this year was a Sir Lard, the son of a mighty rich man from the Principality of Wales, who has 140 ploughs working on his own land. They say that his court costs this prince quite   pound sterling. The other students contribute somewhat towards this, but not very much. This prince, pretending that his baggage had not yet arrived, sends his chancellor as an ambassador to the King, with a letter, requesting two of his maces, which are sent to him and are carried at all times behind his halberdiers before him and his council. He has to entertain the King with many important persons and his entire college at a royal banquet, upholding his dignity as the King himself, addressing him as his brother. He always remains covered, while everybody attends to him bareheaded. He wears a different dress every day; the robes which he wore for the King's visit cost him £350.

63 *Evelyn* reports on 1 January 1661/2 o.s. being 'invited to the solemn foolery of the Prince de la Grange at Lincoln's Inn' and adds 'One Mr. Lort was the young spark who maintained the pageantry.'

All told he is an expensive but short lived king. On the same day we went to look at the Fleet prison, where a very great number of people are held for debt. They go out freely with a warder, who receives his payment for this from the prisoner and stands surety for him. The place has a large wide yard on which is a bowling alley.

On the 12th we went to the bear baiting and bullfight.

On the 16th we went to look at the Inner and Middle Temple.

On the 20th we were to dinner with Mr. Jan Thierry at the Wheatsheaf.

On the 27th we went to look at Bedlam,[64] the lunatic asylum, founded in 1246 by Simon Fitzmary, Sheriff of London.

On the 28th we went to the Old Bailey, the court house, and saw there prisoners in criminal cases being judged by the Lord Mayor and the higher justices and sheriffs.

In the afternoon we went to see the Charterhouse,[65] a very large building and grand in its conception, halls, chambers, kitchens, school, and many other rooms, besides galleries, a beautiful church, and a very fine, pleasant garden with attractive walks.

On 29th January, Sunday, we went to Islington to hear the sermon.

On the 30th we saw four thieves being hanged at Holborn above King's Gate, and six outside at Tyburn. In the afternoon we went to see the French comedy 'Andromeda'.

On the 31st we went with some friends to dinner outside London at the Artillery Garden, for the hanging of the signboard showing the Amsterdam Bourse, which Mr. Jan Thierry had sent over for the ward.[66]

On the 1st February we saw at the Red Bull the English Comedy play 'The Newly made Lord'.

On the 2nd February we were at Westminster Hall to watch the   that is the beginning of the law term, which occurs four times in the year, when all   .[67]

On the 4th we saw the play 'A New Way To Pay Old Debts'.

On the 5th, Sunday, we were at the Lord Mayor's at a wonderful dinner; all the judges were there in their red, fur trimmed robes, and many other officers, altogether some eighty people. In the afternoon we went to the wine cellar to taste the wine and sack.

---

64 Bedlam, a corruption of Bethlehem, originally a priory of St. Mary of Bethlehem, situated just outside Bishop's Gate. Since the fourteenth century used as a lunatic asylum, commonly visited by sightseers. Moved to Moorfields in 1676 (*EoL*).

65 Charterhouse Hospital for old gentlemen, and a school set up in 1661. The school moved to Godalming in 1872 (*EoL*).

66 Artillery Gardens was off Pettycoat Lane. The ward, for which Thierry had sent over a signboard might have been Bishop's Gate Without (*EoL*).

67 The start of Hilary Law Term.

On the 6th we walked with thousands of people to Tyburn and saw there Lord Monson, Sir Henry Mildmay, and Mr. [Robert] Wallop[68] lying in their tabards on a little straw on a hurdle being dragged through under the gallows, where some articles were read to them and then torn up. After that they were again dragged through the town back to the tower. Their sentence is that they are to be dragged through under the gallows on this day every year.

In the afternoon we went outside London to see and to talk to an old man of 114 years, who walked with us through his garden. We also saw Bridewell otherwise the house of correction for prostitutes and rogues.[69]

On the 8th we went to Whitehall and walked to Westminster and round outside through the meadows. Went to the Duke of York's house to see 'The Maid in the Mill' being played.

The 9th February or 30th January old style is kept as a holy day in memory of His martyred Majesty Charles the First. We went to the Tower to hear the sermon there, but nobody was allowed inside.

On the 11th we rented a chamber in Fleet Street near the Temple Bar and St. Dunstan's Church.

On the 12th or 2nd February old style, Sunday, we went, as it was Purification of Mary or Candlemas Day, to the service at the King's Chapel at Whitehall. The music, voices and instruments, were extraordinarily beautiful. The sword was carried before the King, who knelt before the altar and offered in a large exquisitely driven silver gilt dish, which the Bishop of London held out to him, a handful of gold specie. In the afternoon we saw the King dine in great style with the Duke and the Duchess of York.

On the 13th February we moved from Mr. Thomas Hill's, where we had been staying so long,[70] to our newly hired accommodation in Fleet Street.

On the 14th we were the guests of Mr. Boellin.

On the 16th we saw at the Comedy the play 'The Cruelty of Love'.

On the 17th we went to Whitehall and, in the Banqueting House, watched the King healing the King's evil[71] or touching the sick. The King was sitting on a chair, a prayer was read by one of the clergy,

---

68 They were members of the tribunal condemning Charles I, but did not sign the death warrant, so their lives were spared, but they were condemned to this annual penance in 1661 (see Pepys iii, 19).

69 Bridewell Hospital at the time was a house of correction, where punishment was meted out in public. Orphans and young criminals were trained there for various occupation (EoL).

70 Schellinks went there on 6 December 1661.

71 The King's Evil, scrofula, was supposed to be cured by the touch of a King; the ceremony was revived after the Restoration (Pepys i, 182; ii, 74).

then came the sick one by one and kneeled before the King, who touched them with both his hands under the chin and spoke a few words. This sickness is a painfully sore goitre and is hard to cure. After he has touched them the patients come one by one to kneel again before him, and he hangs a piece of gold on a white silk ribbon round each man's neck. After this there is another prayer, and he washes his hands.

On the 21st we saw in the Comedy the play 'Rule a wife and have a wife'.

On the 12th, or 22nd February new style is 'Vastenavond', Shrove Tuesday in England and their Lent or fasts starts and one eats pancakes. Their entertainment then is to throw at the cock. In London one sees in every street, wherever one goes, many apprentice boys running with, under their arms, a cock with a string on its foot, on which is a spike, which they push firmly into the ground between the stones. They always look for an open space and, for a penny, let people throw their cudgel from a good distance at the cock, and he, who kills the cock, gets it. In the country or with countryfolk they bury a cock with only its head above ground, and blindfold a person and turn him two or three times round himself, and he then tries to hit the cock with a flail, and the one who hits it or comes closest to it gets the prize.[72]

The 14th February or 24th new style is St. Valentine's Day, of which here in England much to-do is made by high and low and rich and poor. So it is customary, alike for married as well as unmarried people, that the first person one meets in the morning, that is, if one is a man, the first woman or girl, becomes one's Valentine. He asks her name which he takes down and carries on a long strip of paper in his hat band, and in the same way the woman or girl wears his name on her bodice; but it is the practice that they meet on the evening before and choose each other for their Valentine, and, come Easter, they send each other gloves, silk stockings, or sometimes a miniature portrait, which the ladies wear to foster the friendship.[73]

On the 24th we went to the King's Playhouse to see 'The Alchemist'.

On the same day we went to see the Chancery.

On the 25th We saw at the Duke of York's Playhouse 'The Law against Lovers', which is judged to be their best play.

72 The game of 'Throwing at Cocks' was considered a fair sport in the time of Henry VIII and James I and continued well into the eighteenth century. The duke of Newcastle recommended the game 'Thrashing of hens' at Shrove Tuesday to Charles II as 'one of the divertisements to amuse the people's thoughts and keep them in harmless action'. See Joan Thirsk, *The Restoration*, 1976, p. 184, and also Vernon Bartlett *The Past of Pastimes*; Strutt, *Sport and Pastimes*, p. 292.

73 Both Pepys and his wife took St Valentine's day seriously, arranging the first person to be met to be a desirable Valentine. (Pepys iii, 28–9 and other years on 14th February).

Sunday, the 26th, we heard the Bishop of Gloucester preach, expounding his text, Isaiah c.21, v.11 and 12, very sternly against the Presbyterians. In the afternoon we went to the French service at the Savoy House in the Strand.

On the 28th February there was a dreadfully violent thunderstorm with a gale which at about 9 o'clock in the morning threw over a heavy triumphal arch, which stood close to our lodgings in Fleet Street, causing great damage to the nearby houses, but nobody was hurt by it, as its fall was expected any moment. All the other arches were badly damaged and ruined, and so were many houses and other buildings, and some people got killed and many were injured. The storm was at its worst in the county of Herefordshire, and around there threw down an incredible number of large grain barns and trees etc.[74]

March

On the 4th we went to the Old Bailey or the Law Courts to see the prisoners and hear them being examined and condemned for criminal offences. There were then four condemned to hang, one woman and three men.

Sunday, on the 5th, we went to church at Newgate, a gate where only rogues and thieves are imprisoned, to hear the death or penance sermon for the condemned, who were present there, and were, after the service, spoken to one by one individually and admonished by the chaplain.

On the 6th March we went to Tyburn to see the hanging of the condemned, but the execution was postponed for one month to obtain further evidence.

On the 8th we went to Southwark to see the session or assizes. None had been held there for two years. The civil cases were heard in a small chapel, the criminal cases in a wooden building erected for this purpose. The Sheriffs and the nobility of Surrey come to receive the judges at the foot of London Bridge, with blowing of trumpets, with many constables in new liveries, and other marks of honour.

On the 9th and 10th we were again at Southwark and saw several being branded on the hand, and many were condemned to hang, who then have both their arms tied behind their backs with a thin rope to mark them, but some obtained a pardon from the King.

NB. Nine men and three women were condemned, and eleven branded on the hand.

---

74 'Windy Tuesday': 'perhaps the worst storm between 1362 and 1703' (Pepys iii, 32 (footnote) and note 34 above.

We went walking right to the end of Rotherhithe, and returned by boat to Billingsgate.

On the first of March old style,

being St. David's Day, the day of the patron saint of Wales, when, according to ancient custom, all people born in that principality put a leek in the band of their hats. That is supposed to be in memory of a battle fought and won by them on St. David's Day, in which they wore them as a mark to distinguish themselves from their enemies. So His Majesty and many great Lords and gentlemen, common people, and even lackeys, coachmen, porters, and all kinds of riff-raff and layabouts wear one on their hats.

NB. The office to fix the leek to the King's hat on this day is worth 600 guilders.

We saw some countryfolk carry such large leeks on their hats that their heads hung almost sideways because of them. And so on this day the Welshmen are greatly teased by the English, not only by calling after them Taffey, Taffey, or David, David, but also by hanging out all kinds of dolls and scarecrows with leeks on their heads, and as they celebrate the day with heavy boozing, and both sides, from the ale, strong beer, sack and claret, become short-tempered, obstinate, and wild, so it is not often that this day goes by without mishaps, and without one or the other getting into an argument or a blood fight. Thus it happened this year that near Westminster a Welsh nobleman stabbed an Englishman. So too an English cook, who, for fun, stuck a leek on his hat and addressed, as a fellow countryman, a great lord, a Welshman, who passed by with his suite, who responded in Welsh, which is as different from English as French is from Dutch. When the cook replied sneeringly in English, the lord went for him, the cook fled into his shop and grabbed a spit from the fire and with this attacked the Welshman, who, supported by his servants with their rapiers, all turned against the cook, who was immediately helped by all sorts of rabble, throwing dirt and other things, so that in the end he was compelled to retreat, and, the furore getting greater, he was forced to take to the water, and, although he had got help, the mob, fighting furiously, got into the boat, and if His Majesty had not sent help quickly by water, they could easily have been killed.

Sunday, the 12th March, we went to church at the King's Chapel at Whitehall. His Majesty, the Duke of York, and many of the nobility were there. The Bishop of Coventry and Lichfield preached, his text was Numbers c.26 v., very harsh against the Presbyterians. In the afternoon we went to the service in Westminster, and walked around London.

On the 13th we went to Southwark to see the malefactors being tried; there were four in number, two men and two women, and, as they were brought on a cart from the prison at the Red Lion to the court and were about   miles away, they jumped from the cart like acrobats.

On the 19th to Whitehall, to the King in his Chapel, and heard the Bishop of Peterborough preach.

On the 20th we went to St. Katharine's to see to the provisions, which had been sent to us, and then went to the Tower to look at all that was to be seen, and then went into the Mint, where I struck a silver halfcrown as a keepsake.[75]

On the 24th we were on the ship *The Black Horse*, belonging to Mynheer Jaques Thierry, which had arrived from Barbados. That afternoon we were guests at Ratcliffe with a large company of our acquaintants, came through Hackney, where we refreshed ourselves with some of our companions and returned to London.

On the 25th we went to the upper end of Holborn, and walked outside the City towards Whitechapel.

Sunday, on the 26th, we went to church in Hackney.

April

On the 1st we saw the play 'Love lies Bleeding'.

On the 4th we saw the play 'The Fair Maid from the West'.

Easter day, on the 9th, we were the guests of Mr. Pettecoms, agent of Denmark.

On the 10th, or the 31st March old style, Easter Monday, we saw the Lord Mayor ride in great style in the annual procession to a place outside Bishopsgate called Spitalfields, where on three successive days a sermon is preached in the open field, where a covered pulpit is erected for that purpose, and also some other buildings for the Lord Mayor and the aldermen, all the ladies, and also the whole procession, as can be seen in the attached drawing.[76]

The order of this Procession was as follows:

First came all the apprentices or young trainees of the Bridewell Hospital, shoemakers, weavers, tailors, and all kinds of crafts, dressed

75 The mint at this time was in the Tower. Schellinks gives a detailed description of it on 28 March 1663.

76 Spital sermons were preached annually in the open until 1642, revived at the Restoration; only the Lord Mayor and aldermen sat under cover. Pepys went to listen to the sermon two days later, but got bored (*EoL* and Pepys iii, 57–8). The drawing is not with the MS.

in blue with grey hoods, each with their master, walking in pairs. 2. There follows a large number of old men and women, living on the charity of the Lady Ramsey,[77] with red caps and blue coats, with the letters MR sewn to their dress. 3. Then came a large number of young children, boys and girls, in two and twos, who are brought up and educated at Christ's Hospital, all dressed in blue coats and yellow undergowns; the boys all have belts round the middle and peaked caps on their heads; the 14 years olds are put out to become apprentices to serve one master for seven years. 4. Then followed four surgeons from the Hospital with green and white sashes round their bodies, with the arms of the guild embroidered on them, with white staves in their hands. 5. After that came a large number of governors of the following hospitals, namely Christ's Hospital, St. Bartholomew's Hospital, Bridewell Hospital, and the Hospital of Bedlam, which is very old. 6. Then came the trumpeters playing. 7. Then a large number of officials on foot. 8. Then the City Marshall of London on horseback by the side of the old Lord Mayor. 9. Then followed many sergeants, clerks, and attendants of the courts of the Lord Mayor, all in their coats, walking in twos. 10. Then came the mace bearer with the sword bearer, wearing the large cap of maintenance and carrying the rich sword, its sheath all set with pearls. 11. Then followed the Lord Mayor on his richly bedecked horse, wearing a red tabard, with his precious jewel hanging on a rich golden chain on his breast. 12. Followed sixteen aldermen on horseback, and the two sheriffs behind, in their red tabards, and with their golden chains round their necks. 13. Then came the Lady Mayoress and all the aldermen's ladies and their companions in carriages.

Having arrived at Spitalfield they went to take their places, each according to his rank. For the ordinary public a lot of benches were put on the square in front of the preacher, on which the folk sat under the open sky, or stood around with great jostling. Dr. Godingh ascending the pulpit, had them sing the 107th Psalm, and took as his text Psalm 68 v.13 'Though ye have lien among the pots, yet shall ye be as the wings of a dove covered with silver, and her feathers with yellow gold'. The service over we returned to the town for that day.

On the 11th April the Lord Mayor came with the same following again to Spitalfields.

On the 12th, Wednesday again, but then they were wearing violet coats, and the sword bearer no cap, and only carrying the ordinary sword. Dr. Hebru preached, his text was Hebr. 13 v.16, and they sang the 100th Psalm.

---

77 Lady Ramsey, wife of Sir Thomas Ramsey, Lord Mayor 1577, left various endowments in her will dated 12 January 1596 to a number of charities (*Endowed Charities*, 32; vi, 102).

NB. These three sermons were repeated on the Sundays after at St. Paul's in a service before the Lord Mayor.

In the afternoon we went to the bear baiting.

On the 18th we went to Rotherhithe to the ship *The Black Horse*, where we drank a cheerful round to the health of our friends.

Our journey to Windsor

21st April. At 3 o'clock in the afternoon we went with Mr. Jacques Conjaert from London in a prevoor, passing Lambeth, Vauxhall, Battersea, Chelsea, and Fulham, lying on different sides of the river. The church towers of the last two places are much alike, and, for that reason, are called the two sisters. We went a little further to a place called Barn Elms, which is very pleasant as it lies, planted with very tall elm trees, by the river. We went on land there and walked past Barnes to Mortlake, where we went to the tapestry works and saw there many fine tapestries, amongst them also some paintings by Mantegna,[78] very beautifully done in water colours; it was the ancient Roman Triumph, and is being copied by an Englishman to make tapestries from it.

At Mortlake, a fine, interesting place, many important people have their pleasure gardens by the river, because of its charm and the freshness of the air. We slept there that night.

On the 22nd at 6 o'clock in the morning we walked to Richmond, a very pleasant way. We came across a large fine field called Richmond Green, and saw there the ruins of the royal house or palace, first built there by Henry VII, who gave it this name, which before was Sheen; it was barely completed when he died there, as did Queen Elizabeth. Here the children of the kings of England used to be brought up, but it is now razed to the ground in the recent war on the order of the traitor Oliver Cromwell. King Edward III died there on 21st July anno 1377.

From Richmond we walked along the river Thames. The tide does not come higher than   feet, so that it stagnates here, and the ships have to be towed up the river by the horses. There are many osierbeds, where the boatmen set their fish traps. We came through Petersham and across the river on the left saw a large deerpark called   , which takes four hours to walk round.

At 8 o'clock we came to Kingston, a large market town, renowned

---

78 Andrea Mantegna (1431–1506), Italian painter, whose series of nine large cartoons on 'The Triumph of Caesar' were bought by Charles I in 1627. These are now at Hampton Court in the Orangery. They were apparently borrowed to copy them as tapestries at Mortlake (June Osborne, *Hampton Court Palace*, 1984; Mary Eirwen Jones, *British and American Tapestries*, 1952. E. Bénézit, *Dictionnaire des Peintres*, 1976 ed.)

for its antiquity. In olden times it was called the King's Town, or Kingston upon the Thames. This place was, as most places in England, destroyed in the Danish war. 1) Athelstan, 2) Edwin, and 3) Ethelred were crowned as kings in the market place on an open stage in the year 1) 924, 2) 950, and 3) 978. There is a wooden bridge over the river, and one sees Hampton Court lying on the other side in Middlesex. In Kingston there is good fish to be had. It was market day, which attracts large crowds, and from all directions goods were brought for sale. We ate our midday meal, consisting of fish, at the Saracen's Head at the market. In the afternoon we went to Hampton Court, named after a parish or village called Hampton not far from there, and called Court because of the magnificent beauty of the royal palace, which was newly built by the great Cardinal Wolsey, and since enlarged and completed by King Henry VIII, and is of such a grand conception that there are in it five separate inner quadrangles or courts, all very magnificently and remarkably built, impressive to look at. It has in its largest inner court a fine, magnificent fountain, and is now the most splendid of all the royal palaces in England. We looked at it all more thoroughly at a later date.[79]

From there we went along the river to Hampton town, on to Little Kempton on the left, forward through Littleton to Laleham, went over a stone bridge, and so came to Staines or Stony Stratford, Stony because of the stony street and because there was a ford or shallows there, where people and horses could cross the river Thames.

NB. This is the usage in English with all names of towns and villages ending in ford.

The houses were all built from a certain uncut stone, which is dug or quarried there in plenty, as also at Caversham nearby.

Staines stands on a public highway called Watling Street, which was paved by the ancient Romans; some of it can still be seen outside the village, and also the ford or crossing, but this is now impassable. It lies in Buckinghamshire, 16 miles from London. We stayed there in the Royal Oak by the bridge.

On Sunday, the 23rd April, we left at 8 o'clock in the morning to walk to Windsor, which lies in Berkshire 20 miles from London; we first crossed the bridge and went through the fields to the village of Egham, and on along the river, and so came to Windsor by its deerpark, and went into the town to stay at The Garter.

79 See 7 June to 14 June 1662 below.

Windsor

Near the town is a royal house and castle. Its position can hardly be bettered for such a purpose, as it gradually rises from the town on a hill, from which one has all round an extremely pleasant view, for which reason the king and the princes are often to be seen there. King Edward III was born here, and he newly built there a very strong castle, the size of a small town, well strengthened with ditches and a stone bastion. Here King Edward at one time imprisoned Jean, King of France and David, King of the Scots, having defeated them in 1343.[80] He founded here the Order of the Garter, the knights of which wear on their left leg, a little below the knee, a garter, on which are inscribed in golden letters the following words in French: Honi soit qui mal y pense, and this garter is made fast with a golden buckle, as a reminder of the close bond between them. Some say that this originated from the garter of the queen, or rather of Joan, the outstandingly beautiful Countess of Salisbury, which dropped down while she danced, and was picked up by the king, whereupon all the many bystanding princes and noblemen laughed, but, as the king noticed this, he said to her that it would shortly come to pass that garters would be in high honour and esteem. The greatest, mightiest princes and nobility in Christendom hold it the greatest honour to be accepted into this Order. There have already been about 22 Kings, besides the Kings of England, admitted to this Order, which consists of only 26 Knights. The King is its sovereign, and its members include dukes, counts, etc. In 1343 the King chose from his nobility the most famous and bravest men, who had not many equals, whom he accepted into the Order, according to the following list:[81]

Edward III King of England
Edward his eldest son, Prince of Wales
Henry Duke of Lancaster
Thomas Beauchamp Earl of Warwick
Peter Capit de la Bouche [John de Grailly, Captal de Buch]
Ralph Lord Stafford
William de Montacute Earl of Salisbury
Roger Mortimer Earl of March
John de Lisle
Sir Bartholomew de Burghersh

80 The Round Tower was built in 1343, David II of Scotland was imprisoned there in 1346, Jean II of France in 1356 (DNB).

81 The order of the names is the same as on the face of the map of Berkshire in John Speed's *Theatre of the Empire*, 1611; see also Grace Holmes, *Order of the Garter, 1348 to 1984*, Windsor 1984.

Sir John Beauchamp
Sir Lord Mohun of Dunstene [Dunster]
Sir Hugh Courtney
Sir Thomas and Otto Holland
Sir John Grey of Codnor [Lord Rotherfield]
Sir Richard FitzSimons
Sir Miles Stapleton
Sir Thomas Wale
Sir Hugh Wrottesley
Sir Nele Loring
Sir John Chandos
Sir James Audley
Sir James Eswie [Henry Eam]
Sir Sanchie Dampredicourt [Sanchet de Abrichcourt]
Sir Walter Pavely

On the other side of the river lies Eton, as a suburb, joined to the town by a wooden bridge. Here King Henry VI founded a fine college, which is worth seeing. Next to Windsor Castle is a nice deerpark, but now without game, which were all killed and destroyed in the recent troubles.

NB. Because it was Sunday, we did not see the castle, palace, and church so well, but see the 4th June, when we came there the second time.

On the 24th April we went from Windsor along the foot of the hill to the ferry, where one crosses the river Thames in a scow, and went to the village of Datchet, where we were back in Buckinghamshire, and walked to Colnbrook, also called Pontes, over four canals, over which lie bridges for the convenience of the travellers. This is a large market town. From there we went over Hounslow Heath to Hounslow, a nice market town, and on to Isleworth, a very pleasant place by the Thames. From there to Sion House, belonging to the Earl of Northumberland, a magnificent place, which had previously been a nunnery, which had entirely fallen in ruins because of its great age. It has a magnificent garden with many fruit trees, several remarkable ornamental gardens with very fine, broad avenues, well worth seeing. From there we went to Great Brentford and stayed at the Red Lion.

On the 25th April we went to look at Brentford; as it was Tuesday, which is the usual market day there, there was a great deal of merchandise brought to market, and lots of people come from the neighbouring villages to hawk their goods or to lay in supplies. The great highway passes through this market place. From there we two went on alone, as J. Conjaert had left us the night before, to Little Brentford, from there to Chiswick, which lies in a great plain, and walking on, came to Hammersmith, a nice market. Next we came to

Fulham, or a place of many fowls, where the Bishop of London used to have a beautiful house. After having eaten our midday meal we went from there by water in a prevoor down river to London, where we arrived towards evening. We had so made a very pleasant walking tour, through a very fertile, beautiful countryside and corn fields, saw many excellent orchards, flower and fruit gardens, and it was all the more enjoyable as we had beautiful spring weather.

On the 29th April we saw the three regicides, John Barkstead, lately lieutenant of the Tower, John Okey, and Miles Corbet[82] being dragged on sledges to Tyburn, guarded not only by the regular sheriffs' guard, but this was strengthened by a troop of the King's bodyguard on horse under Sir Philip Howard, the brother of the Earl of Carlisle, but these were still not enough. There was such an immense crowd of people and the throng was so great that the sheriffs were forced to take the malefactors from the sledges and lead them to the cart, which stood already waiting under the gallows. It was noted that on the way Barkstead was eating or chewing something, Okey had an orange in his hand, and Corbet a book, but he was kept from reading by the shouting and pushing and mud slinging crowds. Barkstead, who was very ill, was on the first sledge, and he was also the first to be lifted on to the cart. The hangman took off Barkstead's wig and put the noose round his neck; this was hauled so tight that he could not sit on the side of the cart; as he was too weak to stand the hangman said to him 'You shall have plenty of rope', and made it a little wider so that he could sit down. He then took out a silver flask and drank a cordial from it. Then the others were brought up through the crowd; Okey was the next to be put on the cart; Barkstead said to him 'Welcome, brother', whereupon Okey, seeing him without his wig, embraced him with both arms, and, turning round, said to the sheriff, 'Mr. Sheriff, I hope we shall have the liberty to speak and to pray', to which the sheriff answered that he should not imagine that they were there to listen to them and to hear their excuses for the crime, for which they had been brought there, but if they would confine themselves to speak to God, they should have the liberty to do so. Then Corbet was brought on to the cart, and, after some silence had been made, Okey, who showed himself very courageous and of good spirits, addressed the sheriff and the people with a long oration; after him spoke Miles Corbet, and then Barkstead, who, because of his weakness, made it short. Then Corbet began to pray, after him Okey, and then Barkstead,

82 The three regicides, who had signed the death warrant of Charles I, had fled to Holland, but were arrested there and brought to trial in England (Pepys iii, 45 and 66–7). The drama of their arrest in The Hague in March 1662, took place while Schellinks was in England. See John Beresford, *The Godfather of Downing Street*, 1925, p. 141.

all praying for the King and his Counsellors, and that the Lord God would be as a father to the people and that he would reign here and in the hereafter. Then, as they had finished their prayers, the ropes were well tied above to the gallows, and white linen caps were put over their faces, and, as they all commended their souls to God, the cart was driven from under them. This had been placed in such a way that they all hung with their faces towards Westminster. Barkstead was the first to be cut down and quartered upon the ground. First his heart was taken out from the body and shown to the people by the hangman, calling out 'God save King Charles'. This was then thrown on to the fire, which was laid on for this purpose, and the same was done with his intestines. The same was done with Okey and Corbet, and their quarters were carried in baskets on carts to London, where the quarters of Barkstead and Corbet, after having been boiled, were put on the city gates, and Corbet's head on the bridge. Barkstead's head was put on a stake at the Tower towards the water, and on the King's order Okey's quarters were buried at Stepney in the presence of such a crowd of people, who went with it, that it was almost impossible to get through with the body.

On Sunday, the 30th April, we went to the Duke of York's Chapel at St. James and then went for a walk in the Park.

May

On the first, May Day, we went for a walk through the Town.

On the 3rd the [anniversary of] the King's coronation was celebrated, and in the evening, as it got dark, the apprentices lit bonfires, and friends entertained each other.[83]

On the 8th we were at the Red Bull playhouse to see fencing on the stage with cleavers and swords, which the fencers borrowed from gentlemen. One was a butcher's man and the other a porter; it was dreadful to watch.

On the 10th we went to Westminster and saw there the five lords, namely Lord Buckhurst and Mr. Sackville, the two sons of the Earl of Dorset, Mr. Belasyse, the brother of Lord Fauconberg, Mr. Wentworth, and Sir Henry Belasyse, the eldest son of Lord Belasyse, stand trial before the criminal Judges of King's Bench; one Happy, a tanner from Newington, had been murdered and robbed by them on the highway from Waltham to London; their sentence follows hereafter in English.[84]

(It does not, in either of the two MSS)

83 Coronation of Charles II, 23 April 1661 o.s. (Pepys ii, 83–8).

84 The five were accused, as stated, of having murdered the Stoke Newington tanner on 18/28 April 1662. They were charged with manslaughter, but later acquitted (Pepys iii, 34–6).

The same day we met in Westminster Hall Colonel Lovelies, with whom I was acquainted, who took us to the chamber of the upper house, where the bishops were assembled, because parliament was sitting at the time. From Westminster we went to Whitehall, and were taken by one Jonker Van der Does into the King's garden at Whitehall, which is very interesting and neatly kept. It has very wide, smoothly rolled lawns, and is embellished everywhere with many antique statues. We saw with him also the long gallery with all the rare, valuable paintings by the foremost masters in the world, which are well worth seeing, and saw the King dine with the Duke of York.

On the 11th or the first old style, it is the custom in London that the young folk and others go at night at the crack of dawn with musicians into the streets or in the fields, to dance or to watch the country girls and the milkmaids dancing. They come dressed up in their best, with their pails, in which they bring their milk for sale, draped with all kinds of wreaths and garlands made of bows and frills of silver and gilt tinsel.

We went for a walk in St. James Park, and from there into the King's Chapel, where there was glorious music; the King and the Duke of York came to attend the service, with their great garter jewels round their neck, and his Majesty dressed in purple. Coming from the chapel we went with Mr. Uijlenborgh again into St. James's Park, and saw there the new garden of the Duke of York, which is large and long, next to the Pall-Mall court. The Duke of York came to walk through the park, with the Garter on his left leg. We left St. James's Park by the back exit and walked to Hyde Park, where every year on the first day of May all the nobility from the court, town, and country present themselves in their best finery, on horseback, but mostly in carriages, so that one can see here the most beautiful ladies' dresses, horses, carriages, pages, liveries, etc, which can be seen anywhere in London, everybody trying to outdo the other in their dress in which they appear in public. The number of horses and carriages, which ride in this tour à la mode round a certain square, was too great to be counted. It is the custom that the King, the Queen, and all of royal blood show themselves every year on this parade, but because it started to rain, there was then nothing extraordinary to be seen. It is remarkable how such an enormous number of people of all kinds and conditions come here together, and everything one can want is for sale as in an organised camp.

On Sunday, the 14th May, we went by boat from Westminster to Vauxhall and went from there to Lambeth to the service. This place belongs at present to the Bishop of London, and a new house is being built there next to the church. Here died Canute, the first Danish

King, in 1037 or 1038, in the midst of a drunken revel.[85] From there we walked along the river to London Bridge.

On the 15th we walked to Whitehall, went into St. James's Park and watched the playing in the Pall-Mall court.[86] The King and the Duke of York were walking there.

On the 16th, Ascension Day, we saw the minister taking possession,[87] as is done in London every year as follows: The minister, the church-wardens, and all who depend on the parish inspect all the wards of their parish to see whether any new houses or dwellings have been built, which should have been registered by them for the payment of tax and record these, and also renew the old markers, which are painted on the wall on many different corners and quarters, to mark the boundaries of the parishes. For this purpose all the youngsters of the parish, great and small, assemble in the morning, each with a stick or rod in his hand, and walk two and two ahead, and when a marker is put up or renewed with the date of the year they make a loud noise all together and then go on to the next. This is done to impress on the young memories of the children the extent of the parish, so that they preserve it in the future without loss, and everyone gets a loaf of white bread from the minister. If it happens that two such parties meet, a fight usually ensues.

On the 24th, the day of the landing of the Queen at Portsmouth,[88] all the church bells were tolled in the evening, and bonfires lit.

On the 28th we went to church at Chelsea at the Dutch ambassador's.

On the 29th May we went to Westminster and waited by the door of the Upper House and saw the King himself, taking his leave from parliament to go to Portsmouth to welcome and fetch home his Queen. It was half past eight in the evening before he boarded his barge, which was most expensively dressed with richly embroidered cover sheets and flags. Four trumpeters blew loudly as his Majesty landed at the stairs of Lord   , where, in the inner court, we saw him twice walk close by us. With all the company wishing him good luck he then took his seat in his royal coach, which was ornamented with very magnificent carvings, with six most beautiful stallions belonging to the Duke of Northumberland harnessed to it. He and many other noblemen

85 This is taken from the Copenhagen MS. The Bodleian version says: 'In this place the first King Athelstan, being a Dane, was smitten to death in the middle of a wassail in the year 1037 or 1038'. However, according to DNB, Canute died 1035 at Marlborough, and Athelstane, a Saxon King, died in 940. Hardecanute, a son of Canute, died suddenly during a wedding feast of one of his thegns at Westminster in 1042.

86 Pall-Mall, a game somewhat similar to croquet.

87 The description of this ceremony of 'Beating the Bounds', which appears in the Bodleian MS in the text, is, in the Copenhagen MS, written on both sides of an unnumbered insert.

88 Catherine of Braganza. See 8 June below for her arrival at Hampton Court.

accompanied his Majesty in carriages and on horseback, besides a brigade of horsemen and his runners; a great number of people had come by water and by land to see him, and so he rode to Guildford etc.

On the 30th he went for a walk in Hyde Park, from there to Marylebone and further on to the waterhouse, where we refreshed ourselves, and were shown the channels or conduits to the town, which supply every street and fountain in it.

On the 31st we went to the Moorfields and saw there a tightrope walker perform such lusty capers that his rope snapped and he fell head over heels on to the heads of the crowd. We also watched the wrestling on the uppermost square.

NB. That day £8 sterling were stolen from our trunk which we found still locked; we suspected that somebody, who had visited us that morning, had done it, but had perforce to follow the advice of our friends, to keep our mouths shut.

On the 1st of June we saw a young woman, who had stabbed her husband to death with a tobacco pipe, being burned alive at the stake at Smithfield. She was put with her feet into a sawn-through tar barrel and made fast behind to the stake with an iron chain under her arms and round her breast. A clergyman spoke to her for a long time and reproved her, and said the prayer. Then faggots were piled up against her body, and one laid on her head, and these were covered with rushes, and finally set alight with a torch, first at the back, and soon it was ablaze all round, with the hangman poking the fire with a long rod with an iron hook on it. Nobody could see whether she had any gunpowder round her, neither was she strangled nor otherwise.

Hampton Court Journey

On the 2nd after we had taken our leave from our lodgings in Fleet Street and had sent our belongings and trunks to a Mr. Thomas Douthy's, we went at 3 o'clock by water to Barn Elms. From there we walked through Barnes towards Mortlake and Richmond, where we went to stay at the Red Lion.

Very early in the morning of the 3rd a Mr. John Pelt of Hamburg came to join us. After breakfast we walked through Petersham to Kingston, where we stayed at the Saracen's Head. We went before noon to look at Hampton Court, where there are more than 28 chambers, halls, and rooms, all royally fitted out and magnificently decorated and hung with tapestries, paintings, canopies, chairs, bedsteads, etc. Especially outstanding is the royal bedchamber, where the rich bed or sleeping couch stood, all covered in green velvet, and hung with magnificently embroidered gold and silver borders, fringes, and tassels, also artistically carved and gilded, and decorated on the four top corners with very fine plumes. All the mirrors have fine frames of driven silver, and the hassocks and footstools too are all of the most splendid. In a very long gallery we saw some extremely rare and priceless paintings, mostly by early Italian masters, also another hall, in which hangs nothing but antlers of stags, antelopes, etc, also the picture of the great stag's horn, which hangs in the church of Amboise.[89] Having seen everything we returned to Kingston, and in the afternoon we went for a walk round.

On Sunday, the 4th, we went in the morning to the service, and in the afternoon we walked to Hampton Court, and looked at the garden there, which is very interesting and decorative. In the middle it has a splendid fountain, decorated with several marble statues, and on the right is a very cool walk, so overgrown with greenery that no ray of the sun can penetrate through it. At the end of this garden one goes through a door up some steps to a very pleasant octagonal summer house, which stands on a higher level; from there one has a view over the whole garden; in its middle stands a marble table on a pedestal, and its ceiling is painted with a heaven full of cupids. There is nothing but glass windows all round, and under them are nicely carved benches. Below this place is a deep vaulted wine cellar. From there we went to look at a large number of rooms, amongst them a gallery by the river with a balcony with a very pleasant view. From the garden we went for a walk in the deer park, in which were 700 young stags and roes. King Charles II had a canal dug there, so that one can go by water with the barges right up to the gardens. There are also 15000 young elm trees in straight and circular avenues.[90] This garden is 3 English miles round its walls.

On the 5th of June at 9 o'clock in the morning we walked with Mr. Pelt from Kingston to Epsom, being 5 miles. We got there at midday, and went to stay at one Robin Bird, and were there well accommodated. Epsom is a very famous and very pleasant place, much visited because of the water, which lies in a valley not far from there, which is much drunk for health reasons, because of its purgative powers, and which is being sent in stoneware jars throughout the land. It is a well, and with a wall around raised as a well head, and the ground is paved with bricks. In the middle it has an opening in the ground for the water flow, and the well water, reckoned from there, stands ten spans high and eight spans from the brick floor. This well stands at the back in a

89 On his earlier Journey in France in 1646 Schellinks had seen the giant antlers in the church at Amboise (see Van den Berg, *Introduction* iv, above p. 16 note 65).

90 The 'straight and circular avenues' were there in an eighteenth-century drawing of Hampton Court by Leonard Knijff. The gardens were reconstructed, only the maze survives (Osborn, note 78 above).

small house, in which there are some small rooms, and many people come in there to drink and to shelter from the sun. For this well a yearly rent of twelve pound sterling is paid, which is given to the poor. Those who come there to drink the water give to the person who draws it as much as they wish. Now in 1662 an old man and woman have it on hire.

The practice of drinking the water is from early in the morning until 8, 9, or 10 o'clock. It is drunk on an empty stomach from stoneware mugs holding about one pint. Some drink ten, twelve, even fifteen or sixteen pints in one journey, but everyone as much as he can take. And one must then go for a walk; it works extraordinarily well, with various funny results – probatum est. Gentlemen and ladies have here separate meeting places, putting down sentinels in the shrub in every direction. It has happened that the well was drunk empty three times in one morning; in hot and dry summers, when the water does not get any feed from above, but has to work up from the lower parts of the ground, it has more strength, and the people who observe this come then in such crowds that the village which is fairly large and can spread at least 300 beds, is still too small, and the people are forced to look for lodgings in the neighbourhood. Some stay there on doctor's orders for several weeks continuously into the middle of the summer, drinking daily from this water, and many people take some hot meat broth or ale after the drinking of the water. I have added hereto my drawing of the described place.[91]

Note. Now after we had eaten well in the evening with our travelling companion Mr. Jan Pelt, we went to sleep in a room above his, he staying below; and although we were in a very good house, having been recommended by our landlord and lady from Kingston by a letter, our Jan was so afraid in his room that he barricaded his door and windows. Now around midnight he began to call alarm, also trouble, trouble, as if he were being strangled, knocking from below against the ceiling and calling to us, whereupon we shot up and sprang out of bed and went down, and he opened his door and came up towards us, all trembling and upset, and told us how he had heard that somebody had wanted to break the room open, and that, when he had called out 'Who is there?' nobody had answered. By the noise the man and woman awoke, called out what was happening, and I told them that the gentleman had thought that thieves had wanted to break into the house, whereupon they began to laugh and said that one of their pigs had broken out of the sty and had run through the kitchen along the door of the room, and that the maid had chased it back into its

---

91 Schellinks's drawing of the Epsom Well (*c.*46 × 142cm, *c.*18″ × 56″), is incorporated in the Van der Hem *Atlas*, now in Vienna. See above *Introduction* ii.

sty. But he, being full of fright, did not want to stay anymore below, but crept into bed with us. The next day we had, to avoid this peril, perforce to return to Kingston. On the 6th June in the morning we went to the water well, and each drank three or four pints of the water, as much as the day before, and went for a walk, and at 11 o'clock we returned to Kingston, where we arrived at 2 o'clock, and went again to Hampton Court to look at the gardens and the preparations which were being made inside and outside the palace.[92]

On the 7th in the morning we went there again and watched the play in the tennis court. We also looked at the royal carriage, very artistically and elegantly carved and gilt overall, and covered and hung with velvet. This had been made to carry the Queen in state into London, but it turned out differently.

On the same day six mules came to Hampton Court, elegantly decked with blankets embroidered with the arms of the Duke of York, carrying the Duke of York's baggage. In the afternoon some baggage wagons arrived loaded with his Majesty's and the Queen's belongings. There also came several carriages with Portuguese donnas and cavaliers and the like, who all went to the palace, not just to look at it, but expecting to stay there, but, as no arrangements had been made there for their accommodation, were, to their great annoyance, forced to go by water in boats and in carriages on land to Kingston, and had to manage there as best they could. Now all the rooms and beds, not only in Kingston, but for two miles around, had been commandeered by order of the King, so that it was very difficult to get into an inn or obtain a bed for the night. Even all the baggage at the palace had to stay under the blue sky, and outside the court it was like an army camp, full of tents and huts with sutlers, where one could buy anything one could wish. These donnas or ladies, with tears in their eyes, were put up in the Castle Inn until next day, and this inn was full of horsemen and other officers.

The 8th June or 29th May old style was the anniversary of the day on which His Majesty made his entry into London, and also his birthday,[93] so at 2 o'clock in the night the Duke of York came with his lifeguard and a kettledrum to Kingston, and rode from there to Hampton Court to meet the King. In the morning we too went there and found there the lifeguard of General Monck; he himself went for a walk and to inspect the stables. Before noon six companies of soldiers

92 The arrival of the Queen, Catherine of Braganza. She had arrived at Portsmouth from Portugal on 24 May 1662, when Schellinks reports bell ringing and bonfires. On 29 May he reports the departure of the King for Portsmouth to welcome her.

93 After his exile Charles II arrived from Holland at Dover on 25 May 1660 o.s. (4 June n.s.), and entered London four days later, on 29 May, his birthday (see Pepys i, 157–8 for his arrival at Dover, Evelyn i, 341 for his entry into London).

arrived, who were put in battle order on the ground. The Duke of York arrived by water in his elegant barge. We went to the Chapel Royal to hear the service and specially the music. The Duke of York and Monck were there, and, in short, all the high nobility. Dr. Allestree[94] preached the sermon; he took his text from Hosea c.3 v.5, and very learnedly and longwindedly expounded the installation of David and the exile and restoration of his Majesty. In the afternoon one could see large crowds of people streaming in from London and the neighbourhood to watch the arrival of the Queen.

First came, at irregular intervals, a lot of baggage wagons, packhorses and mules, then came Her Majesty's litter, which was exquisitely decked and embroidered, carried by mules. After that the Duke of York showed himself with his bodyguard over the river waiting there a while until he was sure of His Majesty's arrival, and at last rode higher up. Meanwhile all the way from the gate of the palace to outside the outer gate by the ferry was, on both sides, lined by soldiers, and beside them stood a large number of horsemen and soldiers in battle order in the field. At last came several carriages with English and Portuguese nobles, then some on horseback, followed by two trumpeters, a carriage with some dignitaries, then came the carriage in which sat His Majesty and the Queen, as well as the Duke of York and several other dignitaries; they could not be seen well, as it was 9 o'clock in the evening and they were riding fast, and because of the dust. After them followed the horseguards and several of the suite. Then a salvo was fired, and in the evening bonfires were lit there at the palace and at Kingston.

On the 9th we went again from Kingston to the palace and got into the dining hall, where we saw His Majesty dine with the Queen, while very beautiful music was played. The hall was so full of people and it was so hot that the sweat ran off everybody's face; the Queen's make-up was about to run off with the sweat, so she hurriedly withdrew with the King, and, with all that, had hardly anything to eat. In the afternoon the Duke of York and many of the dignitaries came, also the Law Lords and the Speaker of the Lower House besides others, to congratulate the Queen and to kiss her hand. Also the Lord Mayor, who, on behalf of the City, presented Her Majesty with a sum of one thousand pounds sterling in a very costly embroidered purse. We saw at court very many dignitaries and nobles, also ladies and donnas, English as well as Portuguese, all exquisitely dressed, with their pages and lackeys; all well worth seeing.

94 Richard Allestree (1619–81), Royalist divine, who maintained contact with Charles II during his exile; after the restoration he became Canon of Christ Church, Oxford, and later a chaplain in ordinary to the King, and Provost of Eton (DNB); see 9 July 1662 below.

In the evening His Majesty went with all the dignitaries to the bowling alley, where Prince Rupert played with some dignitaries. Meanwhile the Duke of York came to take his leave from His Majesty and rode with his lifeguards to London. As it turned evening, we heard there a man called the King's cockerel crow very lifelike, he flaps first with his hands as with wings. His duty is to crow at night outside the King's room.

On the 10th we went again to the palace and saw the King touching for the King's Evil with the Archbishop of Canterbury and very many important people in the hall. Then we went to the great dining hall, where everything was well got ready, but according to custom some dishes were served up ceremoniously and immediately taken off again and everything removed. His Majesty dined that time alone with the Queen in his bedchamber, and nobody was allowed in to see them eat, but in the afternoon we saw His Majesty and the Queen at a window eating cherries together.

We went from Hampton Court to Kingston, and at 5 o'clock I went on foot with Mr. Thierry once more to Epsom; on the way we bought a fat goose for 16 pence and had it roasted at our old lodgings, where we stayed again, which was not at all bad.

The 11th at 7 o'clock in the morning we went again to the well and found there again much company, on foot and on horseback, gentlemen, ladies, men and girls, Dutch, French, etc. We each drank six large pints of the water and then went for a walk, but the whole result was but one stool. To follow the fashion we went to our lodging to take there some bread and meat broth. In the afternoon we went to explore the countryside all round, which was very pleasant.

On the 12th June in the morning we went again to the well and found again a lot of people. After having broken our fast with the water we went to wash that down with a cup of warm ale and so went from Epsom to the wonderful place of Lord Berkeley,[95] which is extraordinarily pleasant, the house as well as the garden. This place has a very excellent avenue with many large trees, and a very beautiful gatehouse. Amongst other rooms we saw a very beautiful one full of paintings, and others richly furnished, also a fine chapel and a large hall etc. The garden is very pleasant because of natural hills and dales, adorned with fountains, sculptures, cypress trees, a maze, wildernesses, grottoes, bowers, avenues or walks, summerhouses, a bowling green etc., all in Italian style.

95 Lord Berkeley's house, the Durdans, Epsom, which must have been a substantial establishment at the time, since Charles II dined there on 1 September 1662 with his family and 'an abundance of noblemen', see Evelyn, 1 September 1662. The house was later rebuilt in about 1682 using some materials from the demolished Nonsuch Palace. This house burnt down soon after and was rebuilt again immediately.

From there we went again towards Hampton Court, over the heath, and turned left through a town or village called Thames Ditton, came to the river, went to the ferry and so to Hampton Court, where we crossed over. In one of the tents we saw a chorister from the King's Chapel, who had been run over, lying dead on a table, also a cook, who had drowned while swimming in the river, getting a cramp and calling for help, and the many watermen, who were around, laughing, thinking he was fooling around.

On the 13th in the morning we went again from Kingston through the deer park to the palace and saw the King and Prince Rupert, who had hunted a stag. The King jumped from his horse, and himself opened the stag and took the heart from it.

On the 14th in the morning we went once more to look at the palace, also the Queen's Chapel, where, on a altar, was a heavy silver ciborium and candlesticks.

At about 2 o'clock in the afternoon we went by water from Hampton Court to London, it was very pleasant to sail past all the river places. We went into Sion House, looked at the pleasure garden, which is magnificent, also the fruit garden and others.

Coming from Hampton Court we passed the following places: Thames Ditton on the right and Kingston; on the left the Witsen [Whitton?] Lord Woodman's (?) house; Richmond on the right; Brentford, Isleworth, Hammersmith on the left; Mortlake, Barn Elms, Fulham; on the right Putney; Chelsea on the left; Battersea, Vauxhall and Lambeth on the right.

Thus we arrived at London at about 8 o'clock and went to lodge at Mr. Thomas Douthy's.

On the 15th we went to Rotherhithe and for a change, walked back to London by another way to see it better.

On the 16th we went to Westminster Hall to see Henry Vane[96] come before the court. There were soldiers lining the way from the jetty across the square to the gateway of the hall, and in the hall itself up to the King's Bench, and in the square stood a troop of horse. General Lambert was meanwhile held at the Swan Inn at the corner of the water gate.

On the 19th we saw Mr. Lambert at Westminster Hall standing before the Bar trying to excuse and justify the crimes of which he was accused. He was for all the world not upset about them and did not speak to deny his deeds, but tried all the time to make them appear

96 Sir Henry Vane, a republican, was treasurer of the Navy during the Commonwealth; he was executed on 24 June, but in a less barbarous way than the sentence reads: he was beheaded. The editor of Pepys's Diary says that he was reckoned to be too dangerous to live (Pepys iii, 103–4 and 108–9). Major General Lambert was also a republican.

less serious, and appealed to the King's mercy, by which he won the judges' hearts, and on the 21st, when he was again with Sir Henry Vane before the Bar at Westminster Hall, Henry Vane, after he had made some pleas in mitigation, had his sentence read by the Lord Chief Justice Foster as follows: Sir Henry Vane, you have been indicted of high treason for imagining and compassing the death of the late King, and you have put yourself upon your trial and you are found guilty. It only remains that judgement should be given against you, which is that you be carried hence to the prison from whence you came, and from thence be drawn on a hurdle to the place of execution, there to be hung by the neck till you be half dead, your privy members to be cut off and your bowels taken out and burnt before your face, your head to be cut, your body to be divided into four quarters and your head and quarters to be disposed as His Majesty shall appoint, and the Lord have mercy upon your soul.

As Sir [Henry] Vane was led away he said, 'Him whom men judge, God will not condemn.'

The same sentence was also pronounced over Major General Lambert, but by order of the King this was not carried out but commuted to prison, and Sir Henry Vane's sentence was also mitigated.

In the afternoon we went to the cockpit and saw there several cock fights. There a great deal of money is won and lost by betting. The place is well laid out for the purpose, a circle with a table or round stage in the middle covered with mats, with the devotees sitting around it, with the seats rising up so that they can see above each other.

On the 20th we received instructions from Holland to go post haste to Dover to go with the fleet to the Straits of Livorno, but as we received the letters too late and the wind was from the east we could not do it, as we would have arrived too late.

On the 24th we went to see Sir Henry Vane beheaded on Tower Hill, but got there a little too late, when it was all over. There was a strong guard of soldiers and trained bands in place around the square.

On the 27th we went to the Artillery and saw there very fine drill by the militia, which happen on this exceptional scale only four times a year.

On the 28th we went by river with waterman Oder of Dover to Rotherhithe and walked back.

On the 30th we went with Mr. Jan Thierry and some other friends to Smithfield and bought there two horses for our journey to the west country and found there clear enough proof of the dishonesty of this horse market, as our horses were really nothing special and therefore overpaid by half. Thank God we had no misfortune with them, although they were miserable beasts.

July

On the 1st in the afternoon we went to try out our horses and rode along Holborn to Marylebone, Tyburn, and Hyde Park, from there to Chelsea, where we refreshed ourselves and returned to London, riding round the outside of St. James's Park to Holborn to the stable in Fetter Lane and packed our luggage in readiness to start our pilgrimage the next day, wind and weather permitting.

Journey from London to the west part of England

On the 4th July at 9 o'clock in the morning we mounted our horses and rode from London to St. James's and past Hyde Park on through Knightsbridge and Kensington. Here we met by chance Mr. and Mrs. Parmer, travelling by coach from Windsor, Mr. Parmer on horseback. After greeting each other and a little chat we rode on through Hammersmith and Brentford to Hounslow, from there 5 miles over the Heath to Colebrook, 15 miles from London, and from there to the ferry almost opposite Windsor. We crossed over and got to Windsor at 3 o'clock in the afternoon and went to the White Hart Inn, the largest in the place. The day was, as it happened, the English midsummer's or St. John the Baptist's day and one of the most important fairs at Windsor. There was therefore an enormous crowd of people from all the towns around, and the inns, taverns, dives and pubs were so full of all kind of populace that it crawled. And because of the stifling heat a great deal of wine and beer was consumed under musical accompaniment, of which we got a turn near us during our meal, that is to say, a dance by two couples of country folk. Many nicely dressed up country women and girls too were prettily dancing English country dances. Having refreshed ourselves a little we went to look at the market up and down. It was a fine market, full of all kinds of goods and very many horses.

From the market we went to look at the castle.

Note: We had to take off our spurs as only knights are allowed in wearing their spurs.

At the gate we handed our swords to the guard and went into the church, which is very large and beautifully built, and heard part of the service in the choir. There one sees all round the stalls of the twenty four Knights of the Garter, all with their coats of arms and standards, with their arms emblazoned on them, and their knight's helmets and swords hanging above each of them, all splendidly gilt and artistically painted. On the backs of the seats were fixed numerous small escutcheons, showing their lineages.

After we had seen all this we went to the upper gate of the castle, where two musketeers were given to us as guards. A girl opened the hall and the private chapel for us, and the King's and the Queen's bedchambers, the state rooms, apartments, and a large number of other places, amongst them one with a balcony, from which one has an overwhelmingly beautiful view, as on this side the castle lies very high on the top of the hill.

Having seen all this we rode from Windsor to Maidenhead, where we went to stay at the Bear, 24 miles from London.

On the 5th July at 6 o'clock in the morning we mounted and rode a wooded hilly way, very steeply descending near a place called Henley, which one almost looks into from the height, 7 miles from Maidenhead. From there we rode to a village called Nettlebed and then Benson, then to Dorchester, and so to Oxford, where we arrived at half past four in the afternoon, and rode over Magdalen Bridge over a small river called the Cherwell, the Magdalen College, with its very high square tower, lying on the right hand. We passed through the East Gate up the High Street, a splendid, wide street, full of shops and several colleges and churches, and, as we were there, took our lodgings at the Golden Mitre, a large inn, where we were very well looked after.

On the 6th July we went to St. John's College and delivered a letter of recommendation to a Mr. John Tarbuke, a student, whom we found in the library. He and his companion received us courteously, showed us first the bibliotheca[97] and then the new library, this with a very large and extremely interesting quadrangle, where a bronze statue stands above every gate, one of King Charles and the Queen his wife, lately built by the Archbishop of Canterbury, William [Laud], beheaded in [1645] in the reign of the Protector. The new library or medical and mathematics school is a very long room, which has, as one enters, a large globe on either side and on the far end two skeletons, and a bust of the founder bishop in a niche. From a locked cabinet he showed us some books, Chinese, Arabic, and others, also a fairly large portrait of King Charles I, the hair, the beard, and the lace of his collar, all the psalms of David and some texts from the Holy scriptures, very subtly written with the pen. From there we went to look at the garden, and

97 The Old Library of St. John's College (c. 1596). The New Library, adjacent, was added by Archbishop Laud (1573–1645) as part of the Canterbury Quadrangle in 1631–6 and is now known as the Laudian Library. This still has some of the items mentioned by Schellinks, including the portrait of King Charles I, also noted by Celia Fiennes some thirty years later. The writing has sadly faded. The two globes have been replaced. The two skeletons have been removed, but are shown on a drawing, reproduced in H.M. Colvin, *The Canterbury Quadrangle*, Oxford, 1988. Laud's bust now stands in the staircase, one of his bookcases at the far end (Information kindly supplied by Miss Angela Williams, Assistant Librarian).

The 'Public Library', which Schellinks visits later, is now known as Duke Humphrey's Library at the Bodleian, still reached by a square winding staircase.

then to the buttery, where we drank some excellent beer. At midday we ate with them in their room their college portion: boiled beef and tongue and more. After the students' meal we went to the public library of Oxford, which is large and beautiful, reached by a high square winding staircase, and at the upper end some more steps up is a closed place or bibliotheca presented by one Sheldon, whose portrait hangs there as a memorial. After this we saw the doctors' hall or anatomy. First one goes round through three or four rooms, where all round the walls hang the portraits of old and new doctors, professors, and chancellors, also several life-sized anatomies or flayed figures, and on the ceiling above the walls sundry likenesses of ancient and new authors etc.

The Anatomy is a fine hall, one sees there various strange stuffed birds and fishes, some skeletons and similar things. Amongst other things they show an uncommonly large and heavy stone cut from a man's bladder, and a little square block, with a ring passing half way through it, both the wood and the ring being whole without any joint.

From there we went to look at New College, founded in 1375 by William Wykeham alias Perot, Bishop of Winchester. Here there is probably the most beautiful and pleasant garden, which has in the middle a mount with several graceful ascents, and on the top a seat with a nice view. Up there they keep two tame ravens, one of which happily makes a pleasant noise when one calls or speaks to him. On the lower ground were neatly laid out in box in four quarters the arms of England, a sundial, the arms of the founder, and the arms of a knight, who was a great benefactor of the college. From there we went to look at several other colleges, some very old, and some were new and very beautiful. We also looked at the Physic Garden in which very many plants and rare trees and herbs are grown. A Latin booklet about them can be bought there by the enthusiast from the superintendent, head gardener and keeper etc., who is a Brunswick man.[98] He has a drink of good beer for sale to the visitors, also fruit according to the time of the year. We walked on and looked at the castle, which is completely razed, the only remains are a prison tower by an arm of the river Cherwell, an artificial mount inside old masonry, having above a very strong wall as a rampart, and an entrance to a room near the ground level of the castle. Below one sees the ruins of a fine building which used to be the law court or session house.

On the 7th July we went to Friar Bacon's study,[99] built just outside

---

98 Jacob Bobart the elder (1599–1680) born in Brunswick, botanist, (DNB); a copy of his Catalogue of Plants in the Physic Garden in Oxford, 1648, is in the Bodleian Library.

99 Roger Bacon (c.1214?–94) Franciscan friar, philosopher, experimented in many branches of science, and gained a reputation as a wonder worker, imprisoned in Paris and later in Oxford for his heretical writings (DNB). Friar Bacon's Tower is shown on

the town from which he was banned; this place is in Berkshire. On the bridge or causeway across the marshy fields is an old tower, under which one passes. This is the place where the barges from London arrive and depart. We went once more to look at the castle, and from there to a bridge called the High Bridge and to St. Giles, and on through the fields to Holywell Mill by Holywell Church, and from the other side of the town to the Christ Church Walks, and looked a bit at the College of Christ Church, which was truly the largest and finest, but was badly damaged in the war by the parliamentarians and is not being repaired. It was first founded by Thomas Wolsey, Cardinal Archbishop of York, who at the full bloom of his fame (which was great) laid the foundations of this college, which in his honour was called Cardinal's College. In the year 1546 while the college was being built,[100] he was humbled, and, having fallen out of King Henry VIII's favour, he stopped the progress of the building. When he was summoned to Court he set out from York to London and, as the historians report, killed himself by drinking poison. So all his possessions came to the King, who not only resumed the building, but enlarged it by an old college called Canterbury and another place called Vine Hall or Peckwater Inn, transferred there the bishop's seat from Osney, called this new foundation the Cathedral Church or Christ Church in Oxford, and richly endowed it. In the great tower of the church hangs the largest bell of Oxford, called St. Thomas. In this college studied King Charles II, the Duke of York, and many other nobles.

On Saturday, the 8th July we saw the regular weekly market. After noon we went to St. John's College, where we heard a service with organ music, and then went with the students to look at some of the other colleges.

On Sunday, the 9th July, we went to several colleges to see the chapels, heard part of the service, and went for the sermon to Christ Church College, which is the main church, a very beautiful building, and saw there the vice chancellor Dr. Baylie, the chief justice of the students, and all the doctors of all the faculties, who change in a choir into their tabards and come out to take their seats in their stalls. Before the chancellor walk four or five people carrying staffs or sceptres, followed by the Minister, Dr. Alistree, canon of Christ College, who preached the sermon, very eloquently and erudite, with nearly all the students being present.

In the afternoon we went to the service in St. Mary's, the main

---

South Bridge on the plan of early Oxford in Anthony Wood's *Antiquities of the City of Oxford* (first published 1675, new edn. by Andrew Clark, 1889) but the location described by Schellinks seems to be Osney Bridge and Botley Causeway.

100 The date of Wolsey's humiliation was 1529.

church of the university, where a candidate preached the sermon. The vice chancellor, the doctors and very many students and townspeople etc. were present there again.

At 4 o'clock we went to Christ Church College and heard the service there, which was accompanied by fine organ music and a choir, which was very beautiful.

Note: There are three organs at Oxford, one as mentioned, one at Magdalen, and one at St. John's College. The church and choir of Magdalen is a very interesting and beautiful building, and the painted glass is also not bad.

At 5 o'clock we went to a pleasure house two miles from Oxford called Middlee [Medley], where the students and townspeople amuse themselves; it is only a peasants' pub and lies on a river called Portsmead Stream. On the way there we passed a well or spring called Aristotle or Brouwmen's Well, where people go to wash their eyes with the water, and drink of it mixed with sugar, as also from another spring called Holy Well lying close to the town.[101]

Oxford has eighteen colleges of which four have churches in which there is a service in turns, Christ Church, Merton, New College, and Magdalen College. The mayor and most of the townspeople attend the service at Carfax Church; before the mayor the mace is carried. The council elections are first the councillors, the chamberlain, the bayliffs, the thirteen ward-aldermen, from whom the mayor is nominated.

Oxford

is a very old town, founded by Alfred, King of the West Saxons about the year 872, but the town has been many times destroyed by wars, as again in the recent war. Even so it is a beautiful town, and because of the university and the students, lively and full of trade; more about this in the printed publication.[102]

On the 10th July at 7 o'clock in the morning we rode from Oxford to Gloucester, passed some stone bridges, a paved way through some watery marshes, then over some hills, and came down at Eynsham Ferry, 4 miles, where one is ferried across the river. On to Newlands and Witney, a nice market town, 5 miles; from there, riding over a height we passed Minster Lovell, lying below us in a pleasant valley,

101 Holywell Mill, Middlee, Aristotle Well, and Holywell are shown on the plan referred to in note 99. Middlee, or Medley, mentioned in George Wither's contemporary poem 'I loved a Lass' ('In summer time to Medley, my love and I would go'). Brouwmen's Well or Aristotle: called after Bruman le Rich or de Walton; 'frequented by our peripatetics' (Wood, *Antiquities of Oxford*).

102 The printed publication on Oxford, is *The Foundation of the Universitie of Oxford* by Gerard Langbaine, London, 1651.

and came to Burford, 5 miles, a large market town, where we refreshed ourselves.

NB. From there to Gloucester it is 24 miles, and there are no villages on the way where one could stay, except some lying one or two miles off the road; Northleach 6 miles, and 5 miles further Birdlip, a level and very good road until 4 or 5 miles from Gloucester, where the going became very bad and difficult for a mile or two, coming down the hill between cliffs and rocks. We arrived at Gloucester at 7 o'clock in the evening and went to stay at the Bell, a very good place.

Gloucester

On 11 July we went to look at St. Peter's Church, the Cathedral; this is a very beautiful church, large, with high stone vaulting without any timber; it is in bad repair due to its age and the recent war, but is now being assiduously repaired and rebuilt. It has a very beautiful choir with a Lady's Chapel behind. The services are held in the lower [part of the] choir. In the upper part one sees the tomb of Robert of Artois, the son of William the Conqueror;[103] around the choir are some more ancient tombs, that of Osric,[104] the last Saxon King, the founder of this church, and of King Edward the second, murdered by his wife at Berkeley Castle. He was carried to Gloucester on a cart drawn by twenty four harts, and these are depicted on a pillar next to the tomb,[105] but this picture has almost disappeared over the years. Further one sees the tomb of Parker, the last Abbot of Gloucester, that of Hugh Crawford, general in the Scottish army,[106] and that of Abbot Seabroke, Great Keeper of the College. Then the tomb of the Earl or Baron 2nd High Councillor and Constable of England and his wife,[107] his helmet, with its open end towards the outside, under his head; if one puts one's ear to this, one can hear a sound like the noise of a boiling pot. There are a great many other tombs and sepulchres. Round the choir are twelve beautiful chapels, and above their vaulting is a wide gallery. On the tomb of Bishop Gouldbron in the upper end of the Lady's Chapel three old statues used to stand, which King Henry VIII had broken

103 Better known as Robert, duke of Normandy, d.1134.

104 Osric mistakenly described as a Saxon King, he was Prince of Mercia.

105 Local lore, harts are the badge of Richard II.

106 General Lawrence Crawford, son of Hugo Crawford, killed at the siege of Hereford 1645. The tomb was removed at the Restoration.

107 This tomb in the south aisle was ascribed to Humphrey de Bohun, Constable of England, whose tomb, however, is at the Abbey of Walden. His son-in-law was Thomas of Woodstock, duke of Gloucester, Constable of England, d.1397, who was succeeded as Constable by his nephew, Edward, duke of York, d.1415. The present attribution to Sir John Brydges, d.1437, is doubtful. See *Bristol & Glos. Archæol. Soc.* xxvii (1904), 299. Schellinks's note seems to indicate the Bohun connection.

up and got 15,000 pounds sterling in gold from them.

It is worth mentioning that behind the choir above the gallery there are very tall windows which are lighted right to the bottom, but on the outside, 16 or 18 feet from the ground are enclosed by a wall. One can go from either side through a narrow stone passage to a chapel behind. This passage is called the whispering gallery, its length in its half-circle is 26 English yards or $32\frac{1}{2}$ Dutch ells. The working of this gallery is like this: if on each end of the narrow passage stands a person and one, to locate himself, holds a finger in a certain little hole and speaks very softly, the person on the other end can hear him and answer him, while none of the other persons nearby can hear anything. The following English verse is inscribed in the middle of the wall of the passage:

> Doubt not but God who sits on high
> Thy secret prayers can heare
> When a dead wall thus cunningly
> Conveys soft whispers to thine eare

which means: (*the intended translation into Dutch is not given in either manuscript*)

Under the church or the choir a very large number of human bones are shown.

We then saw the library, a very fine, large building, but, due to the war, with very few books, and empty shelves.[108]

The Church has a very high tower, which we climbed, and saw the large bell which had fallen down. From the top we had a beautiful view. Adjoining the church is the monastery or cloisters, a fine vaulted building, which used to have a water supply or conduit for the use of the monks, but this is now in disrepair because of the war. Besides the Cathedral there are the following churches:

St. Nicholas,	St. Aldate
St. John,	The Trinity
St. Michael,	The Christ Mortimore
St. Mary,	

The town has four gates: Westgate, North-, South-, and Alleÿs Gate.[109] Westgate has a drawbridge over the river Severn, which at high tide is quite wide here. Small ships come up from Bristol and elsewhere to the quay with coal, timber, wine, linen etc. The river Severn is tidal

108 The paucity of books in the library was not due to the war; the library had only been installed in 1656, during the Commonwealth (Information for notes 103–108 kindly supplied by Canon David Welander, Gloucester).

109 Probably Alvin Gate, mentioned in Samuel Rudder's *History and Antiquities of Gloucester* (1781), p. 513.

here and in olden times was larger and used to flow through and around the town, as can still be seen at some houses, which are standing on three strong bridge arches.[110] On the quay stands a breast-high post or round pillar with a copper top on which is this Latin inscription:

> Qui feliciter optat & civitati Glevensi
> Non ut herculleam columnam sed perpucillam
> Hoc pignus amoris est gratitudinis ergo fecit[111]

which is: (*again the translation is not given in either manuscript*)

The town has four market halls, which are handsome buildings in the middle of the street, vaulted and with many columns, and open at street level, where the people can stand in the dry to sell their wares. There is one for butter and cheese, one for rye, wheat, beans etc., one for oats and peas etc., and one for meat and everything else.

Gloucester is a fairly large town and has some fine streets and shops. On the 12th July in the afternoon we rode from Gloucester to Bristol and passed through Quedgeley, 2 miles, then Whitminster, 4 miles, on to Cambridge, 4 miles, and Newport, 4 miles, where, because of continuous heavy rain, we had to put up for the night. We stayed at the Crown with a young merchant from Bristol called Sanders, whose acquaintance we made, and with whom we travelled on.

On the 13th July the rain still continued, so we only set out at 9 o'clock, to Stone, and from there to Thornbury, 6 miles, a large market town and a handsome place, with a beautiful church and tower, and nearby a large castle with many rooms, towers, and gates, belonging to the Duke of Buckingham, Earl of Stafford, Hereford, and Northumberland, so far only incompletely built and further ruined in the recent troubles.[112] We had our midday meal there at the 'Arms of England' and rode from there at 5 o'clock for Bristol, 15 miles, over some great heights, from where one has on the right side a view over the mouth of the river Severn, and beyond it the province of Wales, very pleasant with its hills and fertile valleys. 6 miles on we left

---

110 These can be seen on Speed's map of 1610. See also *Antiquaries Journal* liv (1974), 46.

111 The Latin version given is that of the Copenhagen MS. Rudder, pp. 33–4, writes: 'there was lately a pillar on the great key made of timber, and the following inscription engraven on a brass plate, at the top of it, about two foot diameter.

1650, Qui feliciter optat Civitati Glevensi,

non ut Herculeam Colummam, sed perpucillam.

Hoc pignus amoris est gratitudinis.

In the middle are these arms: On a cheveron three roses, and on a canton an Ulster, to denote they belonged to a baronet.'

112 Thornbury Castle, started 1511, but incomplete when Buckingham was executed in 1521. Roofed in part in 1720 (see Verey-Pevsner, *BoE, Gloucestershire: The Vale of Dean and the Forest of Dean*).

Almondsbury lying below us, then the road became stony and difficult, and at 9 o'clock we arrived at

Bristol

and went to stay at the 'Crown' in the High Street.

On the 14th July it was one year since we left Amsterdam to travel to England.

In the morning we went to look at the town, it is a second London, by the size of its population, and by its merchants, trade, shipping, and streets, and the bridge across the river Avon, closely built up on both sides with handsome houses and shops. There are two places, where at high tide the ships come into the town; at low tide the water runs out, leaving everything dry. In the town the height of the tide is normally 24 to 28 feet, coming in for four hours and going out for six. Because of this rapid movement, the water is very murky, and therefore without fish, except lots of eels. Lower down, about one hour from the town, the water rises and falls 48 feet. One of the places where the ships tie up is called the Quay, the other the Back, and there the bridge lies across the river. To walk along there below is a pleasant walk with high trees and a nice bowling green surrounded by a stone wall. Here ships are being built. It is the end of the Holm where the town is most built up, also a good deal on the other side of the water. The town has four main streets; High Street, where the market is held, slopes down to the bridge; on its upper end stands the cross, which is the highest part of the town, forming there a crossroads with Wine-, Corn-, and Broad-Street. In the middle stands their Tolzey or Exchange. On both sides of the street are arcades resting on pillars. Here stand several posts like pediments of columns, clad on top with copper, and with inscriptions of their founder, on which they used to settle their mutually agreed deals in full.[113]

The town has five gates:[114]

Temple Gate	Redcliffe Gate	Lawrence Gate
New Gate	Christmas Gate	

There is a corn and flour market and there are 19 churches

The College Church [*The Cathedral*]	11. All Saints
2. St. Austins [*Little St. Augustin*]	12. St. Kuirens [*St. Lawrence*]

---

113 The Bristol Nails (outside the later Corn Exchange), on which merchants completed their money transactions, can still be seen. Hence 'paying on the nail'.

114 Millerd's plan of 1671 notes 10 gates.

3. de Ganges [*the Gaunt*]

4. St. Miles [*St. Michael*]
5. St. John
6. St. James
7. St. Philip [*St. Philip & St. Jacob*]
8. St. Peter
9. St. Mary's over a Gate
   [*St. Mary le Port*]
10. Christ Church

13. St. Walbrodas
    [*St. Werburgh*]
14. St. Leonards
15. St. Stevens
16. St. Nicholas
17. The Temple
18. St. Thomas
19. Redcliffe
    [*St. Mary Redcliffe*]

Redcliffe Church lies above the harbour called the Quay on a small height, built there by a merchant of Bristol. It is a glorious building, but the towers were not completed when he died, and on one the spire is only half built.[115] His tomb can be seen in the corner to the right hand side of the choir, where his wife's carved effigy lies, with the following inscriptions carved in stone on the wall above:[116]

Master William Canings ye richest marchant off ye towne off Bristol afterwards chosen 5 times mayor off ye said towne for ye good off ye commonwealth of ye same hee was in order off priesthood 7 years and afterwards deane off Westbury ende died ye 7th off Novem 1474. Which said William did build within ye said towne of Westbury a colledge, with his canons & ye said William did maintaine by space off 8 yeares, 800 handycraftmen besides carpenters & masons every day 100 men, besides King Eduard ye 4th had off ye said William 3000 marcks for his peace to be had in 2470 tonnes off shipping these are the names off shipping with their burthens ye *Mary Canings* 400 tones, ye *Mary Butt* 220, ye *Mary Redclife* 500, ye *little Nicholas* 140, ye *Mary & John* 900, ye *Margarett* 200 tonnes ye *Galliot* 50 ye *Catharyne of Boston* 22, ye *Katherine* 140, a ship in Ireland 100 –

> No age no time, can weare out well woon fame,
> The stones themselves a statly work doth shew,
> From senseless grave we ground may mens good name,
> And noble minds by ventrous deeds we know.
> A lantherne cleer setts forth a candele light,
> A worthy act declares a worthy wight;
> The buildings rare, that here you may behold,

115 The spire of St. Mary Redcliffe was damaged by lightning in 1446 and remained truncated until 1874.
116 Schellinks's version of the inscription is incomplete, and its spelling imperfect. The text given here is taken from J. Britton, *An Historical and Architectural Essay relating to Redcliffe Church, Bristol*, London 1813. See also Edith Williams, *The Chantries of William Canynges in St. Mary's Redcliffe*, Bristol 1950. William Canynges the younger, a major benefactor to the church, d.1474.

> To shrine his bones deserves a tombe of gold,
> The famous fabricke which he here hath donne,
> Shines in its sphere as glorious as the sonne,
> What needs more words, the future world he sought,
> And set the pomp & pride of this at nought.
> Heaven was his aim, let heaven be still his station,
> That leaves such work for others imitation.

His coat of arms was three moors' heads on a silver field. A large number of other tombs can be seen in this church. Bristol is a free bishop's town, all the lands and ground ten miles around the town belong to the bishop, and he has the rents from them, the magistrate has nothing to command or forbid outside the town.

On the 15th July we went all through the town and looked at the market, which is held in the High Street, where everything is for sale.

On Sunday, the 16th, in the morning we were at St. Mary's for the service, and in the afternoon we were the guests of Mr. John Pietersen Reyers. In the afternoon we went to church across the river to Redcliffe, where a Mr. Brind preached an excellent sermon, his text was from Matth. [vi.26] 'What profit...?'

On the 17th July in the morning we went with Mr. John Pietersen Reyers in a small boat with the ebb tide 4 miles down river to Hongerred (?) or the roadstead, at 3 miles is the roadstead for the ships, which come in from the sea and mostly unload there.[117] Downstream the river is very twisting and turning, and flanked in some places on both sides by very high and precipitous rocks, so that, as one travels through the narrow twisting passage, one fears that one will be driven against them, a strange experience. On the cliffs a lot of goats were feeding. At the foot of these steep rocks, several feet under water at high tide, are, almost on top of each other, two springs or wells, one giving hot and the other cold water in abundance and very clear, whereas the river water is opaque and cloudy because of the rapid rise and fall of the tides. As the water had not yet dropped enough, we could not see the wells. Thus came to the roadstead where a large number of ships lay close to the western bank, where the rocks are full of bushes and trees to which they tie the ships. From there we went one mile further to a place called Crackan Pill, a hamlet, where the merchants, shippers, and seafaring men refresh themselves; so we too took our meal there with Mr. J.P. Reyers and his son. From there we saw Kings Road, 6 miles, where the river Avon joins the river Severn. Going back up river with the tide, we came to the hot well and drank

117 *Hongerree* or *Hongerred* not found. King Road is shown in the Severn, downstream from the mouth of the Avon, on a navigational map in Capt. Grenvil Collins's *Great Britain's Coasting Pilot*, 2nd edn. 1723. Crackan Pill is also shown on this map.

from it; the water was milk-warm, but is hotter in winter; a very good ale is brewed from it.

On the 18th July in the morning we went for a walk along the river to the top of the town; in the afternoon we went on foot to the great well,[118] which is a 3 miles walk, got into a heavy rain shower, and went up the hill to Clifton to refresh and dry ourselves. The landlord showed us some Bristol diamonds,[119] amongst them a piece of rock in which were a lot of crystals, by nature very strange with angles and corners as if they had been cut like that, mostly so hard that one can write with them on glass. They were hewn out of the rocks near the hot spring.

Note: By the water near the well the rocks are being cut away to make a roadway for carriages and also a bath.

On the 19th July in the afternoon we rode with Mr. John Pieterson junior, Mr. George Leen and Mr. Thomas Elbridge to Bath, passed through Keynsham, Weston, etc., a pleasant, good road in summer.

Bath

We arrived at Bath, 10 miles from Bristol, at 5 o'clock, and went to stay at the Bear, a very good inn. We refreshed ourselves and then went to see the five baths, the great church, which is very beautiful and large, also the bowling green and the market street etc.

Bath is a small town in Somerset, lying on the river Avon, which here has good fish. It is very famous for its hot baths, which are very healthgiving and a cure for various illnesses and infirmities. People are sent there by their doctors to bathe here mornings and evenings, and to have the water pumped over the diseased parts of their bodies a certain number of [pump] strokes. The principal bath is called the King's bath, the second the Queen's bath, the third the Hot bath, and next to this the fourth, the Cross Bath, and the overflowing water forms there the Lazarus bath, a small place, and outside the Southgate is the horse bath.

The discoverer of the first or King's bath is said to have been King Bladud,[120] who is said to have been a son of   . As a young man he became leprous and nothing could be done to cure him, and he was therefore banned from his father's court, and deserted by everybody. He became a swineherd in this place, which was at that time a waste.

118 Clifton Hot Wells.

119 Bristol diamonds: nodules of quartz, found e.g. in Dulcote Quarry near Wells and elsewhere near Bristol.

120 Bladud, according to Geoffrey of Monmouth, *The History of the Kings of Britain*, legendary King of Britain, father of Leir (Shakespeare's King Lear). Geoffrey of Monmouth, however, does not record the story of Bladud's pigs.

Now it happened that some of the swine which were scurvy, went often to the bog to bathe and roll in a water pool and became quickly cured and sound. Bladud noticed this, followed the swine and found the water pool, being a hot spring rising out of the ground, and dug as best he could a hole in the place in which he could sit or lie, bathed himself there and was cured. So he returned to court, was not recognised, and, as his father had died, he tried to talk to his mother the queen. At long last he was, by his talk and the showing his ring, a gift from his mother, recognised and accepted, and was crowned as king and had the bath built, and also a small place called Swanswick.

On the 20th July, at 5 o'clock in the morning we went with our English friends to the King's and Queen's baths, and found there a lot of people, gentlemen as well as ladies and others.

NB. It is the general custom to go there very early in the morning, and in the evening after the meal. One undresses to the undershirt in one's lodgings, the men put on underpants under their shirt, the girls and women an entire shift; so prepared, one is carried to the bath in a sedan or enclosed chair; at the steps to the water one strips off one's shirt and goes down the steps into the water, where men and women are waiting to help the strangers. All round and everywhere are seats in recesses, also rings to hold on to. If the seat is too low one asks for a cushion, so I was given a stone, soft and smoothed by the water. The water is fairly hot, so that one nearly breaks out in sweat. It is customary to drink some hot wine boiled up with sugar and herbs to prevent faintness. Some people stay in the water for two to three hours. We saw a lady who had pumped on her shoulder and on her head 800 pumpstrokes, and a gentleman 1000 strokes of very hot water straight from the pipes from the first spring. For weakness, headaches, etc. some people get on doctor's orders 1800 strokes pumped on for several days. There are also people in the bath who are ready with knives, scissors etc. to cut people's corns, warts and nails, to earn some money. So too are some people, who, when one steps out of the bath, spread out a woollen cloth to prevent one from having to stand on the stone floor. One then drops the underpants, has a linen sheet and a bathrobe thrown round one's body, enters a sedan chair and is carried back to one's lodgings. There one goes to lie in the linen sheet in a warmed bed, and sweats profusely for one or two hours, whilst somebody dries off the sweat with warm dry towels, and one drinks some mulled wine to regain one's strength. Meanwhile the musicians come, usually without being asked, to entertain the guests and to welcome them. There are always a lot of people there from all over the place, many staying for weeks and months, hence the prosperity of the place.

We ate the midday meal with our Bristol friends, had amongst other things some very delicious artichokes and a large perch, which, however was not prepared the Dutch way. After noon the three gentlemen left for Bristol.

On the 21st July we went around the town inside and out, and looked first at the churches: the largest St. Peter's, Stawles Church, St. James's, St. Mary's, St. Michael's, the Abbey Hospital, St. Catherine's, St. John's, these are the churches. The main streets are High Street, Stawles Street, Cheap Street, Westgate Street; at the end of Southgate Street a stone bridge lies over the river Avon. I went to make a drawing of the town from the heights.[121]

At 4 o'clock we rode from Bath to the town of Wells, being miles, first to Paulton, 6 miles, from there to Chewton 3 miles, then we came over a large heath, and rode up the hill for about   miles; from the top one gets a first view of the town, which lies below in a valley. Down from this hill of stony rocks is a very dreadful, rocky, stony descent, so that we had to lead the horses by hand. At half past eight we got to Wells and went to stay at the George near the Cross with William Fetteyplace and were there well accommodated.

Wells

22 July. Wells lies in Somerset, it is a small town with a bishop's seat, the town has its name from the wells or springs of gushing water, so the church was in olden days called Fountain Church. On account of the many inhabitants, fine buildings and streets, it is the principal town of this county. The cathedral church of St. Andrew is an old and magnificent building. The west front is very unusual, with oval niches from top to bottom and sections separated by pillars, in which can be seen in old sculptures the entire history from Adam to Christ even to the last judgement, and all the remarkable stories from the Old and New Testament. It was in a bad condition because of its great age, as well as the war, but it is all being repaired. Inside the church is very wonderfully built, without any woodwork in the choir area, very strongly supported by stone arches standing in the crossing of the church as a support for the tower. The retrochoir or lady's choir or chapel is very wide and a beautiful building. On the wall on the left side is a clock showing sun, moon, months, days, hours, and minutes. A sitting man strikes with his heels all the quarters, and with his hands the half and whole hours. Behind the choir are the tombs and graves of several bishops. On the north side one goes up some stone steps to the chapter house, where the deacons and canons meet, it is a very fine, beautiful building, circular, with a pillar in the centre on which the vaulting rests. Around the periphery are seats etc.

121 The drawing of Bath is in the Van der Hem *Atlas* (see Appendix I above).

Going up some stairs one comes into the refectory of the clergy, next to it is the Vicars' Close Hall, and also dwellings on both sides for the choristers and others, each dwelling with a little garden. These were built by Bishop N.[122]

Nota Bene: In the church, as one comes in from the front door, one can see on the south or the righthand side, on the wall above the pillars, two stone heads, one a king's and the other a bishop's head as the two shown to you in the attached figure. These are said to have been put there on the instructions of a religious old woman, with a prophecy that, when a king would come to the throne, who looked like this, and also a bishop, who had that appearance, the abbots and clergy would be driven out, and clerical persons would be free to marry, which became fulfilled in the reign of King Henry VIII and Bishop Barber, as these figures looked somewhat like them, so we were told. The present bishop was called Bishop Pearce, the dean Dr. Chriton.[123]

A very large organ was in hand to be installed in the church. Next to the church is the bishop's palace, which was badly damaged; in it is a very beautiful hall. The town or parish church is called St. Cuthbert's Church. In the High street stands a very old, high and graceful stone building or Cross, and next to it a large market and assizes or court house is being built. Besides High Street, there are Sadler Street, Chamberlain Street, Turcker Street, Queen Street, Southows Street, and St. Grop Lane.[124] The principal trade is the knitting of stockings, which are sent out in quantity.

Three miles from the town are the lead mines called Rouw pits, Green ore, Rives leen; and there is always around these places very boggy heathland. The pits here are very numerous and deep. The smelting works are called Priddy mine, Chewton mine, Hostey (?) mine, and Charterhouse mine, and these are there at some distance from each other in the country all round.

122 Vicars' Close, a street built for the Cathedral clergy in the time of Bishop Ralph of Shrewsbury *c*.1348. The Hall closed the street on the cathedral side (Pevsner, *BoE*, *North Somerset*).

123 The story of the two heads, one of a king and one of a bishop, has not survived into modern times, but the heads are still to be seen on the south side of the nave. Schellinks's Bishop Barber, William Barlow (DNB), became Bishop of Bath and Wells in 1548, after the death of Henry VIII. The 'attached figure' does not appear in either of the two manuscripts.

William Piers (Pierce), 1580–1670, bishop of Bath and Wells 1632–1670. Robert Creighton (Crighton), 1593–1672, member of Charles II's court in exile, Dean of Wells on the restoration, succeeded Piers as bishop 1670 (DNB).

124 'Turcker Street' is today's Tucker Street, 'Southows Street' Southover, 'St. Grop Lane' Grope Lane (now Union Street).

The current names of the lead mines are: Rowpits, Green Ore, (Rives Leen not identified), Priddy, Chewton, Harptree, and Charterhouse (Information on this and the preceding note kindly supplied by Miss J.F.K. Swinyard, Area Librarian, Wells.)

We then went to a place called Wookey hole, which is a cave or grotto, into which one goes, each holding a candle. It is quite extraordinary how the water, seeping through the shafts, holes, and crevices, drips from stone cones into fast flowing little streams, and is in a natural way converted into stones by the cold air. We saw a round pool called the brewery, where the fermentation of fresh beer is very realistically depicted in stone. Further we saw the great hall, which was like a church, the dance hall, the dining room, the table, the cellar, the oven, the che   . Also the likenesses of the fence, the witch, the ham, and the organ high up, formed by nature from the petrified water. In a large cave the woman, who was guiding us, made us hear the sound of a cannon by throwing down a heavy stone.

Into this cave, which lies 3 English miles from Wells at the foot of the hills, and has a steep and narrow entry of great depth, crumbling at the sides; people go with candles and torches, taking bottles of wine with them to consume in the cave.

On Sunday, the 23rd July, we were at St. Andrew's for the service, and saw the bishop there, and then went around to look at the town.

On the 24th at 7 o'clock we rode with our landlord to Glastonbury, a nice town. Near Soomer [South Moor] we passed over a long stretch of very good pasture land with all kinds of cattle, which in winter, because of its low situation, is boggy and at times covered with water like a lake, so that in olden times it was called Glaszy Isle. Over this plain rises a round high hill with a tower, on which, it is said, used to be a look-out for the ships. Riding up the height we came to a place on the right hand side called Weary-all Hill or Mount of Weariness, where Joseph of Arimathea, he, who buried the body of Christ, having been sent by Philip, the apostle of Gaul, over to Britain to preach the Christian faith, is said to have pushed his staff into the ground and said 'We are all weary', whereupon the thorn staff immediately broke out into flowers and is said to have flourished there until the recent war of Parliament and Oliver Cromwell against the King, and to have blossomed every Christmas night, but it has now been uprooted by the soldiers as an object of superstition.

From there we came to Glastonbury, 4 miles distant, a place renowned for its very old abbey. We saw there its ruins, as it was totally destroyed by Henry VIII, who had Abbot Whiting hanged in the watchtower on the round hill for his defiance.[125]

We refreshed ourselves there with our landlord, and then took our leave of him and rode to a town called Street, and on to Walton, to Ashcott, to Pedwell, a very good road over the dry heath or pasture

---

125 Richard Whiting, last abbot of Glastonbury, was tried for treason and hanged on Tor Hill in 1539 (DNB).

land, where we saw a lot of cattle, and so came along a river to Burrow
[Bridge].

Riding on a while along the main road to Ling, I was riding on the
footpath high up by the side of the deep, sunken road and Mr. Jacob
Thierry below. On this road he was held up by a man on horseback,
who drew his pistol and asked him by whose authority he was carrying
arms and also whether he had any letters on him. As he got his answer
to this, I noticed that there was some trouble below and called in
English what was going on there, whereupon he rode back a little, saw
me and at once cocked his pistol and said that we must ride back etc.,
and after some arguments we insisted that he should take us to his
captain. So we rode to a farmhouse, where we stabled our horses, and
he rode to fetch his captain from the troop in that area, of whom
several rode up and down the country to catch some rebels. Now after
we had waited for three hours, our fellow returned with his father and
another and with many words and threats took us as prisoners to
Taunton, riding behind us with his sword drawn. As we came to the
castle the guard kept us standing at the gate, as the commander had
ridden out, so we spoke to some other captains, who questioned us,
and when they heard that we were Dutch merchants (as which we had
passed off ourselves), and that our letters were only addressed to
correspondents in the west, they set us free. So we went to stay in the
Three Cups,[126] and the same evening went to look all round the town.

Taunton

lies in a very pleasant and beautiful fertile region, and is for this reason
full of gardens and orchards, pasture land and corn fields. It lies on
the river Tone, over which is a stone bridge, it is a nice and large
market town and one of the most beautiful of this country. It has long,
wide streets, full of shops and spacious market places, graceful high
towers etc.

On the 25th July in the morning I went to the commander of all the
troops, who noted my request for a free pass and also knew what had
happened to us the day before etc, and said to me that we ought to be
able to pass freely, and that nobody ought to hold us up on the way,
although the order in force was different. The alert had arisen from a
denunciation by a servant of Colonel Pym, who wrote to the court that
a conspiracy was in hand, and accused so many respectable persons,
that at once a thousand men on foot and thousand on horse were
called out and put in arms and were cruising through the land, and,

126 The Three Cups Inn, now the County Hotel.

by controlling the roads, had taken 16 or 17 people by the neck and put them into prison at Taunton Castle etc.[127]

So we rode on to Wellington, 5 miles, a fairly large market town. Here we were stopped by the guard, but on hearing that we had spoken to the commander, they let us ride on. 8 miles further we came to Cullompton, and from there over difficult, hilly roads we came in the evening to

Exeter, 154 miles from London

Exeter lies in Devonshire, a county, which has several good harbours, and towards the west rich tin mines. It has many woods and pleasant pastures and gardens, many villages and fine buildings. The ground is arid throughout, and in the whole of England there is no place where the expense to fertilise or to improve the soil runs so high, as it must be maintained with a certain kind of coarse sand, which is taken from the bottom of the sea in the bays and harbours in this manner: In many places we saw these boats, crewed by two men, lying at anchor and throwing out a casting net with an iron hoop on it, which shifts forwards and backwards a little with the tides. When it has sunk to the bottom, they haul it up full of sand and load it into their boats. It is hard work, but many people live by it. It is carried in bags inland on horseback, where it cannot be brought by boat or cart. There the land is covered with it and thereby becomes fat and fertile.[128]

Exeter is a bishop's town and has its name from the river, in old Saxon Ixe, in Latin Exonia. It lies on a small hill, gradually rising to the top, and is surrounded by strong walls and dry ditches, the circumference being $1\frac{1}{2}$ mile. Its suburbs stretch out far all round, it has a fine bridge over the river, and a quay, where ships of 20 tons come in from down river. 3 miles down on this side of the river is Topsham, where the large sea-going ships tie up and load and discharge, and over the river, 8 miles distant, at its mouth, is Starcross, where the ships first anchor. Because of this situation there is good trade there, and there is also always good fish in the market. On Fridays is the great serge or kersey market in the South Street, and much wool and cloth is brought there from the surrounding country. In the High Street the large provisions market is on Fridays. The town has four main streets forming a cross, five gates, and 17 or 18 churches, of which St.

127 There were rumours of disturbances in the West Country in the summer of 1662. See *Cal. State Papers Domestic, 1661–2*, 439, and Evelyn, 20 August 1662. Colonel Pym has not been identified.

128 Composting with sea sand in Cornwall is referred to in the County Reports to the Board of Agriculture, 1818. In Devon and Cornwall some lanes leading from the sea are still called Sand Lane or Sanding Way. See note 131.

Peter's Cathedral is the largest, a very old building, and next to it St. Mary major. On the 24th August[129] the presbyterians were turned out and all the churches given to the episcopals. On the highest spot of the town, near the East gate, is a castle called Rougemont, very old and in ruins, now only used for the annual assizes or law courts for criminal and civil cases.

There was there on the wall of the castle a quarter of the body of a constable, whose other quarters were on the other gates. His execution was particularly gruesome, as, after he had been hanged, he was cut up while he was still alive, and he sat up and said 'Oh, what doeth thou?', shoving his bowels into the wound with his hands. His head we saw later on the town hall of Plymouth. He was found guilty merely on the evidence of two witnesses, who accused him that he was reputed to have said something against the king's person, and he died for this, although he proclaimed his innocence. For it is the practice in England that a person is found guilty on such evidence, be it true or false, unless he brings some other and more numerous persons to give evidence to the contrary, and plenty of such people, called the knights of the post,[130] can be got here for money.

Exeter is governed by 24 persons, from amongst whom year by year a Lord Mayor is chosen, who, with four bailiffs, governs everything. This town has had three Dukes. We lodged at Exeter at the New Inn where we however stayed only one night.

On the 26th July we sent word of our arrival to Mr. Bernard Spark,[131] who had us fetched at once by his servant, and we had to stay with him; in the afternoon we went to look at the town up and down.

On the 27th in the afternoon we rode to Topsham with a party of 15 or 16 people, including Mr. Spark and his lady, a clergyman and

129 It is surprising that Schellinks refers to the important events around 24 August (St. Bartholomew's Day) nearly a month before that day. Perhaps it was the talk of the town at the time. See note 153.

130 Knight of the post: 'A notorious perjurer; one who got his living by giving false evidence; a false bail' (OED).

131 Mrs. Veronica Chesher, Hon. Research Fellow, Dept. of Continuing and Adult Education, University of Exeter, Dr. Todd Gray, Research Fellow, Institute of Cornish Studies, University of Exeter, and other local historians in Devon and Cornwall have identified many of the personalities and locations mentioned by Schellinks, such as:

The Sparks, wealthy merchants in Plymouth in the mid seventeenth century, and the Boones, a principal Dartmouth family, who lived at Mount Boone, just above the town. A note in Schellinks drawing (Hem 41 Appendix I) reads: 'The House of J. Boone Esquire', Hulton connects this to Sir Thomas Boone, who lived in the Manor House of Norton Downay.

William Godolphin had a newly built house in Paul c.1660.

Other valuable information provided by Mrs. Chesher has been marked by * in the relevant notes.

See also June Palmer, *The People of Penryn in the Seventeenth Century*, 1986.

his wife, and some young ladies and gentlemen, and were well entertained with a light repast on a Lubeck ship. In the evening we rode to
the garden of Mr. Spark, and having again somewhat refreshed ourselves
there we rode back to Exeter.

On the 28th we went to look at the serge, kersey, and provisions
market, there was an abundance of wares and people. In the evening
we were the guests of a Mr. John Cooke.

On the 30th we went in the morning to the service in the reformed
church and in the afternoon to the great church.

On the 31st we went for a walk around outside.

August

On the 1st in the afternoon we rode with Mr. Spark and another to
Starcross, 8 miles, passed Alphington 2 miles, and had heavy rain all
the way, but fortunately the water could go no further than the skin.
On the 3rd August the assizes began, and the judges arrived and were
received with great pomp.

On the 4th August at 10 o'clock in the morning we rode from Exeter
to Dartmouth; we rode over the bridge to Alphington and over great
heights with magnificent views all round and far out over the sea, and
came to Newton Abbot, a large market town, 12 miles. From there we
rode to Abbots Kerswell, where we refreshed ourselves, and rode from
there 10 miles on a different road, up hill and down dale on very
narrow, gloomy paths. Here the evening overtook us, and we came at
half past eight to Kingswear opposite Dartmouth, where we stayed the
night, as it was too late to cross with the horses over the harbour which
is quite wide.

On the 5th we crossed over with the ostler but without the horses,
and had them set us on land at the foot of Mount Boone. We had a
letter to a Sir John Boone, Esquire, who welcomed us and put us up
in his house, where we were very well looked after, and we had our
horses brought over into his stable.

Dartmouth

is a small harbour or seaside town, a port protected by two forts, which
lie on either side of the harbour at the foot of the hill. This place has
shipping from all parts and is frequented by merchants. Dart or
Dartmouth lies at the mouth of the river Dart. 'Mouth' is where a
river flows into the sea or into another, larger river. Such a situation
gives the name to many other villages and towns in England, such as
Dartmouth, Plymouth, Portsmouth, Yarmouth, Weymouth, Exmouth,
and many more like it. Dartmouth is divided into four parishes, the

Town, St. Petrock by the castle of the sea, Kingswear on the east side of the harbour, and Townstall on the hill on the west side.

The residence of this Squire Boone is built on a hill, and his garden, orchards and bowling green etc. are all very remarkable, having been dug out of the hill at great expense, and having the most beautiful view that one can wish over the town, the harbour, and all round.

NB. Squire Boone was Cromwell's plenipotentiary in Sweden and was one of the judges nominated for the trial of King Charles, but was not present at the trial.

On the 6th August we went to the great church for the service. In the afternoon we went to church at the castle, and after the service climbed up the hill until we came to a place, where a large compass rose and a sundial of stone were erected, with four stone steps going up from the four sides. There we had a full view of the sea; on the right hand side we saw Start Point, and outside the harbour numerous rocks, on which samphire grows, which is collected at great peril.

On the 7th we went again to the castle and up the hill to the compass; it was mighty hot. After having thoroughly looked at Dartmouth and made a drawing of it, we took our leave from the ladies, Sir John Boone having ridden at 5 in the morning to Exeter for the court sittings.

We rode from Dartmouth at half past three to Moreleigh, 5 miles, and from there together with four young English gentlemen, whom we met on the way; four miles further they took their leave, and we rode on another 2 miles to a place called Modbury, where we arrived at 8 o'clock, and had great difficulties in getting accommodation, as there were horsemen and soldiers billeted there, who were to be shipped from Plymouth to Portugal.

On the 8th August we rode on to Ivybridge, 3 miles, Plympton, a market town, 4 miles, from there to the Laira, where there are bogs, which are flooded at high tide, and it is very dangerous for a stranger to ride through without a guide, (because of the quicksands), although it is one mile shorter to Plymouth; we therefore rode from Plympton St. Mary to Plympton St. Maurice (sic) nearby; in the country is the highway to Plymouth over a very long dyke of slate to below a large, high hill, where very beautiful, thin, blue slates were cut out. So we rode from the east side of Plymouth over several high and large hills of slate, which however was not as good as that below on the Laira. These [slates] are used in the neighbourhood there, and a lot are shipped overseas. We arrived in the town at about midday and went to stay at the Three Crowns at Mr. Pyck's.

Plymouth

has only recently grown by and by from a poor fishers' village to such a very populous and busy large town that it may be compared with a city. Its harbour is so large and convenient that a large ship may, without lowering its sails, sail right into the bay, where there is a very good and safe roadstead and anchorage, protected by two forts against all interference. One of these is at the harbour mouth close to the town, but on the landside very weak on account of the high ground or hill, and only defended by one ditch;[132] but the island or rock, a cannon shot from the town, lying in the west in the open sea, has a very strong fort.[133] These two forts are well provided with cannons, ammunition and men. The supplies to the Island are carried by boat, the access to it is by a very difficult climb, as only from one side is there a narrow awkward passage, where some holes are cut or worn in the rock as footholds, and someone from above has to help to pull one up. Then one comes to the castle gate, which is strongly manned; there is a garrison of 100 men. Formerly the only defence was the old castle close to the town, which is now in ruins, where, in times of trouble or war, the fleeing burghers and country people brought all their goods for a safe refuge and shelter.

Plymouth, on the river Plym, is divided into four wards or quarters. King Henry VI first laid down that the town should be governed by a mayor, and under him each ward to have its own captain and other officials. The size of the town is not large, but it is well known because of the many foreigners who trade or visit there, as well as for its gallant sailors. Sir Francis Drake was born there, and in 1577 set out from this town to sail through the Strait of Magellan, and was the first after Magellan to sail round the world in two years and ten months.

In the afternoon we walked up the hill by the castle on the sea side, from where there is a magnificent view over the sea and all round. Three ships coming from London were sailing into the harbour. Seven ships lay in the roadstead at anchor, of which some were to go to Portugal. In the harbour were many ships, amongst them a captured Zeeland one, brought in by a privateer, but this was, on the king's order, set free and had its goods restored.

On the 9th August in the morning we went to look at the town outside and inside, and at the market which was being held there.

That afternoon we were the guests of Mr. William Innes with Sir John Shilten Knt,[134] who had been in the service of the State of Funen

132 The fort, built in 1592, was replaced in 1666 by the citadel, intended as much to control the city as for a defence against invaders (Pevsner, *BoE, South Devon.*)

133 Drake's Island.

134 The Copenhagen MS has William Innes, the Bodleian MS William Tennens,

and in Denmark, and was now lieutenant governor of the large castle and the militia. Also dining there was a Mr. Peter Toller of Fowey, a brother-in-law of Mr. Bernard Spark of Exeter.

After the meal we went for a walk with Mr. William Innes, looked at the new church built there since the war,[135] and went with him to visit the minister, and then to a stonemason's yard to see some works in marble, of which Plymouth has several hills to the west; this is grey in colour, well structured and hard.[136]

From there we went to the large castle which we inspected below and above. Sir [John] Shilten let us see all the rooms and chambers including the armoury, which was reasonably well stocked; they had that day received from London much new ammunition, muskets and pikes, axes, carts, shovels and spades, pickaxes and suchlike war materials, as reinforcements, to improve the breastworks, and to deepen and widen the ditches on the land side, which were very primitive and shallow; these had to be hewn out of the hard marble rocks. The castle is well armed with cannons, and there is a regular garrison of 100 men.

On the 10th August in the morning we walked along the height of the castle and round the whole hill on the sea side, and came back to the town along the land side.

In the afternoon we went with Mr. Innes's office clerk in a small boat to the island or fortress built on the rock in the sea on the west side of the harbour. We found the access rather difficult; a sergeant came to demand to know what we wanted, led us higher up to the watch, and showed us all the platforms and batteries, very strongly armed with cannons, and what else there was to be seen. After a round of drinks with the officers we came down and went in the boat up river to the seat of Sir   Edgecumbe,[137] lying on the slope of a hill, an extremely pleasant and sumptuous building, inside and out; it has an exquisite hall of very lofty graceful build, and also many rooms up some stairs, from where there is a glorious view over the entire harbour or bay of the sea towards Plymouth. In a polished black marble chimney mantelpiece, one sees, as one stands in the room, the whole town and the prospect as in a mirror or painting. Also in this room we saw some nicely sculpted water basins with waterspouts fixed to the walls. There is a large deerpark full of animals. After we had seen everything and

---

neither name has been traced. Sir John Skelton (d.1672) was Lieutenant Governor of Plymouth and Deputy Lieutenant of Devon (Information from Devon County Libraries, Plymouth).

135 Possibly Charles Church, see Pevsner, *BoE, South Devon*.

136 Devonian limestone, which polishes like marble. *

137 Mount Edgecumbe, built by Sir Richard Edgecumbe *c.*1550; the owner at the time was probably Col. Piers Edgecumbe*. The house was burned out in the 1939–45 war (Pevsner, *BoE, Cornwall*).

had been entertained in the wine cellar with various drinks, we returned from Mount Edgcumbe to Plymouth.

On the 11th August in the morning we rode to Fowey, 20 miles from Plymouth, and passed a place called Cremyll Ferry. A little further we came to a winding road, breaking off terribly steeply at the rocks and it was difficult to lead the horses down from there to the ferryboat below, with which one is set over the inlet of the sea, straight across from Mount Edgecombe; from there we rode down below at the bottom, along the edge of a tidal inlet from the sea, passed Millbrook

miles, then on to Crafthole, an inlet between the dunes. There we rode steeply up to the top of the cliffs, above we had a good, level road and, riding at the great height, found ourselves sometimes very close to the edge, where it was frightening to look down the steep incline to several small fishermen's villages or hamlets lying on the beach at the foot of the hills. All the time we could see from there far out to sea. In some places the road was very frightening and narrow and for long stretches going steeply downhill, especially near Looe, a sea town, 12 miles from Plymouth. There a bight of the sea makes a harbour for fishermen, and there is in this place a fine stone bridge over the inlet. After we had taken our midday meal there we rode at 3 o'clock from there to Fowey, 8 miles on a reasonably good road, came to a crossing or ferry, crossed over at 6 o'clock and went to stay at the postmaster's, where we took our evening meal with Mr. Peter Toller; but as we had a recommendation to him from Mr. Spark, Mr. Toller insisted that we should stay with him; so we left our horses there in the stable, and were bid welcome by his wife and were hospitably treated as long as we stayed.

Fowey

is situated in Cornwall, long famed for the naval battles fought thereabouts as well as for the good harbour which is deep and protected by the surrounding hills against all storm winds. This sea town is so much like Dartmouth, that many skippers, who lay there in the harbour for some time, and had been at Dartmouth before, mistakenly wrote to their masters that they had arrived at Dartmouth, and only found out from their response and investigations that they in fact were not. The forts at the mouth of the harbour, the harbour itself, the hills and the towers and the church and its tower are very much like those of Dartmouth.

On the 12th August we went with Mr. Peter Toller to see the harbour and everything; it was market day, but because of the harvest and the people bringing in their grain, it was not very large; there was good fish.

On Sunday, the 13th August, we went in the morning and in the afternoon to the service, and at noon and in the evening were guests on the invitation of Mr. Peter Toller's father, who entertained and treated us extremely well.

On the 14th August in the morning we rode with Mr. Peter Toller to Truro, 18 miles from Fowey; after we had ridden a few miles we came to pass some low-lying ground which runs dry at low tide and came to an inlet called the Par where we saw for the first time the pilchards, and how they are salted, pressed, and packed. Of this the following memorandum.

About the Pilchards[138]

The pilchard is just like a small herring (without any difference); they appear from the month of July old style and remain to the end of December on this western coast of England such as Cornwall, Devon, etc., and sometimes in such large quantities that it is hard to believe. The best fish is that which is caught in August and September, the first are very small and in the later months they are largest. The catch varies, sometimes the fish is as dead, sometimes it has to be held in the nets by force, sometimes the nets are so full that they have even been forced to cut them open. It even happens that the fish get frightened and drive the net upward with such a force that they slip through under it, but as a rule they are easy to catch. They are caught with seine-nets, two boats to each, and seven men in each. Their wage is half the catch, 15 to 20 English pounds each, for the whole season. Each boat normally carries 15 to 20 hogsheads of fish, each hogshead holds 7000 or 8000 pieces. While we were there they were sold at 12 English shillings a thousand, before this it was not more than 8 or even 5 shillings a thousand, and 5 score or 100 a hundred from the hogsheads at the market, and 6 score or 120 pieces for 100 to the dealers.

When caught they are gutted, salted, and neatly piled up in large heaps for ten to twelve days. They must not be out of the salt for two hours or they are spoilt. Then out of the salt they are packed in hogsheads and pressed and with heavy stones and levers squeezed down. In the bottom of the barrel is a hole where the oil runs out. 10 hogsheads of fish produce normally one hogshead of oil, which runs underneath into a wooden channel and so into a pit, and from there again into barrels. So packed, the pilchards are sent in very large quantities to France, Spain, and Italy, where they are in great demand, and called there 'fumados'.

138 The Cornish fishing and mining industry of the period is described by James Whetter, *Cornwall in the 17th Century: an economic history of Kernow*, 1974.

Note. There is something interesting about the fishing: Some watch-men go up to the top of the rocky hills or on to some high scaffolding and look out to sea to see if there is any fish about. They recognise this by the colour of the water, which appears to be red if there is any fish there. This is said to be caused by the eyes of the fish. As soon as the watcher notices any fish he gives a signal with a bunch of feathers, whereupon the boats go out to sea and he stays and waves and indicates how they are to go and to which side, and how they must set their nets, in short all he would want to tell them by mouth; and they know how to understand him, but cannot see any fish until they drag them on land in their nets. These watchers or signallers perform very strange postures and movements with their arms, head, body, etc., which they work out for the purpose. For a stranger it is well worth watching, it is an art which is not easily learned.[139]

From this place we rode a little further to St. Blazey, where there are smelting houses for tin, and watermills, in which the mineral is stamped and, through copper plates perforated with fine holes, collected in water tanks, after all the dirt is washed out, and so kept to be smelted in the furnaces.

In the mining works they had this practice: Some countrymen or miners go to a certain person, the owner of the land and bargain with him for a licence to dig on his land for tin, he to receive such and such part per hundred pounds etc.

Others work for wages, a master gets 4 shillings and an ordinary workman 3 shillings per week, some more, some less, whatever they can agree. They do not dig the pits straight down, but when they find a tin vein they follow this across or at an angle whichever way it runs. In this manner the mines spread out and some have become frightfully deep.

At the smelting houses the price of the tin was 4 pounds sterling 10 shillings per 100 lb without overheads, and 4 shillings to the King, and another 6 shillings for carriage.

Cornwall

According to some Latin writers Cornubia. It is the westernmost county of England, and the land gets narrower and narrower in the shape of a horn pointing out to sea, and is about 65 miles long and 35 miles wide. All the English tin is mined exclusively in this county, and it is

---

139 The lookout and signaller was called the 'huer' (from French *huer* = to shout). Newquay retains a 'huer hut', restored 1835. Pilchard fishing was described in R. Carew, *The Survey of Cornwall*, first published 1602. The method of signalling is illustrated in K. Harris, *Hevva*, 1983 (Inf. Cornish Study Library, Redruth).

worth noting that in the whole county very little land is waste, because there is an abundance of grain, and that land, which does not produce a crop, is the richer under the ground because of the tin mines, and the poor ground is pasture for the large number of sheep which are there.

The natives of Cornwall have been famous since olden times for their daring, their fearlessness and their bodily strength, and in wrestling and football playing they are the strongest and fastest in the whole nation.

From St. Blazey we rode to Grampound, 10 miles, but when the sea is in the Par, one has to ride 2 miles round it. Through this market town of Grampound we rode another 6 miles to Truro, put up at the Red Bull, and went to look at Truro, which is a very nice place and has a quay, where the ships come up river from Falmouth, unloading and loading tin and other goods. Around this town are most of the tin mountains, of which the best or most famous are called Godolphin Bal;[140] the biggest mine owner in Cornwall at the time was Sir Francis Godolphin, governor of the Scillies.[141]

After we had taken our meal with Mr. Peter Toller and retired for our night's rest, one George Veale from Penzance, an acquaintance of ours, arrived there during the night.

On the 15th August after breakfast we rode, now four strong, to the blow- or smelting houses, but there were almost none working, as no coal had arrived by boat.

We went into one to look at it, it was very hot and interesting to see how the ore is smelted, I cast there something from tin as a souvenir. From there we rode back to Truro, and after we had eaten there with our friends and had remembered all our friends with a little glass, Mr. Peter Toller took his leave, and we rode with Mr. Veale to Penryn, 3 miles, and from there, after some refreshment and having looked at the town, to Falmouth, where we went to stay at the Seven Stars. We let Mr. Bryan Rogers[142] know that we had arrived, and he came to welcome us and drank a glass of wine with us and stayed as our guest.

On the 16th in the morning we went for a walk, at midday we were the guests of Mr. Bryan Rogers, and in the afternoon we rode with

140 Godolphin Bal tin mine employed 300 persons c.1584, according to John Norden, topographer (died c.1625), in *Speculum Britanniae Pars ... Cornwall*, 1610, publ. C. Bakeman 1728. *Bal* (Cornish) = a collection of tin mines.

141 Sir Francis Godolphin (1605–67), governor of the Scillies, from the ancient family long settled at Godolphin near Breage. (DNB).

142 Bryan Rogers was considered in his day, 'the most opulent figure of any merchant in the West'. He imported goods from the Baltic and exported them to London. He also acted as agent in un-loading and re-loading cargoes from and to Amsterdam to circumvent the Navigation Act. He died in debt: see Whetter 1974.

Robert Williams, Mr. Rogers's servant, and Mr. G. Veale to Penzance, 2 miles; at first the road was very bad, stony, rocky, hilly and rough. We passed several deep tin mines, some going 34 to 36 rods down straight into the ground, and also saw on our right hand the Mouvingh Stone,[143] a very large, heavy stone, which lies on two or three other stones in such a way that one can rock it with the hand like a cradle and then keep it in motion with one single finger, which is held to be a great wonder by the English authors. Riding on we got St. Michael's Mount into view; from the height it was interesting to see how it lies in the middle of the sea; when the water recedes one can go dry-shod from the seaside place of Marazion to these rocks. We refreshed ourselves at Marazion and then rode on to Penzance, the westernmost market town of Cornwall, where we stayed at the White Horse at Richard Veale's, vintner, the father of our travel companion, and were well provided for and had good accommodation.

On the 17th August we were prevented by rain from going to Land's End, so we looked at the market. As it was market day for fish and assorted goods, a lot of country people were at the market, everyone, men and women, young and old, puffing tobacco, which is here so common that the young children get it in the morning instead of breakfast, and almost prefer it to bread.[144]

We went to see the market house and the harbour, which lies towards the west in Mount's Bay. Towards the east we saw the Lizard Point across the large bay. In the afternoon the four of us rode again to the Mount and Marazion, stabled our horses and, as the tide was out, went dry-shod over to the stony rock, on which are built an old castle, a nice dwelling house, and a church. We were conducted up there by the mayor of Marazion, our landlord, and first shown the hall, which is very fine and large; from there we went to look at the inside of the church which is in very bad repair. Here the governor or owner of the

143 Schellinks's description of the moving stone would fit that of the Men-Amber (Grid Reference 650322), given in John Norden's *Speculum* and John Speed's *Theatrum Imperii Britanniæ Magnæ*, 1611, but this was described, before 1660, by Peter Mundy of Penryn (British Library, Add. MS 33420), as having been lately seen by him 'overturned from its basis, lying below on one side: Performed, by report, by Captaine Charles Shrubshall and some of his [parliamentarian] souldiers about the beginning of August 1650'. Mundy then mentions a smaller moving stone, $2\frac{1}{2}$ miles to the west of Penryn; like many of these 'logans', this has by now been quarried away (see P. Stanier, *The Work of Giants*, Truro, 1988, and R.M. Catling in *Rep. Roy. Cornwall Poly. Soc. 1908* (1941)) (Inf. Norman Nail, P. Stannier).

144 Schellinks writes 'drinking' tobacco. This now obsolete use of the word was common in several European languages at the time (see e.g. OED). Celia Fiennes, who, c.1698, travelled in Cornwall, notes the 'universall smoaking, both men, women, and children, have all their pipes of tobacco in their mouths'. *Journeys of Celia Fiennes*, ed. Christopher Morris, 1982, p. 204). *

Mount, Mr. John St. Aubyn,[145] came to us, and when he heard who we were, welcomed us with great politeness, took us back to the hall and said that he was greatly obliged and indebted to Mr. Jaques Thierry and a thousand more such compliments, and treated us there to small beer etc. So we went from there into the church and climbed up a mighty narrow stone spiral staircase to the tower of the castle, from where there is a very beautiful view out to sea as well as towards the land side. When we came down again they showed us many rooms and an old chapel. There are a lot of rabbits living in the crags of the rock, and below by the sea is a bowling green, a harbour, and some fishermen's cottages and store houses for pilchards etc. As the tide now came in so quickly, we had to hurry if we wanted to go over on foot, and still had to wade through the water in boots, and Mr. Veale had to have himself carried over by a fisherman. After we had refreshed ourselves we rode again back to Penzance.

On the 18th August, at 8 o'clock in the morning, the four of us set out to ride to the Land's End, 9 miles from Penzance. We passed Newlyn low down by the sea, 1 mile, the residence of Councillor W. Godolphin, Copt (?), 4 miles, St. Buryan, Boscawen Church, Sennen, and St. Leven, 7 miles from Penzance. From there to Land's End we took a boy with us as our guide, and saw there many animals grazing at the outermost end of the land, where the land is very narrow. We rode on our horses as far to the point as the steeply descending ground allowed, dismounted, let our guide hold the horses, and scrambled as far down and as close to the very tip of the rocks as the conditions would permit. It was very perilous, the dreadfully overhanging cliffs, hollowed out by the sea, crazily lying over and on top of each other, and one's head swam when one looked down from the height.

We saw from there, lying 25 miles off the mainland out at sea, the Isles of Scilly, of which Sir F. Godolphin is the governor. On the north side we saw Whitesand Bay, St. Michael's Point, on the south side Schruw(?)-point. A very great number of sea birds live on these sea rocks.

After having seen all this and having cut our names in the ground as a memorial, we had of necessity to turn back from this non plus ultra, as the grim Neptune barred us the way with his green roaring waves, which he shattered to foam on the fearfully steep, steely rocks, beating a threatening hoarse roar from the swirling whirlpools and dismal caverns of the iron-hard cliffs, so as to say 'tournez vous'. So,

145 Colonel John St. Aubyn (d.1684) was captain of the Mount during the Cromwellian period and helped to quell a royalist uprising in 1649. He bought St. Michael's Mount at that time. The St. Aubin family still live there. See John Taylor, the 'Water Poet', in his *Wanderings to see the Wonders of the West* for his description of St. Michael's Mount in 1649. *

making a virtue out of necessity we showed him our heels, running post haste northward towards London to get that into our sights, but as our orientation in this region was rather poor, we, while intending to ride to St. Ives, passed a height called   , and below it got sight of Mr. Veale again, who had parted from us at St. Levan to search for Cornish diamonds, about which people had told us a lot. Now, meeting up with him again, he showed us what he had got for his money, which did not amount to much, and I demonstrated to him that one of his pieces was merely alum.

To this the uttermost westerly region resort mainly quakers and such folk, also supposedly many witches and sorcerers. Now, as we had ridden out of our way and it was very difficult and dangerous to ride through the shrubs and the unbeaten track, and St. Ives was much further off than we had thought, we rode back to Penzance, where we had our midday meal, and rode at 3 o'clock again along the beach to Marazion, stabled our horses, and, as it was high water, which stands then 11 or 12 feet high above the causeway, went by boat to the Mount, had a game on the bowling green and walked all round the rock, and, climbing along the cliffs, came to a cave in the cliffs at the foot of the Mount, in which is a well of very sweet water. This is often flooded by the spring tides and in storms; if one rubs the rocks under the water with one's hand it turns blood red; this water is called St. Michael's well. We crossed back again by boat and lodged with the mayor.

On the 19th August in the morning Governor John St. Aubyn came to pay us a visit for appearance sake, and pretended to be sorry that he had not known that we had stayed there the night, and why we had not made use of his house, all was at our disposal etc., but we had noticed that, when we were about to cross over the day before, he crossed over before us with a large party of ladies and their companions, and when we asked that the boat should come back to take us across, Sir John St. Aubyn enquired who those people were who wanted to come over, and it was explained to him, so that he had well known that it was us, also we had seen him stand at the gate above on the top of the hill, looking at us as we were playing on the bowling green. So now he got a pint or two of wine drawn, which we had to drink with him for friendship's sake, and so we took our leave, he strongly charging me to express his obedient affection to Mr. Jaques Thierry and to urge him to promote the affairs, which he had in hand for him, and about which he had previously spoken personally to him in London, and more of that kind.

So we rode then at 8 o'clock from Marazion to Falmouth, and passed Breage Church, 2 miles. From there we rode to Helston, 2 miles, a nice market town, where it was market day. We ate our midday meal there, and Mr. G. Veale took his leave from us; we had in him a cheerful travel companion, who had kept us company all the way from Truro to here. We then rode with the servant of Mr. Bryan Rogers to Falmouth, passed Penryn again and came in the evening to the inn where we had left our valises, but had on Mr. B. Rogers' invitation to stay at his house.

On Sunday, the 20th August, in the afternoon we went with Mr. Rogers to church which is one mile away in the country; the same minister, who held the service there in the afternoon, held it in the morning at the church at Penryn.

On the 21st we went in the morning with Mr. Rogers to Pendennis Castle, built by Henry VIII, which lies on the west side of the harbour. The throat or mouth of this famous port was armed by him with pieces of cannon on both sides. On the east side lies St. Mawes Castle. At the large castle Sir Richard Arundell was the governor;[146] there lie three companies in garrison. This castle, which is extremely strong, lies on a rock in the mouth of the bay; access to it from the land side is only by a narrow stretch of land, being not much more then one field's width. As one climbs up, one comes to a gate set with sentries, with a drawbridge over the moat of a dry ditch; climbing further, one passes another bridge and a strong gate and watch house, occupied by a strong guard; the governor has a fine house up there, and the castle has many bastions and flankers, well armed with cannons. All round below the rocks on the sea side lies a redoubt for the protection of the harbour, on which we counted 60 metal pieces, all shooting horizontally. In the late trouble it was besieged by 20,000 men who were not able to take it, but had to starve it out, and after the horses, cats, dogs etc. were eaten up, they surrendered, on condition that every soldier should be allowed to go free and to carry with him, besides his gun, rations for three days, to which the beleaguerers agreed etc. We went with the sergeant, who had shown us everything, to his quarters to refresh ourselves and then returned home.

In the afternoon we went to the small castle of which Lewis Tremayne was the governor.[147] He showed us everything, below and above, and all the rooms, chambers, and cellars. We went with the governor to the town of St. Mawes, lying close to the beach, and drank there merrily a round to the friends' and the king's health. This castle lies at a spit by a river, there are two like that in the harbour, and a great number of inlets and creeks, of which three are larger, one of them, called the Fal, runs past Truro.

146 Charles I had promised the succession to the governership of Pendennis Castle to Sir Richard Arundell, royalist soldier and MP. In 1662 Charles II redeemed his father's promise. Arundell later became first Baron Arundell of Trerice and d.1687 (DNB).

147 Sir Lewis Tremayne (Tremaine), whose son Sir John Tremayne figures in DNB, was presumably the governor of the smaller (St. Mawes) castle at the time.

Note. Besides its great width and convenience, this harbour is also remarkable for another thing, namely that it provides this uncommon facility that 100 ships of 50 to 500 last[148] can lie there at anchor, so that the top of the masts of one cannot be seen from any other etc.

The largest and deepest of these rivers is the middle one, reaching not above 12 English or about 4 or 5 Dutch miles into the land, and it is firmly asserted that one could sooner ride to London, which is a distance of 234 English miles, and back to Falmouth, than from the castle near Penryn round all the inlets, bays, creeks, and the three rivers, which do not even go very much inland, to the small castle lying opposite the large one etc.

Falmouth

Gets its name from the river Fal, and was only built since 1648 and 1649, in a place where before that time only stood two or three houses, namely our inn and another tavern, in which, they say that, when the house was sometimes crowded with sailors, jacktars etc. and the old woman could not tap as fast as the people were drinking, she used to say to her husband, 'These pennies come quick', or such like. Some say that this saying comes from the wenches or whores, who were after the travellers coming into the harbour or other such sweethearts. Falmouth is therefore better known all over England by the name of 'Penny-come-quick'.[149]

On the 22nd August in the morning we walked over the heights to Penryn and so I again made in a hurry a rough drawing of Penryn, Falmouth, and the castle. At 5 o'clock in the afternoon we took our leave from the father and the wife of Mr. Bryan Rogers; he personally rode with us for company to Fowey. We first had ourselves ferried across the harbour with the horses and rode over the hills, crossed two more rivers, being set over with the horses, and rode towards Tregony, 12 miles, where we arrived at 8 o'clock. From a height on the way we saw Dodman's Point, and in a defile between the hills we met Mr. Tremayne, the governor of the small castle. In Tregony we stayed at

On the 23rd August at 7 o'clock in the morning we rode from there to Fowey, 12 miles, saw on the way many tin mines, and came to a bight, the Par, where we saw a large number of boats full of pilchards, all caught that day at the crack of dawn, and learned that in 4 to 5

148 A Dutch 'shipslast' was equivalent to 1976 kg, 1.976 metric tonnes.
149 Falmouth received its charter only after the Civil War. The legend of the origin of the name 'Penny-come-quick' is prevalent in writings about the town.*

hours, that is at 3 or 4 in the morning, 800 hogsheads had been caught, each holding 7000 or 8000 fish. We saw there in the storehouses the pilchards being taken out of the salt and packed into hogsheads for pressing out the oil. We got to Fowey at 9 o'clock, went to our former lodging at the postmaster's Kestell, and entertained there Mr. Bryan Rogers, Peter Toller, and his father. After the meal Mr. Bryan Rogers took his leave from us and rode back to Falmouth. In the afternoon it rained very hard, and on Mr. Toller's pressing invitation we went to stay again with him.

On the 24th August in the morning we had ourselves set across the harbour at the foot of the steep high hill, climbed with a great effort to the top, and found there an exceptionally pleasant step-like promenade, level and flat at the outermost edge of the hill, as if cut out by hand. From there one has a very cheerful and splendid view over the harbour, the town, and the entire countryside, also between the castles out to sea etc. Before the war this place was very well kept, there were pavilions and arbours, but now it is neglected. The people used to come up there to banquet and to amuse themselves, but not any more.[150] Whilst there I drew in haste a prospect of the town and the harbour. We climbed down by another steep path and went by the boat to the quay, ate our midday meal at Mr. Toller's and drank one to the health of the Dutch and English friends.

In the afternoon we rode with Mr. Toller towards Exeter, passed 10 miles and rode along some tin mines, where one day, more than 18 or 20 years ago, four workmen came out of the mine to eat. As they sat down and brought out their food, a raven flew in and took the little basket with the food of one of them in its beak and flew off some distance with it and put it down. The man followed him, thinking that the raven would leave it there, but as he came near, the raven flew up with it and came down again a little further off, and the man followed him; when the bird had led him a long way from the tin mine shaft, he left the food there and flew off. Meanwhile the others had finished eating and had gone back to the tin workings, and he went back to the tin mine, eating his food on the way, but when he got there, he found that the mine had caved in and his three comrades had been smothered in it.

Another 2 miles from this place we came to some high stony hills. We rode up to one of these and led the horses up, and saw there the cheesewring[151] or cheese press, one of the wonders of Cornwall, some

---

150 Richard Carew, in 1602, describes Hall Walk, an extensive pleasure ground, as it was before the neglect mentioned by Schellinks. See Richard Carew, *The Survey of Cornwall*, p. 132. *

151 Cheesewring near Minions, on Bodmin Moor (Grid Ref.: SX 258725). Now

fearfully large and heavy boulders lying on top of each other, the smaller below and the larger on top, a very strange sight. The estimated weight of the third from the top or the middle one is 100 or 120 last. There is no other reasonable explanation how these stones have been raised up or got there, than that all the earth or soil between them has been washed away by the flood, since this whole mountain consists of nothing but such large, heavy, iron hard boulders, lying loose upon each other, with nothing but muddy black bog and some greenery and rushes between them. In the high stones on top, which we climbed, there were large holes eaten out by the rain, wind and weather, some of which we found full of sweet and clear water. Because of the great height we could see from up there the sea on both the north and the south side of England, in clear weather one can see Lundy Island on the north.

The descent from this hill was so terribly steep over and through the rocks without any path, that we were afraid that if the horses were to stumble and fall, they would break their necks. Riding a very difficult way for another 8 miles we got in the evening to Launceston in Cornwall. On this road we met so many black-coats or parsons that we did not know what to make of it. Some smoked a little pipe on their horses, others hung their heads. Some were cheerful, others looked very melancholic, some had the newly printed book of common prayer in their hands etc.[152]

In Launceston all inns, taverns, and guesthouses were so full of these fine priests that we had to leave the inn, to which we had gone, as they could not put us up for all our money, and, fetching our horses from the stable, we went with sack and pack to another, where however it was the same situation, and we had to make do with a little poky closet. After we had eaten, four musicians came into the room and wanted to play, if only for a draught of wine. They had come there to this episcopal convocation, hoping to make a fair bit, but, although these clergymen love the organ sounds, at that time they preferred the gargle sound of the cups of sack, which helped them to carouse all through the night, so that they kept their voices, while some of them did not go to bed at all in the night etc., and the poor jackanapes could not get any appreciation of their gut scraping that time; so they played merrily up for us for nothing, and drank a round with us. These parsons or preachers had come there to damn, so that they should not be damned, that is to say, to swear the oath of uniformity, and to

---

extensive granite quarries. Schellinks' drawing of the Cheesewring is in the British Museum (see Appendix I).

152 They were on their way to Launceston, the county town at the time, to swear the oaths required by the Act of Uniformity. See text-note 153.

abjure and forswear the earlier sworn covenant, which had been sworn
or confirmed by most of them, so they kicked so as not to be kicked.
However four or five could not or would not swear against their
conscience, and would rather suffer here than in the hereafter.

The newly printed revised Book of Common Prayer had been sent
the day before to our host and distributed, and he told us that there
had been such a throng for it that they had almost torn his clothes off
his back.[153] On the 25th August early in the morning the bibbers called
for sack, ale, tobacco etc., and, although it was very damp weather,
came like bees out of all the chamber doors and drew themselves up
in position each to ride to his town, so as we were about to mount our
horses, one of these brethren, a pretty tobacco manikin, presented us
with the favour of his company to travel towards Exeter, and rode
beside us, a pipe constantly in his mouth, and his long robe or mourning
coat drawn up round his ears.

Not far from Launceston we passed a stone bridge, which lies over
a running river, which separates Cornwall from Devon, passed a lot of
hills and dales and some villages, and came at 10 o'clock to Okehampton
in Devon, 15 miles, and, as it is from there to Exeter another 20 miles,
we had our midday meal there with our pastor, who was a sponger,
and rode on. From the tops of the hills we had the most overwhelmingly
beautiful views on both sides, and lost our country parson, for whom
we rode too fast. After passing some villages we arrived back at Exeter
at 6 o'clock in the evening, and again stayed with Mr. Bernard Spark,
who welcomed us and his brother-in-law Mr. P. Toller.

The 27th August, Sunday.

Note: All over England this was the last such Sabbath day, on which
the presbyterians were allowed to preach, as by act of parliament it
had been laid down that by the 24 August old style all ministers had
to abjure the Edinburgh Covenant of 1641 and had to follow the
episcopal order of service, to which many preachers could not or would
not consent, although they had taken the oath before. So was this then
at Exeter the last farewell service held by them. In the morning in St.
Mary Major's Church we heard the minister of Bartholomew parish,
his text was 2 Timothy c.2, v.19. In the afternoon we heard in St.

153 By the Act of Uniformity (14 Chas. II, c.4) all clergy were required:

a. by the last Sunday before St. Bartholomew's day (24 Aug. n.s.) to read Morning
and Evening Prayers from the new book of Common Prayer, a revised version of which
was authorised after its suppression during the Commonwealth.

b. to swear the oath of allegiance to the King and foreswear the Covenant.

c. if they were not ordained by a bishop, to obtain such ordination quickly.

If they failed in any of these they lost their living. The short period allowed for
implementation – fourteen weeks – led to great confusion: see I.M. Green, *The Re-
establishment of the Church of England 1660–1683*, 1978.

John's Church in the High Street the minister, Mr. Atkins, his text was I Corinth c.13, v.11; he gave a fine sermon, moving to tears his hearers, young and old.

On the 31st August we saw at St. Andrew's Church[154] the induction of the new Dean, Dr. Jongh; after the end of the morning prayers all the doctors of divinity, the ministers and all the choristers went from the choir, met the Dean at the cloisters and conducted him into the choir, the choristers, all dressed in white surplices, singing, the doctors in their red tabards and hoods etc. There he was installed in his seat by two doctors. He then got up and said a long prayer, and after that they sang beautifully with organ accompaniment. Then he delivered an oration to the congregation etc. and was, again under singing, conducted back to the cloisters and from there to his house, where a splendid banquet was prepared for all the clerical and civil dignitaries of the town. The Dean sent a doctor to invite us three, Mr. J. Thierry, a Mr. J. Seghvelt and me, but we were out for a walk. The bells were ringing from 4 o'clock in the morning until midday as a sign of rejoicing. In the afternoon we walked with Mr. Seghvelt round the town and watched in a field a prize target shooting with bows and guns.

On the 1st September, after we had taken our leave, we rode at 3 o'clock from Exeter, accompanied for one mile by Mr. B. Spark and Mr. Seghvelt. We came through several villages to Honiton, 15 miles, and stayed there at the Golden Lion; this is a market town, and much lace is being made there.

On the 2nd we rode in the morning to Axminster, 8 miles, and, from the hills, saw Portland in front of us on the left (sic), and rode on past Lyme, a small seaside village on our right, on a low hill by the side of a small river called the Lyme, with a man-made breakwater of heavy stones and piles, which serves as a harbour for ships. In the recent war this small place held out for a long time against the king's army. We rode on to Charmouth, 3 miles, and Chideock, 3 miles, and so to Bridport, 2 miles, where we had our midday meal. This place is a well known market town, and, like Lyme, lies in Dorset, between two small rivers, which here flow into each other. The best hemp is grown there, and a lot of ropes and cables are made here. At one time this town had for several years the privilege that all the ropework for the English ships had to be made only there. 3 miles from Weymouth, lying in the sea, is the island of Portland, so called by a noble Saxon, who anno 703 captured and fortified it and did much damage along the entire coast.

From Bridport we rode to Winterborne, 8 miles. There was a heavy

154 This seems an error for the cathedral church of St. Peter.*

downpour of rain with mist and wind, and we had to pass over great heights or hills, and could hardly see four steps ahead of us; luckily we did not get more than wet through, and had enough to do to keep to our path. When the rain had passed we rode on a good level road towards Dorchester, 4 miles, where we went to stay at the Royal Oak, and dried ourselves.

Note: From Portland, which is a stone cliff, the stone of which St. Paul's in London is built, is said to have been taken; the people on the island are strong, and live very long.

Dorchester

is the county town of Dorset but small in size, very famous in olden times. It lies in a beautiful valley, through which flows the river Fram or Frome, over which the ferry or crossing point used to be at Dorchester. It was of old called Durnovaria, and was once a town, as is evident from its old walls. It has three parishes: St. Peter is the largest church, 2. The Trinity, 3. Hallhe [St. George] in the parish of Fordington. It is said that within a radius of 6 miles around Dorchester more than 300,000 sheep are in pasture. Maiden Castle[155] close to the town was fortified in the late war, but now nothing but the trenches are to be seen.

Lulworth Castle is 8 miles distant, Weymouth 6 miles at the mouth of the little river Wey, and on the other side of the harbour lies King's Melcombe,[156] to which one can go with carriages and horses over a bridge which is 80 paces long and 3 or 4 wide.

On Sunday, the 3rd September, in the morning to the service at St. Peter, in the afternoon at the Trinity, then we walked about around the river, in which there is much T [trout?], and looking at the old trenches etc.

On the 4th September we rode at 8 o'clock from Dorchester to Salisbury, which is 30 miles, and passed through Puddletown, 4 miles, Milborne St. Andrew 3, Whitechurch 3, Blandford 2, Gussage 6, Woodyates, 4 miles. Here there was a man, who, when he heard that the king had been beheaded, vowed that he would not let his beard be cut until England had another king again; his beard was $\frac{3}{4}$ ell long. Coombe 6, Salisbury 2 miles. We had our midday meal at the Greyhound at Blandford, a market town, very pleasantly situated in a valley by a river, the way was rather uphill and down dale, but otherwise a very good road. We rode over a corner of Salisbury plain,

155 Schellinks seems to refer to Maumbury Ring, a Roman amphitheatre, fortified by the parliamentarians in 1642 (Pevsner-Newman, *BoE, Dorset*).
156 Melcombe Regis.

a very wide uninhabited heath,   miles long, with few or no houses on it, on which an enormous number of sheep are pastured. Many robberies occur on these plains. Coming from Dorchester we did not see the town of Salisbury at all until we were on top of the hill, which is so close to the town that one is in the town before one knows it, as one has only to descend steeply. We arrived there at half past five and took our quarters at the Antelope, a good inn in St. Catharine Street, and were there well treated for our money.

Salisbury

is situated in Wiltshire, a very pleasant and fertile county, in a well watered valley. There is a most magnificent cathedral or main church with a very tall pointed spire and two transepts.

Roger Bishop of Salisbury[157] built the church like this, and the work took longer than that at the temple in Jerusalem, which was over fifty years in hand. There are in it as many pillars, great and small, as there are hours in the year, as many windows as days, as many doors and chapels as months. Some scholars think that this was done from the notion that not one month, day, nor hour should be allowed to go by without some devout duty. In the church and behind the choir are many tombs, next to it is a very beautiful cloister, a spacious and beautiful building. Nearby is the bishop's palace, an excellent house surrounded by water on all sides. On the other side of the church is the bell [tower], standing separately, high and strong. The bishop's house was much damaged in the recent war, but is now being completely repaired.

Salisbury has 4 churches, namely the main church, called the Lady's Church, 2 St. Thomas, 3 St. Edmund, 4 St. Martin. The present Bishop was Dr. Hensmans.[158]

There are five gates [sic], namely: Winchester, Castle, Close, and Harmen Gate. The principal streets are these: High Street, Catherine Street (Antelope), Dragon Street, Endless Street, Love Street, Green Croft Street, an arcade, Castle Street, Fisherton Street.[159] In this town which is not very large, there are easily 70 inns or hostelries for travellers, and at least as many ale houses or taverns. In every street is a channel of running water 7 or 8 feet wide, or clear, sweet water. In

157 The cathedral was built by Bishop Richard Poore (see note 164). The separate bell-tower (campanile), part of the thirteenth-century buildings, was swept away by James Wyatt *c.*1789; this, with his work on other cathedrals, earned him the name 'Wyatt, the destroyer' (Pevsner-Cherry, *BoE, Wiltshire*).

158 Humphrey Henchman, bishop of Salisbury 1660–63.

159 Dragon Street (in 1455: Drakehall Street), now St. John and Exeter Street; Love Street is Love Lane (Inf. Monty Little, librarian, Salisbury).

these channels 3 or 4 stones or wooden blocks are set at many places to step on, to cross over the water; the horses go through in the middle and the wheels at the sides of these stepping stones in the water.[160] There is also a fine, spacious market place, where on market day all kinds of goods are brought for sale, especially good fish and fruit.

On the 6th September we rode at 8 o'clock in the morning, with a guide on foot, from Salisbury to Wilton, 2 miles, the river Wylye flowing alongside in many channels.

This place was formerly the chief town of the shire or county, which is called Wiltshire after it, but it is now only a small village, but still governed by a mayor. In this town is the house of the Earl of Pembroke.

We left our horses at the Bell Inn and went with the landlord or innkeeper to look at this house, one of the servants showing us round. We came first into a great hall, and were led into the large vaulted cellars, where we refreshed ourselves. From there we went up and saw many fine chambers and a long gallery full of paintings, mostly portraits, of many great noblemen of England in Queen Elizabeth's time, also all the ancestors of the Earls of Pembroke, and very many old portraits of kings of England and other nobles. Further we saw some chambers, mostly very richly furnished with beds and other fittings. From there we went up to a large flat roof covered with lead, from where there was a very fine view over the splendid pleasure garden as well as over the country. Next we came to the new part of the house, which had burned down some years ago, and had been much more beautifully rebuilt like new. We saw there some magnificent chambers splendidly decorated with painted ceilings, especially the dining room or hall which is very magnificent and exquisite. In it hangs a very old, excellent painting, a Cebes scene.[161] Further we saw a room, painted all round

160 Evelyn, Pepys, and Celia Fiennes mention these runnels, which were in the middle of most streets.

161 The south range of Wilton House was rebuilt by John Webb with the advice of Inigo Jones, after a fire in 1647-8 (Pevsner-Cherry, *BoE, Wiltshire*).

The 'Cebes tableau' (Pinax) is a book, attributed to Cebes, a pupil of Socrates (see Plato's *Phaedo*), in which he describes a visit to the temple of Kronos (Saturn), where he sees a picture, an allegorical representation of the dangers and vicissitudes of life (comparable to Bunyan's *Pilgrim's Progress*), which is pointed out to him, scene by scene, by a venerable old man. The book was current at Schellinks's time, and translated into many languages (Dutch in 1615); it was in use as a school text book, and was the subject of many pictures (see e.g. R. Thomson Clark, *The Tablet of Kebes*, 1909, and Reinhard Schleier, *Tabula Cebetis...*, Berlin, 1973).

The painting at Wilton House was seen amongst those in the Hall by Aubrey in his *Natural History of Wiltshire*, published posthumously in 1697, where he describes it as 'a very large picture, and done by a great master, which the genius describes to William, the first earl of this family, and lookes on him, pointing to avarice, as to be avoyded by a noble person.'

The hall was destroyed by fire *c.*1705, apparently with all the pictures.

with nothing but hunting and park scenes etc., and some other rooms with other decorations. Then we were shown a chamber, exquisitely prepared for His Majesty.

Then we saw the chapel belonging to the house. Thus having seen everything we went down some very elegant stairs, and went with the gardener to see the gardens, which are extremely elegant, interesting and pleasant, with a wide avenue or promenade throughout its whole length with many cypress trees along it. First there are four flower beds with fountains in the middle, then some steps, flanked on both sides by four stone lions, two on each rise, then on both sides a maze with stone statues. Then two fishponds, where a lot of carp are kept. There follow two parks with cypress and fruit trees and in the middle of the promenade a bronze gladiator on a pedestal, then on both sides in the corners again two sitting stone lions. Then one comes to a pavilion, in Italian style, its front with marble statues in niches and a balustrade above, and on each side a curved stair, and the stone railing on top built like shells so as to let the water flow down on both sides. Above on the roof are water pans in which fish are kept. The water, led there in pipes, feeds all the water works in the grotto below. There is a very splendid water work set with historical statues in marble half relief all round, also a Mount Parnassus or nightingale song at the side of the large chamber. The ceiling and all the walls are covered with rocks with a lot of statues between etc.

In the middle of the large chamber stands a small table with a pipe coming up through its stone foot; on this table stand all kinds of water works, which dowse the unsuspecting onlookers.[162]

After we had seen all this, we went to our horses, passed by the armoury which too was also burnt down and has now been rebuilt much better, well equipped out inside, but is not shown to everybody, but only to important people etc.

We refreshed ourselves and then rode to Stonehenge, 6 miles, all the way over level, flat heathland with sheep, but on either side in the

162 The gardens and grotto, which Schellinks describes, were created for the fourth Earl of Pembroke by Isaac de Caus c.1632. They extended on the south side of the house. The grotto was in the centre of a colonnade, closing off the north side; it contained elaborate waterworks, also described by Aubrey, and by Celia Fiennes, which were apparently designed to wet unsuspecting visitors. The 'nightingale song' appears to refer to the noise made by water, producing 'the melody of nightingerlls and all sort of birds' (Celia Fiennes, c.1682). The front of the grotto had fine carvings in stone. Inside were low-relief marble sculptures, said to have been brought from Italy. The gardens were totally reconstructed in mid eighteenth century, when the colonnade and grotto were moved to a new position east of the house. Later the front of the grotto was moved by Samuel Wyatt to what is now known as the Park School House, when the low-relief sculptures were incorporated in the Italian garden loggia (Aubrey's *Wiltshire*; Celia Fiennes, *Journeys*; *Country Life*, July/August 1963, 206–9, 264–7).

distance hills with corn fields. As one comes within sight of the stones they look like a gentleman's house or building down below. We rode to them on the horses and dismounted.

Stonehenge

On Salisbury Plain, 6 miles from Salisbury, is a threefold round circle, or three separate rings, of erect, unworked, very heavy stones, some of them 28 feet high and 9 to 10 feet wide and very thick, two standing in the ground and lying over them on top like a gate. The circle, measured outside round the stones, is 300 feet. The stones are difficult to count, as some have fallen and lie on top of each other. The ancient writers of history called it chorea gigantium or giants' dance, and it is now one of the wonders of England. The writers and opinions on it differ widely, some say that these stones stood originally in Ireland, and were brought here with the help of Merlin, a magician, others that they were erected by a certain Aurelius, king of the Britons, whose nobles were murdered there on one day of assembly in the reign of Vortigern, his country's scourge, about AD 475, through the treachery of the Saxons.[163] In their memory Aurelius had this stone circle erected, and it is said that he and two of his successors as British kings and many of their nobles are also buried there with their weapons of very old fashion, large and broad.

Not far from there one sees the ruins of an old fortification supposedly built there by the Romans.

Note. The stones of Stonehenge are rough and grey in colour. Many think that they are made of sand, gravel, burnt lime etc. and have become hardened by time and weather. However that is, there are no stones to be found on this heath or plain for many miles around. Some think that they have been hewn like this from one rock.

From Stonehenge we rode to Amesbury, a town in a well-watered valley, 2 miles away. There we made our midday meal and then rode back to Salisbury, and in passing saw the castle,[164] of which now nothing is to be seen but some ruins of ditches and walls; it is dug out of the hill or rock, and was in olden times the strength of the town, but when the town burned down, it was rebuilt on new ground a mile or two away, in a well-watered valley, where it stands to this day.

163 Vortigern, 'a haughty tyrant' (DNB), king of Britons in the fifth century, is said to have invited Saxon tribes to help defend his kingdom against the Picts. His son and his nobles were massacred by Saxon treachery. Ambrosius Aurelianus, a contemporary leader, is said to have conquered part of Vortigern's kingdom during a campaign to control the Saxons (DNB and EB).

164 Old Sarum. Bishop Poore, in 1219, obtained permission to abandon the uncomfortable hill-top site and built a new cathedral in the valley.

On the 7th September we could not go out much because of heavy rain in the morning and afternoon. Towards evening I went quickly to make a sketch of the town.

On the 8th September we rode at 9 o'clock in the morning from Salisbury to Winchester, 20 miles, passing Stockbridge, which is in Hampshire, 12 miles, and on to Winchester, 8 miles on a good road, and went to stay at the George. In the afternoon we went to look at the cathedral and also the town.

Winchester

Is situated in Hampshire in a fertile and pleasant valley at the foot of the hills; it has a surfeit of water because the river runs through it in several places. It is about $1\frac{1}{2}$ miles in circumference, has 6 gates with suburbs, and has the following churches: the Cathedral called Trinity, 2 St. Thomas, 3 St. Lawrence, 3 (sic) St. Maurice; these are now in use. In former times, when the town was larger, there were 16 churches; of these the following still exist: St. Clements, St. Mary Kalender, Colbrook, St. John, and St. Michael, and the hospitals of m̅ Symons (?), St. John's, St. Mary Magdalene, on whose day a fair is held there. There is also St. Cross Hospital, sisterhouse,[165] Wolvesey the bishop's see, and the Monastery. The gates are named after the four quarters of the wind. and besides them Durngate, Kings Gate, gentleman's house called Abbey, Eastgate house and squire Paulet's house.[166]

This town, which prospered in Roman times within its wide walls, which are now, like the castle, badly damaged, is large but only thinly built over. The High Street is the largest and best street for shops and houses. The main church is a very lovely building, very long, with its screen of white stone, with niches on both sides, in which stand the lifesize statues of King James and King Charles, very artistically cast in copper, and above in the front two recumbent angels, and the choir itself very neatly and interestingly carved in stone all round.[167] There

165 St. Cross Hospital was founded in 1136 as almshouses for men. Cardinal Beaufort's foundation (about 1445) was intended to include accommodation for 3 sisters, but it is doubtful whether that was ever carried out (VCH *Hampshire*, ii, 196). Miss Elizabeth Lewis, Museums Curator, Winchester, suggests that Schellinks may refer to St. John's House almshouses, which were on the east side of the High Street in 1554.

166 Squire Paulet, a relative of the Marquis of Winchester; his house stood on the site of 75 Hyde Street.

167 The stone screen, attributed to Inigo Jones, was removed by Gilbert Scott *c*.1875. It was shown in the first guide book of the cathedral (1715), reproduced as the front cover of *Winchester Cathedral, an Anthology*, 1970. The statues of James I and Charles I now stand inside to the left and right of the west door. Secondary sources about the cathedral state that these figures, by Hubert Le Sueur, were sold during the Commonwealth for £10 to a Mr. Newland in the Isle of Wight (see note 172 below), who hid them in his garden.

are many monuments of ancient bishops and Saxon kings and other
nobles, and choirs and retrochoir, also a chapel in which King Philip
was married to Queen Mary anno [1554]. In the large choir one sees
on both sides, standing above on a ledge, some bone chests:[168] on the
right hand the tomb of King Edmund with this inscription towards the
inside next to the choir:

> Edmundus Rex obit A.D.M.

on the other side or outside the choir one can read:

> Que herã, retinet, Edmundus sui ipe Christe.

At the Restoration Bishop Buppa bought them back for £100 (*Winch. Cath. Records* 37
(1968), 45–52, inf. from John Hardacre, curator, Winchester Cathedral).

168 The remains of Saxon Kings and Bishops, removed from the earlier Minster,
were placed in eight chests on top of the newly erected sidescreens of the choir *c*.1525.
Cromwellian soldiers desecrated four of these, the contents of which were, at the
restoration, placed in two new chests, those furthest away from the altar. Schellinks
mentions these two chests, at that time uninscribed; the inscriptions were added between
1684 and 1692.

We have given in the text the version exactly as written in the Copenhagen MS. The
version recorded by Ball in 1818, rearranged in the order used by Schellinks, is as follows:

(King Edmund)
'The inscription on each side is as follows:

> Edmundus Rex, obit A.D.M.
> Que theca hec retinet Edmudu suscipe Christe
> Qui vivente patre regia sceptra tulit'

(King Edred)
'The title and epitaph, which is alike on both sides of this chest, runs thus:

> Edredus Rex, obit A.D. 955
> Hoc pius in tumulo, Rex Edredi requiescit,
> Qui has Britonum terras rexerit egregie.

(King Kenewalch [Kenulph] and King Egbert)
'On the one side this chest is inscribed,

> Kenulphus Rex, obit A.D.M. 784

on the other,

> Egbertus Rex, obit ADM. 857.

The epitaph, which is alike on both sides, is as follows:

> Hic Rex Egbertus pausat cum
> Rege Kenulpho nobis egregia munera uterqz tulit'

(King Kinegils and King Ethelwolph [Adolphus])
'It is inscribed thus, on the one side:

> Rex Kyngils, obit A.D.M. 641

on the other,

> Adulphus Rex, obit A.D.M. 859

The epitaph is the same on both sides:

> Kyngilsi in cista hac simul ossa jacent et Adulphi
> ipsius fundator, hic benefactor erat.'

The version given by Vaughan in 1919 differs somewhat from the above. It appears
that the inscriptions were repainted on a number of occasions. See Charles Ball, *An
Historical Account of Winchester with Descriptive Walks*, Winchester 1818; John Vaughan,
Winchester Cathedral, its monuments and memorials, London, 1919.

qui vivente Patre Roma sceptra tulit

next: Edredus Rex obitt Ao 955

on the other side:

Hoc Piner in tumulo Rex Ed Requiesit qui has Britorum terras Rex erdit Egregie

Below near the bottom at the foot of the pillars:

Nicholai olih Winton Episcopi

next to this:

intus est Corpus Richard Willhelmi Conquestorie Fili et beorne Ducis

on the left hand of the choir inside one can read

Egbertus Rex obit 837

on the other side

Hic Rex Egbertus Fausut cu^n rege Kenulph nobis Egregia Munero Vteræ tulit

next to it, to be read inside

Rex Kijngils 642

on the other side of the tomb

Kingilhi in cista Has sivul ossa jacent Adulphus, ipsus Fundator Hic Benefactor erat

In the choir stand two tomb chests without any inscription.

In the chapel behind the choir is the sepulchre of Richard Weston, Earl of Portland,[169] his figure in copper lying on a decorative marble tomb.

We saw the funeral of one Dr. Standeley,[170] coming from his home, which was near the church, with all the choristers, dressed in white, walking singing before the bier with the coffin with his armorials hanging round it; then followed his friends, gentlemen and ladies together, each with a branch of rosemary in the hand. They brought the body into the choir and a service was held and a funeral sermon

---

169 Richard Weston, earl of Portland, treasurer to Charles I, d.1635. The tomb is in the Guardian Angels' Chapel, DNB.

170 Dr. Edward Stanley, headmaster of Winchester College before 1642, when he became a Prebendary of the Cathedral. He died in 1662 (Vaughan). The text is more likely Job 5 v.26.

preached by a Doctor, his text Job 5 v. 56 [26] and the rite of earth to earth, dust to dust, etc, nothing to nothing. Then during another long piece of music led round the grave and then, kneeling down again, another prayer was said.

In Winchester is a beautiful college,[171] which William Wykeham, Bishop of Winchester, had built there.

On the 9th September in the morning, walked round and through the town, and drew the view from the hill as a memorial.

At half past three in the afternoon we rode from Winchester to Southampton, 10 miles, arrived there at 6 o'clock, and went to stay at the Dolphin, the largest inn, but had such a bad service there that we moved the next day to stay at the Star.

On the 10th in the morning we heard the service, and in the afternoon went for a walk, crossed by the Itchen ferry, and went a pleasant road to Weston, where we took refreshments with some Southampton people; then we walked round there, and went back again by the ferry.

On the 11th there was heavy rain. At 6 o'clock in the evening the Bishop of Winchester came into the town and was met and accompanied by the gentry; sitting in his carriage, he was welcomed in front of Holy Rood Church and the town hall by the aldermen and the mayor, and conducted to his lodgings at the mayor's house, while all the church bells rang like possessed. There was not enough accommodation in the town for all his large suite. The Bishop came there to introduce the new order of service and to change and abolish the old customs.

On the 12th September, after a sermon by the Bishop, the ministers were confirmed and the people blessed by the laying on of hands.

Southampton

lying in Hampshire, a fine, populous town, is an independent free town. It has an old citadel called the New Castle, lying on a height within the town, but in ruins. It has five gates, East, West, South, Bar, and Watergate, the West and East Quay at the water side, and seven churches, Holy Rood, St. Miles, the French Church etc., and lies on an inlet from the sea.

On the 12th in the afternoon we boarded the packet boat with our horses and sailed to the Isle of Wight, together with many other passengers and another four horses. It is a distance of 20 miles, but due to the good following wind we got there at 3 o'clock. We passed by Hampton along the New Forest, which is 18 miles long from Lipp [Lepe] to Downton, is full of deer, and belongs to the king. King

171 Winchester College, founded 1382.

William of Normandy had in this place all the towns, villages, houses and churches over a range of 30 miles pulled down and destroyed, and all the poor inhabitants driven out, and made it a forest for wild beasts. And also past Calshot Castle, which lies on a spit of land and is at high tide completely surrounded by water. We sailed to West Cowes, disembarked, and went to stay at the Three Feathers, where we met a merchant, Benjamin Newland,[172] and drank with him and the governor of West Cowes Castle with good cheer the health of all our friends in Holland; the name of the governor was Colonel Tourney.

On the 13th September in the morning we went to look at Cowes. In the afternoon came Lord Culpeper, the governor of the Isle of Wight, with a troop of horsemen and a lot of clergymen, gentlemen, and others from Newport, to welcome the Bishop of Winchester and to conduct him to Newport. The Bishop came from Southampton by water, and as he passed, Calshot Castle fired off all its cannons. Meanwhile we looked over West Cowes Castle from top to bottom.

We saw the bishop disembarking near the castle and being welcomed by the governor of the Isle of Wight and many gentlemen and country clergy, while all the cannons were fired off. He then went into the castle and from there rode with governor Culpeper, the Dean and others in a carriage 4 miles to Newport, accompanied by the horsemen, noblemen, ministers, and many others, so we joined them for the pleasure of the ride and to increase the escort. When they approached Newport the garrison of Carisbrooke Castle fired off all their cannons. As they came into the town the mayor and aldermen in their tabards stood ready to welcome the Bishop, the militia being under arms. The Bishop took his lodgings at Lady N.N., a widow. We rode back the same evening to W. Cowes, and Mr. Newland and the governor were again with us at our lodgings.

On the 14th September in the morning we were ferried over by Benjamin Newland's boat to East Cowes, where all the dwellings and

---

172 C.D. Webster and James O'Donnell, Isle of Wight Record Office, have kindly supplied us with information on the Newlands, a large family of seventeenth-century merchants, including a pedigree. Robert Newland (d.1637) was a main stockholder in the I.o.W. plantation in Virginia. Amongst his sons were:

a. William (1605–60), father of Sir Benjamin (c.1633–99), M.P. for Southampton 1679–99, who in 1672 was accused of acting as agent for the Dutch (Henning, *House of Commons, 1660–90*, iii. 135–6).

b. Benjamin (1607–71) the elder, father of Benjamin the younger (c.1636–c.1724). The latter is recorded in 1660 as owning considerable property, including two quays and two wharves at East Cowes and Whippingham (Feet of Fines, Hants., Trinity and Michaelmas 12 Chas. II). He seems to be the Benjamin who looked after Schellinks while in the I.o.W. One of his nephews, Isaac, was described as a 'Duch merchant'.

c. John (1619–59), the Newland who was involved in the unsuccessful escape plots of Charles I from Carisbrooke Castle; see note 175 below.

warehouses were built by him, including a small church.

NB. The Duke of Gloucester had given Benjamin Newland an assurance that he would bestow on this place the privilege of freedom for all foreign ships etc, but due to the Duke's early death this did not happen.[173]

This Mr. Benjamin Newland has a very fine house there, and warehouses and wharves for building and repairing ships etc.

Mr. Benjamin had bought for the sum of 125 pounds sterling the two metal statues, which stand in front of the choir in Winchester Cathedral, and which used to stand there and had been pillaged by Cromwell's soldiers. He had buried them in the ground, and refused large offers of money for them. When the king returned he presented the statues to His Majesty, who ordered him to return them to the Bishop as they were stolen church property, so he mentioned the sum of money which he had paid for them and was given 100 pounds, and he was going to approach the present Bishop for the balance.

We were entertained with an excellent breakfast at his house, and after that we crossed over and rode with him again to Newport. When we got there we went to the church; the service was over and the Bishop proceeded with the confirmation of the people and blessing by laying on of hands: there was such an immense crowd of people who, without any order, jostled each other as if they were to get money.

Note: When I saw that every Tom, Dick, and Harry were confirmed by the Bishop by the hundred, without any examination or distinction, I joined the end of the crowd and pushed into the choir and received the blessing from Bishop Morley of Winchester.[174] After the blessing was done, he delivered a long oration to the listeners in the church about the episcopal authorities' present form of service, after that he went to the St. George Inn and held there a large banquet with the governor, the mayor, and many others. Meanwhile all the militia remained at arms.

On the 15th September in the morning Mr. Newland came to our inn, the Bull, to ask us in the mayor's name whether we would like to go hunting with him; this we declined, as our horses were not fast enough.

So we walked in the morning with Mr. B. Newland to Carisbrooke Castle, which is quite old but still strong, lying in the heart of the Isle of Wight.

Note: I spoke to governor Culpeper in Dutch and requested to have

173 Henry, duke of Gloucester (1639–60), youngest brother of Charles II. He was, with his younger sister Elizabeth (who died in 1650, monument in St. Thomas's Church, Newport), at Carisbrooke Castle from August 1650 to late 1652 and there most likely met Newland, a fervent royalist.

174 Bishop George Morley had been appointed a few months earlier.

the honour to look at the castle and everything. So the custodian showed us everything, the highest bastion or keep, going up 92 steep steps, on whose top were eleven pieces of cannon mounted on naval gun carriages. We also saw the king's prison chamber,[175] which was not large and not a very pleasant room. In front of this chamber was another in which lay the guard; he also showed us the window, where a new iron bar was set in. King Charles or somebody else is said to have eaten away the iron with strong water to give him a chance to escape by this way. We also saw some very deep water wells, the chapels, and a bowling green, the most beautiful in England, large octagonal and absolutely smooth and level. Then we had some refreshments with the custodian, who treated us to wine and venison pasty.

We returned to Newport and engaged a man who was to ride with us to show us all over the island. We left at 12 o'clock and came to Niton and from there to Onderweath (?), just across the island towards the south; there we were at the beach and could see a long way to either side along the island and the shore. From there we rode up St. Catherine's Hill, a very high hill on which an old chapel seems to have stood. There was still a tower, in which a watch is kept in wartime, and a fire at night. From this hill we could see almost all round the island as it lies in the sea. Riding steeply down from the hill we came to the cottage of a countryman, who treated us well, and when we wanted to pay him, he would not accept anything, so we gave something to the girl, and rode on to Chale, then to Brightstone and from there to Charwell, passing by the seat of Mr. John Dingly, and then, riding back 2 or 3 miles, came to Shorwell, where we stayed at a country pub, the only accommodation which was to be found. It was clear that, as there was no inn in any of the other villages, and that nobody would be willing to put us up, we would have to manage in the woods, or make do with one or the other haystack, so we made a virtue of necessity.

On the 16th September we rode in the morning from Shorwell back to Brightstone and from there to the village of Brook, and down to a plain called Brook Green, from where a broad ditch, 2 or 3 miles long, runs towards the sea, which, in summer, is without water and almost dry. In the ground, or rather on both sides of this ditch, 25 or 30 feet, and nearer the sea 50 to 60 feet down below ground level, one sees and finds some very large hazelnut trees with their branches, leaves and nuts, which are fully grown. There is no other explanation, how

175 Charles I was imprisoned in Carisbrooke Castle from December 1647 to November 1648. There were several plots for his escape, in all of which Newland was involved. In one of them acid was to be used to cut a window bar (see J.D. Jones, *The Royal Prisoner*, 1964. Inf. R.E. Brinton, Carisbrooke Castle).

they could have got so deeply into the ground, but that they were covered with earth by the deluge, which prevented the air from reaching them, and in this way they were preserved for ever. We took two men and a boy with us with a shovel and two pickaxes, but did not have much trouble with digging, as we found them in the ground, trees, branches and nuts, in the loose, broken ground. We found many so fresh and hard, as if they had not long been lying there, but most of the nuts broke up if one did not handle them gently like rotten wood. We took some of them with us as a keepsake. At a gentleman's house very close to this place they show the antler of a deer, which was also found in this ground etc.[176]

From Brook Green we rode across several fields to a high hill, steeply breaking-off towards the sea, which we rode up with difficulty and then led the horses along the outermost edge of the precipitous cliff as we could find no other way. It was frightening to look down, and very dangerous because this chalk hill had at and under the edge a lot of holes and cracks, and lumps sticking out.

At last we reached some level ground, where we had a better road, rode down a little to a fisherman's hut at the foot on the beach, and we rested a while. The hills we had come over were called Freshwater, 15 miles. We climbed up another hill called Needles Point, which is the extreme point towards the west. These Needles are protruding chalk hills which have some points or pyramids on their seaward ends, which are cut off from the large hill. We went to the highest point and saw from there the island north and southward almost all round us, with Yarmouth in a plain 4 miles away. The north side of the Isle of Wight was mostly low boggy ground. From the top we went to the tip of the island and so returned over the height, a heath for sheep, and, coming back to our horses, mounted and rode right through the middle of the island, passing many parishes and several high hills, on which a lot of sheep were pastured, and water holes in the valleys for watering and washing the sheep.

So we came back to Carisbrooke and, as we were so high up, let the castle lie on our right below, although the castle itself is on a reasonably high hill.

At 1 o'clock we were back at Newport, held our midday meal, and, with Mr. Newland, drank a round to the health of our friends.

176 Fossilised plant remains, which 'were first noticed by Thomas Webster (in 1816)', see H.J. Osborne White, *A Short Account of the Geology of the Isle of Wight*, HMSO, 1921, p. 171.

The Isle of Wight

Vecta or Vectis Insula belongs to the county of Southampton and extends from east to west 20 English miles in length and 10 or 12 in width, 3 or 4 miles from the mainland. The Emperor Vespasian was the first to conquer it, the inhabitants are considered to be courageous soldiers, well trained and tough. The Isle is said to be able to put 4000 men into the field. It has 36 settlements, villages as well as some with castles. The Bishop of Winchester has the ecclesiastical authority over the island. Its soil is fertile, and it supports a lot of rabbits, hares, partridges, pheasants and other game. It has a small forest, and two deer parks with stags and hinds. A line of hills runs through the middle of the island, on which very large numbers of sheep are pastured, whose wool is highly esteemed by the clothiers. Corn grows there in abundance, as well as other produce and fruit. Thousands of sea birds nest there in the cliffs of the sea rocks.

Opposite Yarmouth lies Hurst Castle, and somewhat further Sandwich and Peserley Point (?).

Note: On the western and southern side of the Island all the trees and bushes are bent towards the east and north by the wind, and are so bare that the bent branches appear shorn like palms.

On the 16th September we had our midday meal at Newport and then rode back to West Cowes to rest in our lodgings.

On Sunday, the 17th September, wind and weather were so favourable that we decided to cross over from the Island by a large sailing boat. We first informed the governor of the castle and asked for his permission, which he gave us, and sailed over at 9 o'clock with our horses. At 11 o'clock we landed at Hill Head, 9 miles, and rode from there along the beach, missed the way, and, as the tide came in, did not dare to take any risk, stuck to the higher ground and turned into a country lane and came to Basing Stock [Alverstoke ?], 4 miles. From there we rode to Gosport, 4 miles. This town lies on the other side of the harbour, and we took a small rowing boat to cross over with our two horses. Now as the sea came in very fast and the wind blew up hard, the boat tossed and the horses got frightened, and we were in very great danger of overturning the boat; we had to hold the horses as still and quiet as we could by force and threats, and landed at Portsmouth at 2 o'clock. As the town was closed while the service was on, we went to stay at the White Hart in the suburb called the Point,[177] where we refreshed ourselves a little. After the service we went for a walk in the town and looked at it, saw the King's lodgings and chapel,

---

177 This is clearly not the White Hart in White Hart Street, which is within the walls; Mrs Sarah Quail, City Records Officer, informs us that the Blue Posts on Broad Street, i.e. on the Point, was formerly called the White Hart.

which has a platform, but it is not large. There is a wooden footbridge from the town wall to the entrance of the King's Lodging. We saw the town walls and outworks, well provided with cannons, and well manned with guards. The walls consist of wooden stakes, inside and out very thickly covered with earth. In addition a very strong watch is kept night and day at the three gates, and there is also a watch on the church tower, who, by the sounding of a bell, warn how many on foot and how many horsemen are approaching, and put out a flag on the side to indicate from which direction they come. In 1662 there were 5 companies in garrison, mostly old, experienced soldiers. The governor was Charles Bartholee,[178] to whom we had to send that evening our names and lodgings in writing. From the town walls on the side towards the sea we saw three or four large ships lying in the roads, one of which set sail that evening for Tangier, with its governor the Earl of Peterborough[179] and other officers and soldiers on board.

On the 18th September in the morning we spoke at our lodgings to an Englishman who had lived a long time in Utrecht and had married a Dutch woman there. He kindly went with us to show us everything worth seeing. So we went first to the shipyard or docks, which are like the locks in Holland, but are only open at one side towards the water, dug into the ground, dry at low tide and very deep, and when the lock-gates are opened, which is only done when a ship is finished, the water comes in so high with the tide that the ship becomes afloat and is so taken mid-stream to sea. In the same manner they bring in the ships with the tide for repair, strutting them to the sides, and when the water falls, they close the dock with very strong gates and inside struts, and, if still a little water comes in, they keep it dry by means of a pump.

In this dock was the ship *Phoenix*, in which the young Tromp was taken by surprise before Livorno, which was being completely rebuilt, and with her lay the *Gloucester*. In mid-stream and in the harbour lay a large number of ships, amongst others the *Vogelstruÿs*, the East India ship taken in the war between Holland and Oliver Cromwell, which had been turned into a derrick and lighter to unload goods from incoming ships, also many naval cannons were stored in it while they were not required at sea. There lay also by the store the ship *Monck*,

178 Sir Charles Berkeley (1629/30–1665), of the Somerset (Bruton) branch of the Berkeley family, a favourite of Charles II and the Duke of York, later Viscount Fitzhardinge and Earl of Falmouth, lieutenant-governor of Portsmouth 1662–5, killed in the battle of Lowestoft: *The Complete Peerage of England* v.246 and 407–9, and Pepys, *Companion*. He was succeeded by his younger brother Sir William Berkeley, lieutenant-governor of Portsmouth, 1665–6 (DNB).

179 Henry Mordaunt, second earl of Peterborough, governor of Tangiers 1661–2, see DNB; Pepys iii, 110, 172 etc.

just arrived from Tangier,[180] whose captain was the same who took the King of England over [to France] after he had lost the battle anno [1651]. As soon as the King had come back to the country, this man presented himself to His Majesty, who recognized him and made him a sea captain.[181]

In this large shipyard we also saw a very fine, long rope-walk which was very busy.

When we had seen everything we went back to our lodgings and after our meal walked round the town on the outside of the ramparts and also to the sea fort,[182] lying on the beach a cannon shot from the town.

On that day the governor had given secret orders to divide the garrison into several detachments, to search all houses in the town and the country around and collect all the weapons which they could find. This was carried out, and towards evening the troops of the main guard came to the parade ground by the King's Lodging and brought the weapons there, pikes, muskets, pistols, carbines, swords, battle axes, etc., which were laid down before the governor and other officers and all registered.[183]

Portsmouth

is a small but strong and famous town, one of the arsenals of England. It has a very fine, long street full of shops, and there is a nice market house. There are many other streets with very neat houses, only one church, and three gates, namely Pointgate, Quaygate and Towngate. On the 19th September at 9 o'clock in the morning we rode from Portsmouth to Chester [Chichester], 14 miles away, passed Kingston, Cosham, a redoubt manned by a guard, rode over a stone bridge there, on through Farlington and Bedhampton to Havant, a large market town, 7 miles, and from there through Emsworth, Nutbourne, and Fishbourne, to Chichester, where we went to stay at the Swan. After a meal we went for a walk through and round the outside and inside of the town and looked at everything. We went to look up one of our acquaintances, Mr. James Bollen, but he had left there and had gone

180 As part of the dowry of Catharine of Braganza, Tangiers became British in January 1661, potentially an important base to control Algerian piracy, but troubled by continuous attacks by the Moors, tying up large forces (cf. Pepys, *Companion*, 407).

181 After the battle of Worcester Charles II eventually escaped to France from a creek near Shoreham, in a coalbrig *Surprise*, captain Nicholas Tattershall; Arthur Bryant, *King Charles II*, 1933, pp. 33–9.

182 South Sea Castle.

183 Portsmouth was republican, hence the collection of arms; a number of town councillors were dismissed in 1662 (*VCH Hampshire*, iii, 178).

into the country, so we found the verger who carries the mace before the bishop when he comes to church, and this person showed us everything.

Chichester

in Sussex. This county borders on the sea all along its south side, but has few or no harbours; the coast is 60 miles long, all of sand and rocks. Along its centre it has high marl, limestone, or chalk hills, where corn grows in plenty because of the fertility of the soil. At its north side are lots of woods and iron mines with marshy pools which drive the hammer mills. The middle part [of the county] is the most fertile.

Chichester lies in a level plain, the town is quite large and walled. It has four gates, and four long streets called after the four winds, in the middle of the Cross roads stands a market house of stone, supported by pillars all round, and here the market is held. On this stone market house the bishop has or had the intention to erect a bronze statue of King Charles, and this was in hand. The Trinity or main Church is not large, but a fine building, much like that at Salisbury, mainly the spire which however here is straight, whereas that of Salisbury is twisted above.[184] This church was built by an apprentice or pupil of the master of the other about the year 1050 or thereabouts. This master came once, when the church was nearly finished, to look at the work, and when he went with his disciple along the passage above the pillars, he pushed him out of jealousy down from the top, so that he fell to his death, and lies buried at the right side of the choir, where this story can be read on a stone tablet as a memorial. Then one sees nearby the pictures of all the kings and queens of England up to Charles the First, and all the portraits of the Doctores Theologiæ. Also the story how Henry VIII removed all the clergy. The present bishop is Henry King.[185] The town has five more churches. Chichester was built by Cissa, a Saxon, the second king of this province, and is therefore called after him.

On the 20th September at 9 o'clock in the morning we rode from Chichester to Guildford,   miles, passed Lavant 1 mile, Singleton 3

184 The ancient spire of Chichester Cathedral blew down in 1861, the present spire is a replica built by Gilbert Scott. The story of the apprentice, killed by his master out of jealousy, is told of other places, but has not survived at Chichester; there is no memorial tablet now (Inf. Dr. Mary Hobbs, Chichester Cathedral).

185 Henry King (1592–1669) was elevated to the see of Chichester in 1642, the day after the House of Lords deprived the bishops of their vote. When Chichester surrendered to Parliament in 1643 he lost his episcopal estates and found refuge with friends in Buckinghamshire and there assembled his poems, published in 1657. At the Restoration, he returned to his see (DNB).

miles, Cocking 2, Midhurst 2 miles; this is a large market town, and we had our midday meal there; the way was pleasant, but difficult to find. We rode on to Chiddingfold,[186] from there to Haslemere, Milford and Godalming, and on to Guildford, where we arrived at 6 o'clock and went to stay at the Golden Angel.

Guildford

lies in the county of Surrey, a large market town, well known and prosperous due to the passage and transit of travelling people. There are many excellent inns and taverns, it is populous, has many streets, three churches in which services are held, etc. Next to the town, up on the hill, lies an old castle, but badly dilapidated; next to it is a bowling green, from where one has a very pleasant view over the river and the country. There is a stone bridge over this river. The king had put in a garrison of foot and horse to forestall any revolt.[187]

On the 21st September in the morning we went to look at the town and the castle, and after breakfast we rode from there at 8 o'clock to London. We passed Ripley 5 miles, Cobham 5 miles, Kingston 5 miles, and had our meal in the inn called the Castle, but they ought rather to hang out the scissors or the candle snuffer.[188]

After our dinner or midday meal we rode from there, went round behind the great park [Richmond Park], over the common or heath, and came to Putney,   miles, where we had ourselves set over by the ferry across the River Thames to Fulham, and rode from there through Chelsea to London, where we arrived at 6 o'clock, and went round by Holborn and stabled our horses again at the Lily in Fetter Lane.

Thus we had, thanks be to God, happily completed our journey to the west, fortunately without any misfortune or even any inconvenience, although we had miserable, clumsy, stumbling horses and travelled most of the time without a guide, on criss-crossing, twisting, and winding roads, which were sometimes for a stranger not easy to find. But enquiries and vigilance were our signposts, and every main town our lodestar and welcome haven. It served us throughout that we had

186 The road from Chichester to Guildford, shown on Ogilby's road map of 1675, runs through Midhurst, Chiddingfold (an important place at the time), Milford, and Godalming. The route Schellinks describes, via Haslemere after Chiddingfold, may infer that he got lost.

187 On Tuesday, 26 August (5 September 1662 n.s.) a Royal Commission had dismissed the mayor, six magistrates, and the town clerk, for 'refusing to take the oathes' (*Court Book*, Guildford Muniment Room, p. 140r, Inf. Matthew Alexander, Guildford).

188 A Dutch colloquialism; the expression indicates that Schellinks feels himself badly done by.

such wonderful weather, and were never held up or hindered by wind or rain on our entire journey.

The journal of our journey to the Northern part of England

Anno 1662, the 2nd October New Style at 11 o'clock we rode from London to Cambridge. From Bishopsgate we rode to Newington, Tottenham, High Cross, Edmonton, and Waltham Abbey; we came along a large, long wall of a deerpark, where a very beautiful house of the king used to stand, which was however destroyed by the soldiers in the recent war.[189] We passed several more villages, and met a lot of coaches and people who came from Stourbridge fair.[190] Because of the rain which had fallen the roads were deeply rutted and filthy. We fell in with a presbyterian preacher and reached Hoddesdon at 4 o'clock, 17 miles from London, and had some refreshment there. From Hoddesdon we rode by ourselves (the pastor riding to Ely) to Much Hadham 6 miles, where we stayed the night at the King's Head.

On the 3rd October it rained heavily, so that we only left there at 9 o'clock for Little Hadham, and rode from there over very bad, clayey, deep and little-known by-ways to Audley End, where we refreshed ourselves and after our midday meal went to look at the splendid house or palace of the Earl of Suffolk, built anno [1603], a wonderful building, of many halls, rooms, chambers, and cellars, the like of which we had not seen in England apart from Hampton Court.[191] In front of the very wide house, surrounded by its walls, is a splendid front garden full of trees; as one comes in through the gate, one comes to a fine inner courtyard, with colonnades of stone pillars all round, covered on the top with lead, a promenade with artistically made stone balustrades, on which can be read on both sides these words in letters carved in stone:

189 Theobalds, near Cheshunt, enclosed by James I, sold during the Commonwealth and largely demolished. Pevsner-Cherry, *BoE*, *Hertfordshire*, p. 360

190 Stourbridge fair, near Chesterton, north east of Cambridge, was the largest in the world, according to Defoe, who describes it in detail in his *Tour through England and Wales*, 1724.

191 The house of Audley End was substantially altered in the early eighteenth century and partly demolished *c*.1721; of the structures described little is now to be seen; an etching by Winstanley (1676) shows the house as Schellinks saw it: On either side of the great court were arcades, above which the stone parapets were pierced to form letters, clearly readable against the sky. On one side the letters formed the motto of the Garter (partly sketched by Schellinks at the top of the relevant page of the Copenhagen MS), the text on the other side read: 'Prudentis est in consilio fortunam semper habere' (see William Addison, *Audley End*, 1953). As in other places, Schellinks's copy of the Latin text is imperfect.

Honi soit qui mal ÿ penze,

and in Latin:

Prudentis est in concilio unam semper habere

Besides some other rooms we saw an exceptionally large, long and wide hall, in which the ceiling is very preciously and artistically decorated in plaster or stucco with many allegorical figures in half relief and half round. The floor, as in most of the other rooms, was covered with rush mats. There was also a most magnificent stone table, white alabaster, beautifully cut out and through and inlaid with very precious stones of various colours, which is valued at 2000 pounds sterling or 20 thousand guilders. We saw the chamber in which King Charles and his Queen had been staying some time and had been sumptuously entertained.

Then we were shown a gallery of portraits of the ancestors of the Earls of Suffolk, and of many kings, of Henry VII, Henry VIII, James, Charles I, Henry IV of France, Queen Elizabeth and many other kings and nobles. Below is a large hall, a large beautiful bowling green, a fine garden, a very large kitchen, wide, long, and high, with a great many hearths, ovens, and stoves, which is attached to, but is not reckoned part of the house. The house has 140 fireplaces and very curious and decorative chimneys, standing like pillars in an orderly manner on the house, sometimes 2, 3, 4, and 5 gathered together. Then we were led by the keeper into the cellars which have very high vaults resting on pillars; one of these cellars is very much like the church of St. Faith below St. Paul's in London. The cellarmaster entertained us with very good old beer and showed us in another room a model of the whole house, very prettily made of paper, as a hobby, by a nobleman. In the great storm of February 1662 many of the chimneys and other ornaments of the house were thrown down, and many of the rooms much damaged and spoilt.

Above the house is a large walk floored with lead, with several pavilions or chambers with a very fine view over the whole countryside.

At 4 o'clock we rode from there to Saffron Walden, only a mile from Audley End, a very large market town, populous, situated in a fertile part of the county of Essex. All round there saffron is grown in open fields, many of them surrounded by a fence against animals. From there we rode into Cambridgeshire, and as the evening overtook us, we managed to get to Whittlesfordsbridge and good accommodation, still 6 miles to Cambridge.

On the 4th October at 8 o'clock in the morning we rode from there to Cambridge, had, because of the rain, very miry roads, came at 10 o'clock into the town and went to take our lodgings at the Lion, right opposite the entrance to St. John's College.

Cambridge

is one of the most famous universities in the world; it is situated in Cambridgeshire on the river Cam, which, turning eastwards, divides the town into two parts, causing it to be called Cam-bridge from the stone bridge, which lies there over this river. There is nothing lacking but better air, which, because of the vapours from the bog lands, is somewhat unhealthy, especially in summer time, when it is rather heavy and murky.

There are many different opinions about the first beginnings of this university. The historians differ much, but the principal ones agree that Sigebert King of the East Angles was the first, who, about the year 630 or 636, founded the various houses and hostels for students to educate them, and gave them great privileges and freedoms, of which some are still in existence. Pope Honorius I too granted them many freedoms, which [Pope] Sergius confirmed.

Since that time the light of this academy was much eclipsed, due to manifold troubles, wars, and quarrels between the Britons, Romans, Saxon kings of this region, and Danes and Normans, and was by the barons' war totally extinguished, but, even if the destructions were many, so were the reconstructions by one prince or the other, so that in the end it has risen to such a magnificent height. Much honour has been done to this place by sons and kin of kings, who were counts thereof.

Cambridge has 16 colleges, namely:

1. St. Peter's College or House [Peterhouse College], founded anno 1280 by Hugh de Balsham, Bishop of Ely.
2. Clare Hall or University House, founded anno 1326 by Richard Badew, Chancellor [of the University].
3. Pembroke Hall, founded anno 1343 by Mary de St. Paul, Countess of Pembroke, Baroness of Veisser and Mountenant, daughter of Guydo Chastille.[192]
4. Corpus Christi College, founded anno 1351 by Henry Monmouth, the son of Henry de Lancaster.[193]
5. Trinity Hall, founded anno 1353 by William Bateman Do. of Law, Archdeacon of Norwich and Bishop of Cambridge.

192 Marie de Valence, daughter of the Count of Châtillon and St. Pol (Pevsner, *BoE, Cambridge*, where most data on the founders of the Colleges are given, sometimes differing from Schellinks's dates, who obtained his information from Gerard Langbain's *The Foundation of the Universitie of Cambridge*, 1651).

193 Corpus Christi College was founded in 1352 by the guilds of Corpus Christi and St. Mary (Pevsner). Monmouth, i.e. Henry, duke of Lancaster (d.1361, DNB under Henry of Lancaster), was the noble patron, who obtained the royal licence for the college (B.D.G. Little, *Colleges of Cambridge*, 1973).

6. Gon[ville] and Cai[us] College, founded anno 1353 by Edmond Gonville, rector of Terrington and Rusworth.

7. King's College, founded anno 1440 by King Henry VI named Henry of Windsor, King of England and France.

8. Queens' College, founded anno 1448 by Margaret Andegavensis,[194] daughter of René Duke of Anjou, titled King of Sicily, Naples, and Jerusalem.

9. Catherine Hall, founded anno 1475 by Robert Woodelarke, Do. of Theology, [provost of King's].

10. Jesus College, founded anno 1496 by John Alcock, Bishop of Ely, Chancellor of England.

11. Christ College, founded anno 1505 by Margaret Countess of Richmond,[195] mother of King Henry VII.

12. St. John's College, founded anno 1508 by Margaret, as above.

13. Magdalene College, founded anno 1519 by Edward Stafford, Duke of Buckingham, Earl of Stafford, Hereford, and Northampton.

14. Trinity College, founded anno 1546 by King Henry VIII.

15. Emmanuel College, founded anno 1584 by Sir Walter Mildmay, Chancellor [of the Exchequer] and treasurer and privy councillor of Queen Elizabeth.

16. Sidney Sussex College, founded anno 1598 by Frances Sidney, Countess of Sussex.

The number of students, with the professors and officials, without various young students, who are not nominated in one of the colleges, but accepted out of charity, was 3050 in 1622. This was much reduced by the plague of 1629, when many went to Oxford and elsewhere, and was only 2850 in 1651.

There are 13 churches in Cambridge, namely:

1. The University Church or St. Mary [the Great]
2. St. Michael's
3. All Saints
4. Holy Sepulchre
   or Round Church
5. St. Clement's
6. St. Peter's
7. St. Giles
8. Trinity
9. St. Andrew's
10. Little St. Mary [the Less]
11. St. Botolph's
12. St. Bene't's
13. St. Edward's

St. Andrew's is outside the gate towards Barnwell.

To the south east, close to the town, are some hills called Gog and Magog, on the top is a large fort with threefold trenches, now partly ruined, in which prisoners are being kept.

194 Margaret of Anjou, 1430–82, wife of Henry VI.
195 Lady Margaret Beaufort, countess of Richmond and Derby (d.1509).

On the 4th October we went in the afternoon with a Mr. Key, a glazier, to see eleven of the colleges. In King's College the chapel is of such size and so magnificent and beautiful of build that it is considered that there is none more beautiful in the whole world. King Henry VI intended to make the college equally outstanding, but because of his untimely death King Henry VII completed the unfinished part of the stonework on the outside of the chapel, and King Henry VIII had the glass, stalls, and floor and everything brought to perfection, and gave it a royal coat of arms, confirmed by an act of parliament, a lily of France and a lion of England, to show that it was a royal work.

First we saw the choir, then the library, which is on the right in a stone chapel; the books there were chained, most of them there from bequests. From there we climbed up to the vaulting, which is all of stone, extremely artistically made. The chapel is without any columns between the roof, [which is] covered with lead. In the vaulting is a large space, and at the side are covered passages round the outside of the chapel. Mr. Key and myself went along the turrets and jointed lead on the roof, from where we had a beautiful view over the whole of Cambridge and could see the Isle of Ely.

Trinity College, which is the most magnificent of the colleges, has a very large, beautiful court, with a splendid fountain in the middle, the water springing from several sculptures. It has a large, wide and high refectory or hall, a very beautiful chapel, and has upper promenades, and fives or tennis courts, such as many colleges have, surrounded by walls and open at the top. We went to the buttery and were treated to college beer.

Next we went to St. John's College, the most beautiful after Trinity, and there saw the library, which is very long and beautiful, with unchained books on both sides, which was founded by Margaret, the mother of King Henry VII; her portrait hangs there, very old but very well done; she is kneeling in front of a table on which lies a book. Above the entrance door hang three portraits, John William, Bishop of Lincoln, Keeper of the Great Seal,[196] Sir Ralph Hare, Knight of the Bath, and Bishop Thomas Morton, a great benefactor of the College. At the other end stand two globes on white marble tables, next to it another inlaid with various stones; there are also some smaller pieces which look like paintings, amongst them a palace, very neatly and skilfully executed, and further some strange ground glasses to look through.

On the 5th October we went for a walk in and outside the town, and went again to the King's Chapel. The vaulting, which is very high,

---

196 John Williams, 1582–1650, bishop of Lincoln, later archbishop of York, studied at St. John's and made substantial contributions to the Library (DNB).

is half-round and on its underside so artistically worked in stone to the amazement of the observers. The walls, inside and out, are covered everywhere with coats of arms of King Henry, well worked in stone, and there is in this chapel such wonderful stained glass as cannot be found elsewhere in the whole of England; behind the choir the whole Passion, very artistically executed.

From there we went on their footpaths across a stone bridge over the river Cam, crossed some fields, and came from the rear back to Trinity College and saw the students playing in their tennis court. In the afternoon we went to look at the remaining five colleges, some of them were very fine; we also saw the schools of the university. *Note*: Outside Emmanuel College we saw the master or professor pack his books and household goods on to a cart, as he had lost his post because he would not agree to conform with the acts of the bishops.[197] At St. Michael's Church we saw the church wardens or elders with their sidesmen or assistants taking the oath of conformity before the Vice Chancellor, who read it out to them. Many tried to get a few days respite so that they could read the newly drafted articles and would know what they were affirming etc. but they got short shrift.

As we had seen all the streets, markets, and everything at Cambridge, we rode from there at 11 o'clock on the 6th October to Newmarket, 10 miles, passing Stourbridge Common, lying to the east of Cambridge, where the market or fair, which begins on 8th September old style, was just over; this is the largest fair in England, judging by the crowd of buyers as well as sellers, and the mass of wares which are brought there to market. From there we rode close to Quy [Stow cum Quy] and came to a large sandy heath called Newmarket Heath, but green enough to pasture sheep. We came to a great raised dyke with a dry ditch extending a long way, called the Devils Dyke. There are only some narrow gaps as a passage to ride through. So we got to Newmarket, and rode from there 7 miles to Barton, or because of the water mills Barton Mills, where we broke the journey. On our left hand we saw the Isle of Ely and the minster or great church with its lantern of lead or clock house on it and its high square tower.

This Isle of Ely, William the Conqueror could not subject, and the peasants in their white smocks carried on ploughing their fields in spite of him.

From Barton Mills we rode to Brandon, 7 miles, a good road, sand and heathland, full of rabbits. We got to Brandon in the evening and went to stay at the Red Bull.

---

197 William Dillingham was deprived of the mastership on 24 August 1662 for refusing the oath ordered by the Act of Uniformity; his successor was William Sancroft, who had resigned his tutorship at the College during the Commonwealth, and later became archbishop of Canterbury (DNB).

On the 7th October at 8 o'clock in the morning we rode to Lynn 18 miles, passed by Weeting, Methwold, Stoke, Wereham, Stradsett, Setchey, and so to Lynn-Regis in Norfolk. Norfolk or Folk of the North, is a large, flat region, which sustains a lot of sheep and rabbits; it has 27 market towns and 625 villages.

Lynn, 84 miles from London,

is called Old Linne or Linnum Regis, King's Lynn, is fairly large, encircled by a deep ditch and a wall, and is divided by 2 little rivers, which are crossed by 14 or 15 small bridges. It has a very good harbour, the Great Ouse river flows into the sea there, forming an inlet. The place is very favourably situated to provide several counties around it with grain and coal, which arrives there from Newcastle in large quantities. For this reason many merchants live there, and there is much trade and business in this place because of this situation. There are some fine houses and these four streets are the principal ones: the High Street, Chequer Street, Grass Market and Broad Street. There are four churches, including St. Margaret Major, St. Nicholas, and St. James South Lynn, but in the last there is no service. On St. Margaret's Church is an erection standing on the crossing of the church or the roof, called the lantern, having a gallery, from which one has a very fine view over the town, the harbour, and the countryside around.[198] Outside the town is a Dutch sawmill or two, in which some Dutchmen live. There are two gates, East and South Gate, and also New and Old Gany Gates, which are wicket gates. Behind the Customs House[199] is the common guard, the harbour wharf on which at all times some millstones are being kept; if they fail in this they would loose their charter or freedom. There is a very large market place, in which a market is held on Tuesdays, and [another market] on Saturdays in the High Street.

On Sunday, the 8th October, we were at the service at St. Margaret's, the text was Cor. 1 v.13.

In the afternoon we went round the town inside and out, and to one of the sawmills, the Dutchman there was very ill and we visited him at his bedside.

198 The south west tower of St. Margaret's crashed in 1741, and the crossing tower, a lesser version of the one at Ely, had to be replaced (Inf. from David Lloyd to Soc. Prot. Anc. Build.)

199 The Customs House at the time was on the west side of Tuesday Market. The current Customs House was built as an exchange or merchants' meeting place in 1683 and converted to a customs house in 1718. 'Common guard' is the Common Staith Yard; the story of the millstone does not appear to have survived. See Henry Bell's 'Groundplat' of c.1680.

On the 9th in the morning we went to visit Mr. de Jongh of Rotterdam, a Dutch merchant who lives at King's Lynn and met there also a Mr. Kruyt from Rotterdam, and were treated by de Jongh to absinth wine etc.

Nota: On this day the installation of a new mayor took place. It began with a service at St. Margaret's for the outgoing and the new mayor and all the aldermen. We went beforehand into the court chamber and saw the old and the new mayor, dressed in carmine red coats, enter to the playing of musical instruments, with the recorder walking in the middle. King John's sword was carried before them, and four maces, followed by all the aldermen and other officials. The sword was set in its place, which is a carved gilt hand fixed to the wall behind the mayor's seat. The mayor and the aldermen went into the council chamber, and after some time they all came out, and the old or outgoing mayor took his seat with the new mayor on his right and the recorder or pensionaris or treasurer on his left, and on both sides the aldermen etc. At another, lower table sat the clergy and other officials, secretaries, and clerks. The recorder rose and delivered a long speech, praising the good government of the outgoing mayor, and commending the new mayor. Then an official stood up holding the statute or charter book and read the oath to the new mayor, who repeated it word for word after him; another official held the gospel book, on which the mayor laid his fingers and kissed it four times after the reading of the four oaths.

Then the old mayor exchanged his seat with the new mayor and handed to him the sword and the town's seal and wished him good luck. The new mayor handed the sword back to the sword bearer, thus confirming him in his office, then the four mace bearers delivered to him the maces and the keepers of the gates and of the prisons their keys, which he returned to each one into his hands. After all this was done he was with all the pomp conducted to his house.

The name of the new mayor was John Burd, his house was across the River Ouse.

We then went to see the rooms in which three days later the great banquet was to be held.

In the afternoon we went to look at the town and at the common guard, went up some stairs to a platform, which is built there to look over the river and harbour out to sea for the incoming and outgoing ships. We saw sixteen ships come in from Wells, a small seaside hamlet, and go out from Wells over to Iceland to load salt fish and bring it over. We then went to visit Mr. de Jongh, who was at the King's Head. There we were joined by Mr. Kruyt and Mr. Anthony Slade, and Mr. Blauw, the brother of Alderman Blauw, who had come over with us from Holland on the packet boat, and we drank their health.

On the 10th October we went in the morning with Dirck de Jongh, Kruyt and Slade to the new mayor's house, where Mr. de Jongh asked to have the honour of seeing the ancient drinking cup, which King John presented to the town in the year 1199, together with the sword from his side, in grateful memory. When the whole country rebelled against him at the revolt of the barons and nobles, and he had lost several battles, and was fleeing from place to place and was everywhere refused admission, he was taken in and protected by them of Lynn, and when he left, he presented them with his sword and this cup. Intending to march further north he passed over the Wash, which is 16 miles to Lincolnshire.

This Wash is like a wide, sandy beach, which, because it is so flat, becomes very quickly submerged in the sea by the incoming tide. Moreover it is riddled with wells or quicksands, and as solid ground cannot be found, and the tide is coming in so fast, the travellers sink in, horses and all, and cannot be saved. For this reason one has to employ a guide.

Now, as the king was with his treasure, arms, and baggage on the Wash, some horses and carts sank in the quicksand and the sea came in, and almost everything was drowned and lost, and he and most of his people only escaped by the skin of their teeth, and whilst he stayed at the abbey at Swineshead,[200] he died of sorrow, some say that he was poisoned, drinking ale from the very cup we saw.

This ancient cup is silver gilt, its style very old and strange, covered on the top by a lid. The cup was also set in several places with precious stones, but many of them have been stolen by one or the other; in many places are enamelled pictures of male and female saints and other decorations more.[201] This cup has attached to it an annual allowance to show it to the spectators or strangers with the following ceremony: First the cup is filled with sack and then the lid is put on. Then it is handed to the visitors, who have to take off the lid. When the drinker has drunk, he turns the star, which is above the foot and below the cup, three times, then three times the other way around the drinking cup, and then the lowest part of the foot three times the other way. After that it is again filled and covered and handed over to the next drinker, who performs the same ceremony and hands it back. After that we were shown the unsheathed sword. It is wide and has a hilt like a broadsword, and is very heavy, and its hilt is of fine silver. On its crosspiece the following Latin words can be read on one side: Encis hic donum fuit Regis Johanes sua ipsius latere datum; on the

200 King John died at Newark Castle in 1216.
201 The sword and cup are still part of the civic regalia. The figures on the cup are now thought to represent hunters.

other side are these words: Vivat Henricus Octavus anno regis tua 20.[202] This sword, covered with a rich scabbard, decorated with the arms of the king, the town, and England, silver gilt on both sides, is carried before the mayor when he goes to church or to the council. After we had seen all this, we went with the Monsieur to drink our farewell with a glass of absinth wine.

After our midday meal we climbed to the lantern of St. Margaret's Church and looked inside the church at the very small library,[203] established in 1632 by Mr. John Wollier, who gave 53 pounds towards it, Mistress Joan Atkin 10 pounds, and Master Tom Atkin 10 pounds. They showed us an 18 lb cannon ball, hanging in an iron band, which was shot from Cromwell's camp on Sunday, 10 September 1643, during the service, and had flown past and between some people without killing or hurting anyone. The verger showed us five large silver flagons or tall jugs, two goblets, and two dishes to serve the Holy Communion, which had been presented by mayors, aldermen, and ladies anno 1615, anno 1616, anno 1616, anno 1632, anno 1632.

NB. 16 miles from Lynn is Old Walsingham, and also New Walsingham. A farmer, ploughing his field, found 18 burial urns, in which the Romans had buried the ashes of cremated corpses; many of these were broken by the plough.

At one o'clock in the afternoon we rode from King's Lynn to Norwich, 30 miles. We passed Gaywood, 1 mile, Gayton 4 miles, Litcham 10 miles, Mileham, Stanfield, Brisley, Elmham, where we went in the evening to stay at the King's Head.

On the 11th we rode at 8 o'clock from Elmham 12 miles to Norwich, passed Billingford, Bawdeswell, Attlebridge, Lomert Brecke, Drayton, and so to Norwich, the road being over much boggy ground, and the somewhat higher ground full of rabbits. At Norwich we went to stay at the King's Head at the market, opposite the cross or market house,

202 The version of the inscriptions on the sword are as noted by Schellinks in the Copenhagen MS. The correct version, given to us by Dr Paul Richards of King's Lynn is:

ENSIS HIC DONUM FUIT REGIS IOHANNIS
A SUO IPSIUS LATERE DATUM
and on the other side
VIVAT REX HENRICUS OCTAVUS
ANNO REGNI SUI 20

Dr. Richards suggests that the story about the millstones might have been promoted by the Corporation to justify its monopoly of the trade in millstones.

203 The Bodleian MS says 'very beautiful'. Schellinks must have seen the still extant first catalogue of the library, from which he took the details about its founders as recorded by him. The story of the cannon ball survives, the ball used to hang in the entrance of Hampton Court across the street (Information for notes 199, 201–3 from Jane Lineham, Principal Librarian, King's Lynn).

an excellent inn. After our midday meal we went to speak to a Mr.
Vinck, an old man of 80 years, who, although of Flemish descent, was
born there, and had a very large hosier's shop.

Norwich

in Norfolk, is a famous, old town, pleasantly situated on the slope of a
hill along the river which protects its lower side, and elsewhere
surrounded by strong walls with towers and twelve gates. The town is
3 miles in circumference, is very populous and prosperous, and has
beautiful churches, houses and streets. There are 32 parishes, served
by 52 chapels and churches; the largest and main church is Christ
Church, after that St. Andrew, St. Peter, in whose tower is a carillon,
which plays at 4, 8, and 12 o'clock, St. Stephen, St. Gregory, and St.
Laurence, these are the largest. The Dutch Church is St. Peter Hungate,
the name of its minister is Dr Elison,[204] and at that time there were
only 100 communicants. The hospital behind Christchurch is a large
establishment. The Market Cross or Market House and the cloisters of
the main church are judged to be the most beautiful in the whole of
England. There is a large house or palace, the Duke's House, belonging
to the Earls of Arundel, which has a fine bowling alley.[205]
   In the hospital a hundred men and women are regularly maintained.
On a hill in the middle of the town, from where one has a fine view
over the town and the countryside, is the Castle, which houses the
prison, and where the assizes or high court sessions are being held.
Guildhall is the Town Hall, where on Saturdays and Wednesdays the
court for burghers and countrymen is sitting; inside is the New Hall,
where the new mayor holds his feast, near the beautiful Market Place
and Market House. The principal streets are St. Stephens, St. Giles,
St. Bennets, St. Magdalen, which is half a mile long, St. Martin,
Coneysfort Street, Bear Street; Coneysfort Street is one English mile
long along the water, where the wharves are, where the ships, coming
up from Yarmouth, load and discharge, bringing much fish and coal a
journey of 30 miles because of the twists and turns of the river. Regular
ferry boats from Norwich to Yarmouth sail daily, mostly in the evening,
similar to the Breukelen boats in Holland; every passenger pays a fare
of 12 pence, a very convenient service for travellers.

   204 Theophilus Elison, who had succeeded his father Johannis Elison (1581–1639), as
Minister of the Dutch Reformed Church, Norwich. In 1634 Rembrandt painted lifesize
portraits of Johannis and his wife, now in Boston (U.S.A.) Museum of Fine Arts. See
Gary Schwarz, *Rembrandt*, 1991.
   205 The Duke's House: Tudor palace of Henry Howard, duke of Norfolk, between
the river and Charing Cross, now demolished. Evelyn was shown the plans for its
restoration and extension, but thought it a 'wretched house' (see Evelyn, 17 Oct. 1671).

The names of the twelve gates are:

1. Culser Gate	7. Hayhow Gate
2. Bear Street Gate	8. St. Martin's Gate
3. Langbrazen door	9. Possharp Gate
4. St. Stephen's Gate	10. St. Augustine's Gate
5. St. Giles's Gate	11. Bishop's Gate
6. St. Benedict's Gate	12. Conisfort Gate.

The river is the little Ouse,[206] flowing into the sea at Yarmouth, where it is very wide. It rises near Lopham from a rising fountain or spring, divides into two channels and gets larger and larger by the influx of other brooks. The one branch runs through Brandon and flows at Lynn into the sea, the other branch, the Great Ouse, runs in the opposite direction through Bungay and Beccles and flows into the sea at Yarmouth.

Bishop Renaulds of Norwich and Dean Dr Krafts had the church and the very large and extensive cloisters, restored as new.[207]

In the afternoon we went to look at the town generally, and first saw in a square the militia under arms exercise and drill. Then we went up the castle hill and looked at the ancient castle from the outside; there were a lot of prisoners there, who called very loudly for alms. From the hill we went to the cathedral or Christchurch, which is very old, large and long, with massive, thick pillars, and a very high spire standing over the crossing, that is the middle of the church. Inside the church there is nothing special to be seen. There are some old bishops' tombs; on the right hand side, near the door, there is a drawing of a skeleton on the wall with the following inscription in English:

> All you that do this place pass by
> Remember death for you must dye
> As you are now even so was I
> And as I am so shall you by

Below this, at his feet, are the following lines:

> Thomas Gooding here to staye
> Wayting for God's judgment daye

It is said that this person is, by his request, buried or immured there in the wall in an upright position.

In front of the altar, in the choir, is the tomb of Bishop Herfort,[208]

206 Schellinks is here mistaken: the Little Ouse rises near Lopham, and does not come near Norwich (Inf. Barbara Green, Norfolk Museum Service, who also drew our attention to 2 drawings by Schellinks of Norwich. See Appendix I).

207 Edward Reynolds, Bishop of Norwich 1661–76; John Crofts, Dean 1660–70.

208 Bishop Herbert: Herbert de Losinga d. 1119.

the founder of the church. Next to the church is a chapel which houses the school.

On the 12th October we went out at Bear Street Gate and up the hill, from where one has a beautiful view over the surrounding countryside. Going down the hill we came to the river near Conisfort Gate, went through the gate and along the long street to the end, saw the Crane Wharf and the ferry boats etc., and went again to the large church. In the afternoon we went through Bishops Gate and over the bridge, and climbed up Monastery Hill; on the plateau on top a maze is cut neatly in the ground and out of the grass. Next to it stands an ancient chapel, but after the fire there is nothing left of it but some ruins. Some years ago a cripple spread a rumour that a large treasure was buried there. Near this Monastery Hill is a well.

A large number of Dutch craftsmen live at Norwich, who have taught the English the weaving of all kinds of cloth, and Norwich is famous for the quantity and quality of the cloth which is produced there. The churches are all built of closely fitted, straight and smoothly knapped flint, nice to look at. Much of the surrounding countryside is a swampy bog on which lots of geese are raised, and the higher ground is sandy and full of rabbits.

On the 13th October at 9 o'clock in the morning we rode from Norwich to Yarmouth, 16 miles, and passed the villages of Thorpe St. Andrew's and Blofield. It became so foggy that we could not see four steps in front of us, and we came to much bog and flooded land, passed a stone bridge over the river, and rode a very long way through the water, everything being flooded as far as we could see. We came through several villages and through Caister, 2 miles from Yarmouth, where we arrived at 2 o'clock and, being strangers, took our lodgings at the Golden Angel at the Market Place; we enquired for Dr Ubelmans, and heard that he lived at a Mr. Roaus's at Caister. As we did not like the look of the inn, we rode out of the gate back to Caister. When we got there, I knocked with my cane on the door, and Dr. J. Ubelmans, who was in his study at his lodgings, looked from the window, appeared surprised. He came straight down and bid us welcome, invited us in, stabled our horses and treated us to wine and beer, and showed us his lodgings, study, garden etc. Towards evening we rode again to Yarmouth and, on Dr. Ubelmans's recommendation, went to stay at the Three Feathers, the largest inn in the town.

Yarmouth

in Norfolk, has a good harbour and is well known because of its fishing industry and shipping. It is a fair town, well protected by walls and built up, strong by nature and the art of man. There is only one English

church which is large and has a high tower. Half of the church was
partitioned off and the part, where the Independents used to hold their
services, nailed shut at the time by order of the Bishop of Norwich and
the Dean. There are two very long streets, 1 mile long, the one called
Dean Street, and the other Middle Street, with many alley ways and
cross streets, large and small; the quay is as long as the town and the
streets along the river, where a large number of all kinds of ships lie
along the wall. It is a wide street, much like the Teer Thuin at
Amsterdam between the Camper Jetty and Schreijers Hoek,[209] only
better. Along it stand fine houses. The Dutch church is above a
warehouse near to the middle of the quay, a reasonable establishment.
The market place is fine and very wide and long, where there is market
on Saturdays. No other county in England has three such [market]
places as at Norwich, Lynn, and Yarmouth.

On the 14th October we went to look at the quay, but, because of a
heavy mist, there was a very bad smell there, mainly because of the
vile odour of the new herrings, which were being smoked at all the
warehouses, as it is now the end of the year and the fishing season. So
we returned to our lodgings and refreshed ourselves. The stench is so
bad that somebody who is not used to it would become ill. After this
we went out to look at the market, which we found to be very large
and full of all kinds of foodstuffs, fruit and goods, and there were many
buyers and sellers. From there we went into the church, where a service
was being held for the bishop, magistrates and country clergy and
church wardens etc.

After the sermon the bishop went into the choir and all ministers
who agreed to conform were confirmed in their ministry. He also
accepted the oaths of all the churchwardens and persons belonging to
the church.

In the afternoon we walked around, and Dr. Ubelmans, who had
not been long with us, went back to Caister.

On Sunday, the 15th October, we went in the morning to the Dutch
church. As the Holy Communion was to be served, there were in the
church many Dutch fishermen, who come over in the herring season
to sell their fish. Dr. Ubelmans's text was Acts 8 v.37; in the afternoon
it was Psalms 50 v.14; his sermons were wonderful.

After the service we took a walk round the town on the outside and
also to the beach; it was dead quiet, and we saw a lot of fishermen at
sea, and ships sailing northward.

On the 16th Dr. J. Ubelmans came in the morning to visit us in our

209 Teertuinen, a quay on the west side of Amsterdam, where the merchants dealing
in pitch and tar, important shipbuilding materials, had fine houses. Their wares were
stacked in barrels in front of their houses.

lodgings, had breakfast with us, and joined us on a walk. After that we returned to our lodgings and drank to the health of our Dutch friends, got ready, and went over the harbour bridge, where Suffolk begins, and mounted, took our leave and rode at one o'clock from there, and had a very pleasant road all the way. First we rode to Gorleston, over the harbour mouth by the sea, where a great many herring fishers sailed in and out. The weather was very good, and we rode along the sea coast to Corton, Lowestoft, Pakefield, and Benacre, where we stayed comfortably in a country inn by the roadside.

On the 17th October at 8 o'clock in the morning we rode on to Ipswich, 28 long miles, passed many villages, the main ones were Blythburgh, East Bridge, Snapebridge, Woodbridge, and stopped for refreshment at Eyke, a little short of Ipswich. For 18 miles of this way we had from the height all the time a view of the sea on our left hand side. At 4 o'clock we arrived at Ipswich, having had very heavy rain for an hour or two, but got wet not further than the skin. We went to take our lodgings at the Griffin at the market place in Mary Town Street, a good inn, where we had a cheerful fire lit and dried our soaked pilgrims' togs and treated ourselves to make up for it.

Ipswich

is a fine, spacious, well watered town, situated in Suffolk, lying somewhat low in a watery valley. It is the hub of the county, surrounded by orchards, and was formerly well walled. It has a reasonably good harbour, is well populated, and there is much trade here, mostly in drapery. The quay is a large place, where ships arrive from sea from Harwich 6 miles up with the tide; large colliers go with every high and low tide up and down the river, for 2 pence one can go by them. Here in this town are twelve churches, namely:

St. Mary-Le-Tower Church is the largest,	
St. Matthew,	St. Margaret,
St. Lawrence,	St. Joham Tope,[210]
St. Stephen,	St. Peter,
St. Clement,	St. Nicholas,
St. Mary at the Elms	St. Mary at the Quay

The Streets are full of shops, the largest is Mary Tower Street, St. Matthias, St. Lawrence etc., the gates are Old Barr Gate, Barr Gate, Bull Gate, a small gate. The market place called Cornhill is not large, so also the Butter market. The streets and the houses are fine. We went

---

210 St. John the Baptist, a medieval church, now disappeared, see Roy Tricker, *Ipswich Churches, Ancient and modern*, 1983 (Inf. Hilary Platts, Suffolk Libraries).

to see everything, outside as well as inside the town. The great Cardinal Wolsey was born here.

On the 18th October, as we had looked at everything in Ipswich we rode from there to Colchester, 18 miles, and passed several villages; at one place called White Elm stood an elmtree in front of an inn,[211] which was coated all round with plaster; from there it is 5 miles to Stratford [St. Mary], a very nice and large village, where many drapers and weavers live. It lies in a very pleasant valley, 8 miles from there and still 5 miles from Colchester we came to a bad road through wet clayey ground, and came to Colchester at 4 o'clock and stayed at the King's Head.

Colchester

the County town of Essex, is pleasantly situated on the top of a hill extending from east to west, is walled, and is adorned by several churches, of which some have lately been destroyed. It is an ancient town, it seems to have got its name from the river Coln, which flows past it. Many writers and the inhabitants declare that Flavia Julia Helena, the mother of Constantine the Great,[212] was born and brought up in the town of Colchester. It is famous for its good oysters, cloth, and baize.

Note: The fair or the large market day of Colchester is on 13th October Old Style.

On the 19th October at 10 o'clock in the morning we rode from Colchester to the oyster beds, about $3\frac{1}{2}$ miles distant. We came to the village of Fingringhoe, and riding half a mile further, one comes to a marsh of flooded land or bog, about 4 or 5 miles from the sea and four miles wide, which is flooded at every spring tide, that is every 14 days, so that one can sail all over it with large boats.

In this Fingringhoe marsh are a great number of large ditches and pans dug out about $1\frac{1}{2}$ to 2 feet deep when the land is dry. In these pans they sow the oysters thinly, so that they do not lie on top of each other, and within 14 days they grow green beards from the sun and the stagnant water.[213] These the English consider the finest and so slurp

211 White Elm, on Ogilby's map of 1675 (*Road from London to Yarmouth*), between Copdock and Capel St. Mary.

212 As to the legend of Queen Helena and Colchester see Edward L. Cutts, *Colchester*, 1898.

213 In the seventeenth century in the Colchester area oysters were placed in special pits, as described by Schellinks, to cause them to turn green by a growth of innocuous algæ. Such oysters used to fetch a better price in some markets. This practice was discontinued in the nineteenth century: see P. Morant, *History and Antiquities of the town of Colchester*, 1748; P. Benton, *History of Rochford Hundred*, 1867–88.

them up; the holders or keepers of these oysterbeds, who are four in number, buy them [the seed oysters] from the fishermen coming from the sea. This marsh belongs to a Mr. Fryer, who lives at Wivenhoe, a sea town, who allocates the parcels of ground. When the oysters in the beds are sufficiently green, they open a dam or little wall of clay and drain the pans. When they are dry they go and collect the oysters in baskets or hampers and take them on horses to the market, or send them in small and large barrels by boat. In some of the beds are only large oysters for boiling, frying, stewing, or pickling, in others are small ones for eating raw. They also keep some filled baskets in the water, ready counted, to be able to send them out quickly to the gentry or whoever orders them. So when we came with our horses to the pans we dismounted and tied up our horses, and one of the keepers conducted us and explained everything to us, and opened there several fresh for us. Because of the warm sunshine many oysters were lying there gasping, and we drew our swords from the sheath and put the tip of the sword in between the shells and they pinched these so firmly together that they adhered so strongly to the tip that we could easily wash off the clay from them. We did this too with our knives and also caught some with our hands; they tasted wonderful, being so fresh, and, as we now had thoroughly seen everything, we had a portion brought by the servant into the keeper's house and together ate them raw, boiled, and fried, dipped in flour in the English manner.

So we rode back to Colchester and went to look at the fair, which had started that day. There was an incredibly large crowd of people, country folk, gentry and all, and the taverns, inns, alehouses, pubs and beershops were so full that one could barely get anything to drink. The musicians played merrily everywhere, and in the market was plenty of everything to buy on sale.

On the 20th October at 8 o'clock in the morning we rode from Colchester to Chelmsford, 18 miles, and passed the following towns: Lexden 1 mile, Stanway, Kelvedon, Witham, a market town, Hatfield [Peverel], and Boreham, and arrived at Chelmsford at 12 o'clock, soaked through by rain. We ate our midday meal there at the Red Lion, and at 3 o'clock we rode on through Ingatestone to Brentwood, 10 miles, where, because of the continuing rain, we went to stay at the Crown, a good inn, 15 miles from London.

On the 21st October we rode at 9 o'clock in the morning from Brentwood to London. [Earlier] the landlord had shown us a very long fine boxwood shove [halfpenny] table, wide and smooth to play on. The gentlemen from London and from the country come there and stay for 3, 6, or 8 days at a time to gamble away their money.

Brentwood is a nice market town. Next we came to Romford, also a market town, 5 miles, Chadwell 1 mile, and at a horse pond at a bend in the main road, the straight road to Barking is on the left hand. The story goes that at this watering place, which is called Seven Kings, seven English Kings together watered their horses at the same time,[214] and that some of them are buried at Barking, which, because of that, is said to have been called Bury Kings, that is burial place of kings.

So we took the road to Barking, 4 miles, and got there at 11 o'clock, and went to the Black Bull to have our midday meal. There was the annual fair and the market day together, and there were lots of people gathered as in Holland at a country fair. We went to look at the market and the town, which is famous because of the fishermen who live there, and because of the convenience of the creek or harbour by the river and the brook on which it lies.

From Barking we rode to Ilford, Stratford, Langton, Bow, and Mile End, then through the suburbs of London past Whitechapel to Aldgate, where we arrived at about 3 o'clock. We had (thank God) again completed this our journey without having had any trouble from robbers or otherwise, and, considering the time of the year, had luckily had very good weather throughout.

Now we were back in London and had planned to depart forthwith, but we found and received other instructions, namely that, as it was so late in the year, we should stay over the winter and also to wait for the sitting of parliament to apply for the naturalization of Monsr Jacob Thierry.[215]

On the 25th October at 10 o'clock in the morning we rode with Mr. Adriaen Boddens, Mr. J. Seghvelt, and Mr. Samuel Hill to Greenwich, and looked at the King's House, now in somewhat better order than when we saw it anno 1661 on 7th September. On the hill in the park behind the house two avenues of trees had been planted from the bottom to the top, and near the top of the hill, where it was too steep to climb up, steps had been cut into the ground to walk up in comfort.

On the river side all the old buildings of the palace are pulled down to the ground, to make, to begin with, a large level area; His Majesty, who takes great pleasure in the place because of its beautiful situation by the river, and the outstandingly pleasant view from the hill over the

214 The legend of the seven kings, watering their horses here, goes back to Saxon times. Seven Kings Brook crosses the road nearby. See G. Tasker, *Ilford Past and Present*, 1901; P.H. Reaney, *Place Names of Essex*, Cambridge 1969 (Inf. I. Dowling, Redbridge Central Library).

215 James Thierry was British born, baptized in the French Church, Threadneedle Street on 26 December 1603; his son, Schellinks's companion, was born in Holland, baptized in the Oude Kerk, Amsterdam on 3 May 1648. Naturalization at that time was by a Private Act of Parliament (7 J.I.c.2). Young Thierry was included in Killigrew's Bill of Naturalization (15 Car.II.c.34), which had its first reading on Thursday 12 March 1662/3, sent to the Lords on 6 April 1663 and was passed by them on 21 May 1663.

park, is planning to have a magnificent palace built there.[216]

We had our midday meal in the Ship Tavern, a very large inn, and at 5 o'clock in the evening we rode back to London.

On the 29th we went to Westminster and walked round the outside of the town.

On the 31th we saw at the Cockpit the play Friar Bacon or the Great Magician.[217]

On the 4th November we changed our lodgings, and went to stay in Cornhill, at a stationer's, right opposite the entrance of the Exchange.

On Sunday, the 5th November, was an alarm in London and at the Court. All were called to arms, the trained bands, hamletts (?), auxiliaries, the King's, Duke of York's and Monck's mounted bodyguards; all posts were manned, and the guards rode through the town to the sound of kettledrums and trumpets; so too went the militia, but quietly without beating the drums. Many people were taken by the scruff of their necks, and assemblies of anabaptists, quakers, and fifth monarchists[218] raided, and many men arrested. For several nights there were ten thousand men on guard in the town besides those at the Court and at Southwark; at daytime the watch was somewhat less. The alarm had been caused by the discovery of a great treason plot, which later came to light from the confessions of the prisoners, about which more later.[219]

On the 7th we went to the Guildhall and saw there the installation of the newly elected Lord Mayor. First we saw the great preparations which were being made there for the holding of the festivities; all the halls and rooms were hung with tapestries, and a raised dais was erected and a very large number of tables were put up, and in the kitchens all were very busy with preparations for the making of venison pasties and the like.

216 The new Palace of Greenwich by John Webb was only partially completed. The 'King Charles's Block' was later extended to form the Royal Naval Hospital. See Pevsner-Cherry, *BoE, London South*, and note 21 above.

217 For Friar Bacon see note 99.

218 Fifth Monarchy Men, a religious sect, believing that the second coming of Christ was imminent, who repudiated allegiance to any worldly government. They were considered a threat to the throne. (OED, *Evelyn* 10 August 1657, see also notes 228 and 229 below).

219 Pepys reports on 26 October o.s.: 'All this day soldiers going up and down the towne, there being an alarme and many Quakers and other clapped up; but I believe without any reason, only they say in Dorsetshire there hath been some rising discovered'. In view of later events (see 1 January 1663 and note 229 below, and Pepys iii, 236) Pepys obviously underestimated at the time the seriousness of the disturbance. See also *Hist. Manuscr. Com. Rep.* 7/1, 463. As to Dorsetshire see 24–25 July 1662 above and note 127.

The procedure at the installation is as follows:

On Simon and Judas day, which is 28th October Old Style at 8 or 9 o'clock in the morning some of the aldermen and the sheriffs come in their violet lined tabards on their richly dressed horses to the old Lord Mayor's house (all those who are to dine with him that day); from his house they conduct him to the Guildhall, and there in the council chamber await the new Lord Mayor, who with the other aldermen, is dressed the same way and on horseback, each Lord Mayor with his company or guild before him; after they have been some time together they come out into the Orphans' court, where they put on their mantles or great gowns and so go all together to the Great Hall or Hustings Court and take their seats in order on a raised platform, the old Lord Mayor in the middle or highest seat, the new Lord Mayor on his left. In front of the Lord Mayor stands a small table covered with velvet, on which lies a large cushion of the same material. When they are all seated, with the aldermen on either side, the town crier calls out, ordering everybody to keep silent; then the Town Clerk kneels down in front of the table and from the old charters reads the oaths to the new Lord Mayor, who, standing on the other side of the table, and (with the old Lord Mayor still sitting in the middle seat) repeats the oaths word for word, and after each of the three oaths kisses the Gospel. Then the old Lord Mayor rises and gives over the highest place to the new Lord Mayor and congratulates him. Then comes the Chamberlain, makes his reverence by bowing down three times, and delivers to the Lord Mayor the sceptre, keys, and the very richly and heavily embroidered purse, the sceptre of   , with agate stone, very preciously worked. He also delivered the great silver seal. He is followed by the swordbearer, who makes the same reverence, and, kneeling on one knee, hands over the sword. After that the Chamberlain approaches and receives everything back, and so also the swordbearer the sword. etc.

Then they all rose, took off their gowns, left the hall, and mounted their horses, and the old Lord Mayor escorted the new Lord Mayor to his home, and there took his leave, leaving with him the aldermen who were to dine with him. The old Lord Mayor rode with the remaining aldermen to his house, with the sword carried before him, which, after the meal, is brought to the new Lord Mayor.

On the return from the Guildhall they kept to this order: In front went several attendants, then followed the grocers, 19 or 20 pairs, members of the old Lord Mayor's company, all in their gowns. Next several attendants, the Marshall on horseback, then 9 or 10 pairs of clothworkers, following in order before the new Lord Mayor, Sir John Robinson, Knight and Baronet, who was of the clothworkers' company.

Before him the sword and the mace were carried. Then came the two Lord Mayors on horseback, with the new Lord Mayor on the right hand, and then followed the twelve aldermen and sheriffs all on horseback, all the horses with their trappings etc.

The following day was the Lord Mayor's triumph or show.

On the 29th October, that is the 8th November New Style, this Triumph was performed in London with several glorious scenes and pageantry on water and on land at the expense of the clothworkers' company in honour of Sir John Robinson, Knight and Baronet, Lieutenant of the Tower of London, Lord Mayor of the mighty City of London.

The order of this Show.[220]

At 9 o'clock in the morning the persons assigned to the service of this great show assembled at the Clothworkers' Hall, namely:

1) All the Masters, wardens and their assistants in their gowns faced with foyns.
2) Then the livery men in their gowns faced with Budge and their hoods.
3) 60 Foyns bachelors in their scarlet gowns.
4) Then 50 Budge bachelors in their scarlet gowns.
5) 50 gentlemen ushers or bailiffs in velvet gowns, each with a golden chain over their shoulders round the body and a little white staff in the hand.
6) 13 other gentlemen to carry the banners and pennants, 11 in velvet coats, 2 with jerkins, each with a sash in the company's colour round his body.
7) Then the sergeant trumpeter and 36 others, 16 of the King's, 4 of the Duke of York's, 4 of the Duke of Albemarle, General Monck's, the sergeant had a sash of the Lord Mayor's and one of the company's colours round his body.
8) Then the drum major of the King or the chief drummer, who had the company's sash crosswise round his body, then another 4 of the King's drummers and also 5 pipers, then 7 drummers and 2 pipers, all these in coloured leather doublets and, except the king's men, with black sashes round the body.
9) The City marshals also with the company's sashes and 6 attendants.

220 The details of the Lord Mayor's procession in 1662 are given in John Tatham, *London's Triumphs ... in honour of ... Sir John Robinson*, printed for H. Brome, London 1662. Schellinks may have used this. We have translated his version, but it is clear that this does not exactly correspond to Tatham. Cf. notes 59 and 60.

10) The Foot marshal with the like sashes and 6 attendants.

11) The Master of Defence with the like sash, accompanied by 10 attendants.

12) 48 pensioners or wage drawing persons, all in new blue coats and red high caps with a white cord or ribbon with a bow on it, each carrying a banner or standard.

13) 48 other hired men, also in blue coats, long white sleeves and black flat folding caps, each having a javelin in one hand and a target or shield in the other, on which were painted the arms of their benefactors.

14) *Note*: All the gentlemen who carry the banners, the sergeant trumpeter, the drum major, every drummer and trumpeter, piper, the several marshals, the master of defence and their attendants had each a bow in the company's colours on his hat.

Thus dressed and all assembled

they are divided by the Foot marshal into seven groups, two by two, starting with the lowest, namely

The standard bearers, before them went two drummers and one piper, one gentleman carrying the company's arms.

2) Then followed six trumpeters, two gentlemen carrying the arms of the governors and patrons of the company; after them came the old retainers in their long coats, and in the midst of them two drummers beating the Switzer's march.

3) Then three drummers, one piper, two gentlemen in velvet coats carrying two banners, then six gentlemen ushers.

4) Then followed six trumpeters, two gentlemen carrying banners, eight gentlemen ushers.

5) Then the Duke of York's and General Monck's trumpeters, eight in number, two gentlemen carrying banners, then twelve gentlemen ushers, then the entire livery.

6) Then followed the drum-major, four king's drummers and pipers, two gentlemen, [one] carrying the banner of the Lord Mayor and the other the City banner, then twelve gentlemen ushers, then the Court of assistance.

7) Then followed the sergeant trumpeter and sixteen of the king's trumpeters and a kettledrum in His Majesty's livery, three gentlemen carrying the banners of the King, the Duke of York, and St. George, went throughout three cornered formation, twelve gentlemen ushers, then the master and wardens of   .

When they all had taken their places in the procession in this order, two by two, and the Lord Mayor and the aldermen and sheriffs and all their attendants, they went to the Guildhall and from there the usual way to the Three Crane Wharf in the Vintry,[221] where they boarded the barges and landed at the Westminster stairs. As he passed, the Lord Mayor was met by a pageant, set up on the water by the gentlemen of Trinity House. After he had landed at Westminster and had completed all the usual pledges and ceremonies in each court, the Lord Mayor came to the Exchequer bar, where the Lord Chief Baron addressed him with an oration. After this was done, he and all the companies went to their barges and sped to Baynards Castle, where the bachelors stood ready in order as in the morning, and where the Foot marshal awaited him; and when they were all assembled, the two parties marched up St. Paul's Wharf Hill and so to the churchyard. The gentlemen of the artillery, all in full dress, also attended the Lord Mayor as their president and paraded. Near St. Paul's school the Lord Mayor was greeted by the first tableau, a model of the Tower of London, with people on both sides, boys sitting minting coins, and others as guards protecting the gate. As the Lord Mayor got there he was saluted and addressed with an eulogy by a person mounted on a horse like a soldier. Meanwhile small cannons were fired from the Tower.

When this speech had ended they went to Cheapside and at its west end the Lord Mayor was greeted by another scene, a representation of cloth making, nicely displayed, each worker performing his craft, beginning with the spinner, and under an oaktree in the middle sat an overseer with a cheerful face seeing to it that everybody performed his task properly. A little further was another display, a large ram, gilt all over, which is the crest of the company's arms,[222] on which sat somebody playing the bagpipes. The overseer or old master represented one Jack of Newbury[223] and was dressed in very old-fashioned clothes. This person greeted the Lord Mayor as he approached and addressed him with an eulogy, and when this was ended two old women workers started to sing and the others of the workpeople answered each verse with a refrain.[224]

Near Lawrence Lane was the third tableau, a merchant ship, fully fitted out; in front of the ship was a sea lion with a triton on its back, playing music. Behind the ship followed a gilt camel loaded with

221 Three Cranes or Vintry, a tavern deriving its name from three timber cranes on Vintry Wharf to unload wine (*EoL*).

222 The Lord Mayor installed in 1662 was Sir John Robinson, Lieutenant of the Tower of London (where there hangs a portrait of him), a member of the Clothworkers' Company.

223 Jack of Newbury, another name for John Winchcombe, the weaver from Newbury, who 'was wonderous well beloved of rich and poore' *The pleasant History of John Winchcombe*, by T.D. (Thomas Delaney), ninth edition 1633.

224 The song is included in the description of the procession referred to in note 220.

merchandise, led by an Asian, a reference to the Lord Mayor's trade.
The Asian too addressed him with a speech about the prosperity of the
merchant trade. After that came the Lord Mayor and the invited guests
to the Guildhall and held there the great banquet, while the companies
went to their halls to refresh themselves. After the meal they were again
arranged in order by the foot-marshal, but the hired men had now
torches in their hands instead of the javelins, to conduct the Lord
Mayor and aldermen and the company in the evening from St. Paul's.
When they were all assembled again they departed for St. Paul's
Church, and, in Cheapside, near a nicely made silvered model of St.
Paul's Church, the Lord Mayor was addressed by a Civilian or
one dressed like that, with a speech mostly about religion and the
reconstruction of the church.[225] There was another display, a completely
gilt carriage drawn by two gryphons, which are the supporters of the
company's arms. In the coach sat Patience, Prudence, Fortitude, and
Temperance. Up behind sat Vigilance, on her head a helmet with the
figure of a cock, and her dress set all over with eyes.

In this manner the Lord Mayor and all his suite went to St. Paul's
Church, and all the displays went to the clothworkers' hall, where they
were set up close to each other. The company's trumpeters, drummers,
and the hired pensioners formed a lane, to let the Lord Mayor pass
through, and as he came into the middle of the displays, he was once
more addressed by the four speakers, by Jack of Newbury, the soldier,
the Asian, and the Church; after that the silkworkers and other displays
were led off and put away, and all the companies went to their lodgings.
The Lord Mayor heard the service in St. Paul's, and in the evening
came from St. Paul's by torchlight and went with the aldermen and
the Grocers' and Clothworkers' Companies and many other followers
through Cheapside, Poultry, and Cornhill, all the pensioners and hired
persons in blue coats carrying torches, and so they conducted the Lord
Mayor home. All the time the precious sword of Justice was carried
before the Lord Mayor, the sword bearer wearing the cap of maintenance on his head. From the Lord Mayor's house everybody went to
his own home etc.

It was wonderful to have seen in the morning all the barges on the
water or the river, vying with each other to be the best decorated and
decked out; on a platform by the river, behind the King's court at
Whitehall, stood his Majesty with the Duke of York and the King's son
and many great Earls and Lords and watched from there the display

225 The need for restoration work to the old church was recognized from the time of
James I, and money collected. Some work was carried out under Inigo Jones, but during
the Commonwealth it was greatly neglected (*EoL*). The great fire of 1666 destroyed the
old church entirely.

on the water; His Majesty was in a happy mood, and all who sailed by showed their respect, and their salutations were immediately returned by him and by all the nobility who were with him etc.

I saw all this great and pleasant show in the morning from the water, as I had myself rowed in a boat close to the platform, on which the King was standing, remained there for some time, watching the mutual salutes of the passing companies as well as of the King and the nobility, sailed to Westminster and across to the cannon, and from there back to St. Paul's Wharf, disembarked, went to Cheapside and took a place and from there saw everything well, and in the evening went again to our lodgings in Cornhill opposite the Exchange.

On the 5th old or 15th December [sic: November] new style in the evening the gunpowder plot, or the anniversary of the gunpowder treason of the year [1605] in the reign of King James, is celebrated in London; many bonfires are lit all over the town in celebration, and a great lot of fireworks are let off and thrown amongst the people.

On the 17th December we again changed our lodgings and went to stay with Mr. Cambies in Broad Street, where we had lodged the year before with Mynheer J. Thierry and another.

On the 19th we went to Hackney, on the way back we saw in a field a group of people, some of them standing a little higher on a small mound. We went nearer and saw that they were Quakers. A young fellow delivered an admonition, and as soon as he had done, a 12 or 13 years old boy started. He read his text, and, whilst he was preaching, four soldiers came from the next field; at this the little hedge-preacher stopped his sermon and started to pray with the congregation etc. It started to rain, and we had to look for a good shelter, but we saw that the Quakers cared little that they got wet; the fire in the town was too hot for them.

On the 27th November the anniversary of Queen Elizabeth's coronation was celebrated with bell ringing and the lighting of bonfires in the evening.

On the 29th we saw the procession of the Oxfordshire countrymen in Cornhill.[226] A service was held for them in   , after which they all marched two by two to   where they were to have their celebrations together. In front went   .

[3 lines blank]

Note: This is in London usual with most

[6 lines blank]

---

226 Oxfordshire Countrymen procession. The Copenhagen MS has, at the end of this passage, several blank lines, where Schellinks seems to have intended to make some observation on this ceremony. No record of the occasion has been found.

On the 5th December we went for a walk to Islington and Newington, there was a hard frost and fine weather.

On the 7th December the ambassador of the Grand Duke of Muscovy, Alexee Michaelrich,[227] Emperor of Great, Lower and White Russia was most magnificently received in London. There were three ambassadors, the Grand Duke and governor of Toulskij Peeter, the son of Simon Prozorofskij, 2. The governor of Coarmeski Juan, son of Offonasseij Zelebouskij, 3. The councillor Juan Stephano. The chief ambassador was unwell from the hardships of the journey, and had for this reason remained at Greenwich, and was not in person at the state reception on this day, but went in one of the King's row-barges by water direct to York House, which had been requisitioned and prepared for him and his suite.

The order of the Ambassadors' reception

On the previous day the drum had been beaten throughout London to warn everybody to be ready at 7 o'clock the following morning, to wit all the trainbands consisting of six companies and also the auxiliaries consisting of six companies, which are in six colours, namely 1. white, 2. yellow, 3. green, 4. red, 5. blue, 6. orange, one regiment's company of each colour. All these six regiments of trainbands consist of house-holders, and the six regiments of auxiliaries of young men and apprentices. On the morning they all gathered at their assembly points and were set to line both sides of the streets through which the ambassadors were to pass. The Tower Wharf was the great assembly point of the mounted companies of the guilds and also of many companies on foot. The King's bodyguard arrived there too, and when they were all assembled they were joined by the Lord Mayor, the aldermen, and the sheriffs in their scarlet tabards and with their golden chains round their necks, on horseback, with the trumpeters before them, and rode over Tower Hill to the gate and so to the Tower to receive the ambassadors, who arrived by water and disembarked there at about 1 o'clock in the afternoon and were welcomed there by the Lord Mayor, and then rode into the town in this order:

First came the trumpeters and kettledrum with the King's lifeguards, mounted and in arms. Then followed the 24 companies of the guilds,

227 Tzar Alexis had sent four envoys, Prince Peter Semenovic Prozorovskj, Ivan Af'anas'evic Zeljabuzskij, Ivan Davydov, and Jurij Ivanovic Nikiforov, to congratulate the King, and negotiate trade and loans, who, on his orders, were received in state. They were put up at York House (between Charing Cross and the river), and had an audience with the King on 29 December 1662. See L. Bittner and L. Grosz, *Repertorium der Diplomatischen Vertreter alle Länder*, 1936, p. 435, and Pepys iii, 267–8 and iv, 173; Evelyn, 29 Nov. 1662.

the most distinguished and senior officers all on horseback and dressed in plush or velvet gowns, everyone a golden chain over his shoulders; each company had two or three trumpeters before them, and behind them rode the standard bearers of the company, then 18, 20 or 30 men of each company, behind them followed the aldermen and sheriffs, and the King's coach with the two Russian deputy-ambassadors and the Lord Mayor with them. Behind some more coaches followed 20 or 24 Russians on horseback with falcons on their hands, then some more coaches with Russians and others and all kinds of attendants, and were conducted by the company to   [York House].

On the 12th December we went by water to Rotherhithe. The river was full of ice, as there had been a hard frost; we went on foot to Greenwich and returned in the evening to London in the company of Mons. D. Camby.

On Sunday, the 24th December, in the afternoon to the service at St. Paul's Church and heard the organ playing.

On the 25th I went with Messrs Pouldoun and Denham, our fellow lodgers, to the parish yard, a place next to Newgate, where persons of some consequence are imprisoned and are at their own costs reasonably well treated etc.

Note: These two young merchants had lain there in prison on a false accusation by one Mistress Olivier, whose husband had been convicted of counterfeiting. The judges had promised him a pardon if he would disclose who had received his false money from him, and his wife, to protect him as long as she could, brought first one and then the other into trouble, and they had to wait in prison for the sessions for their examination and the judges' pleasure to declare them innocent etc.

Anno 1663

On the 1st January new style the four condemned traitors, Thomas Thongue, George Philips, Francis Stubbs, and Nathaniel Gibbs were hanged and quartered at Tyburn.[228] They were brought to trial on 21 December at the Old Bailey, the session house, and were, largely on the evidence of witnesses, in particular the Lord Mayor and a preacher Hill[229] etc., found guilty of high treason. In particular [that they] had intended with their co-conspirators to murder His Majesty, as well as

228 Thomas Thonge, George Philips, Francis Stubbes, and Nathaniel Gibbs were involved in the plot on 5 November (q.v.), and tried with others on 18 December (*Mercurius Publicus* of that date). See also note 219 above.

229 William Hill, a parliamentarian, lost his living at the Restoration and became involved with a number of fanatical plotters against the King. He turned informer, and as a result of his evidence the plot was discovered, the culprits arrested late in October, and four of them hanged at Tyburn (DNB).

General Monck, the Lord Mayor, and all who were of the King's blood, and the greatest of the nobility, to change the government, temporal and spiritual, to their desire, to hold up the King in Whitehall, and Sir John Robinson, governor of the Tower, in his coach on the way to the Tower, to take the Tower by surprise, and to capture Windsor Castle by bribing a constable and a sergeant.

They had, to dispel all suspicions of evil intent, spread forged letters everywhere, warning that everybody should be on his guard, as the papists were planning a general massacre of the protestants. Also the above named G. Philips, being a herald painter and a sergeant in the trainbands, would try to obtain the password from the other officers and thus lead his detachment to the Exchange and murder those who were on guard there etc. They had also said that they knew how to get at the weapons of the artillery and to capture them. They had had their grand council, out of whom six heads were chosen, who were to disperse over the different provinces, and should all be generals and other senior officers besides. With these and many other planned attacks etc. they were charged before the judges, General Monck and many from the nobility, in the courthouse. They were to have put their attempt into effect on All Hallows Day, if they had not been discovered. Their heads were put on stakes close to the Tower on the town side, but their bodies were, by the King's favour, buried.

On the 2nd January we went to the bear baiting with Mr. D. Cambij.

On the 4th, Christmas day old style, we went to church in St. Paul's and heard the music and sermon; in the afternoon we heard the service below St. Paul's and then went to see the heads on the stakes near and at the Tower.

On the 6th we went to the two temples or colleges to see the gambling. In the night seven people, all the family of Monsr Du Laan, merchant, died in a great fire in Lothbury.[230]

This being the English Twelfth Night or Three Kings [Epiphany] we made merry in our lodgings with our friends.

On the 7th we were with all the family of Miss Camby the guests of Mr Korchnij.

On the 18th and 19th we went with company to Lambeth and returned through Southwark.

---

230 Pepys, on 29 December o.s. (when he heard of it), comments on 'the strange burning of Mr. Delaun, a mercant's house, in Loathbury', who, with his whole family perished in the fire. The mystery was the greater, because the house was new and brickbuilt, which was rare before the great fire. (Pepys iii, 296).

March

On the 7th we saw at Tyburn eleven people being hanged, three of the King's bodyguard, two women, and one negress or coloured woman.

On the 9th we saw in the Comedy the play The mad Hamelot.[231]

On the 11th, Sunday, we went with Mr. Camby to church at Stepney.

On the 14th we heard Dr Sheldon, the Bishop of London, preach at the King's Chapel at Whitehall, his text was John 6. v. 14: 'Behold thou art made whole, sin no more etc'.[232]

On the 16th we went to Stepney through   to Blackwall, there had ourselves ferried across the river, and went to Greenwich and on to Deptford. When we got there we went to the King's Yard or shipyard, where we saw one of the docks, in which they enclose the ships so that they remain afloat even when the river is at low tide.[233] We saw the little boat, a ketch, in which the King fled from England to France anno 16.. [1651].

I went there and looked at everything. From there we went through Rotherhithe to London.

In the evening we went to the dancemaster of Mr. Jacobi to see a ballet being danced; there were many gentlemen and ladies there, and seven musicians played.

On the 17th, which was assizes day at Southwark, we went there to see the malefactors condemned. They were ten in number who were condemned to hang, and 14 were branded in the hand with the letter T for Tyburn.

On the 18th we went to church at Stepney.

On the 19th we went with cousin Dentier[234] through Southwark to the court, expecting the condemned to be executed. There was a great crowd of people, but the execution was postponed for further orders, so we went from there to Bethnal Green etc.

On the 23rd March we were at Westminster to see some of the members of the lower house with Mr. Jacobi and Mr. Smith about the Naturalization.

On the 24th we went with cousin Dentier in the afternoon for a walk to the Jack of Newbury.[235]

---

231 Pepys saw Shakespeare's 'Hamlet, Prince of Denmark' in Davenant's version, which was the only one licensed at the time, on 24 August, 27 November, and 5 December 1661 (Pepys ii, 161, 221, 227), and on 28 May 1663, when he again much admired Betterton's performance (Pepys iv, 162).

232 Gilbert Sheldon (1598–1677), a royalist, imprisoned during the Commonwealth, became bishop of London soon after the restoration (DNB). The text 'Behold, thou art made whole: sin no more' is John c.5 v.14.

233 Deptford Dry Docks founded 1513 by Henry VIII.

234 Cousin Dentier: See *Introduction* iii.

235 Jack of Newbury, an inn named after this popular character, see note 224.

On Sunday, the 25th, in the afternoon thunder and lightning.

On the 28th we went to the Tower to see the new money mint of the French mint master Blondeau,[236] which operates with a mill or stamping press. We saw the silver being melted and being cast in moulds into long flat bars, then in another place, through the rolling mill below, on the highest floor flattened by two round nearly touching steel rollers (in the manner of the drawing of gold). From these long flat bars blanks of the correct diameter and weight are pressed out by a screw. These are then passed to another man, who puts these round discs, 30 to 40 together, into a hollow steel mould, which encloses them all round and also presses them equal. At the same time they are pressed absolutely flat on both sides by two tools pressing against each other. Then they are annealed, and at another place scoured and boiled white. When all this has been done they are brought to Monsr Blondeau, who, in secret and without any other help, embosses the letters on their circumference. Thus they are brought to the large press, which is steadily being pulled back and forth by three men, and one person sits two or three steps down in the ground, and steadily puts the unminted blanks on to the die, and knocks the minted coins from it, all proceeding very quickly.

After I had seen it all I changed two of these new crown pieces for 10 shillings and drank with one of the workmen a pot of ale or two.

We then went to see the lions and the leopards, eagles etc. In the afternoon we went with Monsr de la Ruwaard to Exeter House[237] in the Strand, the lodging of the French ambassador, where we saw a monk, a Franciscan friar in his habit and heard him preach.

On the 30th we went by boat with company to Whitehall and at the Banqueting House saw the King touch many people for the King's evil. After that we saw His Majesty eat with the Queen, together with the Duke of York.

From Whitehall we returned to London Bridge to the Old Swan.

April

On Sunday [1st April] in the afternoon we went for a walk with cousin Dentier to Stepney, from there to Mile End and on to Bow. There we refreshed ourselves and went to   , and from there to Hackney, rested and refreshed ourselves there and returned to Westminster.

236 Pierre Blondeau, engineer to Cromwell's mint, returned in 1662 to be responsible for minting milled money, introducing his new process. Pepys ii, 38–9. Denis R. Cooper *Coinmaking*, 1988.

237 On the north side of the Strand, previously known as Wimbledon House, Burghley House, and Cecil House. After the restoration Queen Henrietta Maria had a chapel there (see EoL).

The 12th April.[238] We had originally been instructed that we should first travel to Dover to go to Italy by boat. The convoy for Spain and Smyrna was to come specially close to Dover and signal with some blank shots that we were to come on board, and would fly flag and pennant and so hail us. But all our friends had advised us against this journey by sea, and also [the convoy] did not arrive; we had written about this, and we now received orders that we were free to start the journey by land through France to Italy. We therefore took our leave everywhere from all our friends and acquaintances, and got everything ready, which we would need for this journey, and had a meal prepared for some of our best friends and acquaintances, to which we invited the following persons:

Mr. Jan Thierry	Englishman
Thomas Douthy	idem
Mr. William de Peyster	Dutchman
Eduwart Smith	Engm
Mr. . Cambij	Engm
Gorge Crescy	Frenchm, Paris
Monsr Ruwaart	idem, Bordeaux
Dentier	Fleming
Mr. Barents Sr.	from Hamburg
Mr. M. Barents	do
Mr. Pey or Prins	Engm

and us two, all together 13 persons.

Our friends made merry and drank three or four rounds of large rummers of wine to the good success of our journey, whereupon we took our leave from them and both sides wished the other all the best. This parting meal we had on Margaret Hill by Billingsgate in the Three Tuns tavern.

On the 13th April 1663 we took our leave from our friends at our lodgings and went with all those who were to see us off to Southwark to the posthouse. At half past twelve we mounted the horses to ride post to Rye in Kent, 60 English miles by post from London.

The first stage, being 20 miles, we rode mostly a gallop, and passed Lucum [Lewisham], $3\frac{1}{2}$ miles, Linnits (?), Bromley, 10 miles from London, Farnborough, 4 miles, Shoreham, 6 miles, together 20 miles, got there at 4 o'clock in the afternoon and stayed there the night.

Note: At Farnborough we went down on foot from a very high hill, leading the horses down.

---

238 The following entry for 12 April does not appear in the Bodleian MS, which has here two blank pages, and continues in a different handwriting, starting with a summary of the farewell meal given in detail below.

On the 14th in the morning we had rain and a very stiff east wind; we rode from there at 8 o'clock and had all the way a deep, dirty road, mostly up and down hill, so that our horses had to go in single file. After 7 miles riding we passed first Tonbridge, then Woodgate, 5 miles, Lamberhurst, 6 miles, Stonecrouch, 3 miles, all being very long, this is the second stage, where one changes the horses. As the postmaster had nothing but two thin, wretched curs of horses we decided to stay there and to refresh ourselves a little and to get some rest, the more so as the bad weather with rain and wind continued incessantly.

On the 15th April the weather continued with wind and rain, but we nevertheless resumed our journey and found the road even worse than before; we passed the village of Hawkhurst, 4 miles, Newenden, 8 miles, and after riding another 8 miles came to

Rye

at about 12 noon, and went to stay with the postmaster at the Mermaid, a good inn.

On the 16th we presented our letter of introduction to a merchant called Monsr Louis Gilliart and enquired about the possibilities of crossing. The weather meanwhile continued very variable, with rain and an easterly wind, so we went to look at the town and everything, up and down.

Rye

is a small seaside town in Kent, and has a good harbour. Its walls were first built by William the Conqueror.

On the 18th April 1663 we went for a laissez passer, which we got and paid for in accordance with an order of parliament, 3 shilling 3 pence English, for ordinary customers for both of us. I affix hereto the original paper, reading in English as follows:[239]

[front]

> Rye. These are to require you to permit Mr William Shillings and Mr (crossed out: James Shery) duchmen to passe into ffrance and this shall be your warrant.
> Witness my hand the eight daie of Apprell 1663
> John Dalleholl
> To his maisties seur (?) at the water side

---

239 This document, on a smaller size of paper and different handwriting is bound in with the pages of the Copenhagen MS. It appears to have a seal on it.

[back]

Rye[240]

There was three persons of us agreed for fower pounds; whereof one was ordered for London; and he gave the boats mr content, soe our two pds deducted out of fower pounds is:

two pounds thirteen shill & fower pense ster: to which the mr of the shallop agreed.

Witness: this 8/18th Apl 1663 Michaell Oarman

Note: At Rye we had arranged to sail with another gentleman from Rye to Dieppe in France in a French shallop, open on top without any cover, but our companion received orders to travel to London and paid the boatman, so that we had to travel alone, and paid for both of us 2 pistoles. As there is only little traffic in this place, their charges are high, and the boatmen are the worst rogues and swindlers in the world, as we were to find out to our detriment.

On the 18th in the evening we boarded our miserable boat, and had a favourable wind, but in the night the wind turned and dropped completely, and it started to rain and we were in a miserable situation, as the boat, the sailors, and the weather played in unison. On the 19th in the morning it was still raining and little or no wind, so that we made little progress. We got sight of the French coast, but it became dead calm, so much so that the boatmen had to take to the oars, and in this way we at last reached land at Dieppe at 6 o'clock in the evening and thus finally, to our relief, set foot on French soil.

France

Note: When we had taken lodgings at Dieppe at the Bastille, a large inn in La Grande Rue, we had the greatest difficulties in the world with our boatmen, because, when we wanted to pay them the agreed fare, and indeed a good tip besides, they were not satisfied with that and insisted on the full fare for us and the gentleman, who had travelled to London and had already paid them, as can be seen on the back of the laissez-passer. In the end and after the intercession of friends and also of our agent, Monsr Mell, we had still to satisfy them by a payment of 30 guilders. Without their intercession we would have had to pay them even more.

NB. Such thievish rogues are all the boatmen along the coast, but

240 This is written in a different hand on the reverse of the document referred to above.

especially at Dieppe, who ferry over the travellers and strangers and take them on land from the ships or bring them on board; and the workmen or baggage porters are not a whit better as we, to our sorrow, can testify.

The Journal continues as described
in the Introduction
with their travels
in Europe.

INDEX OF PERSONS

Numbers in Roman refer to pages, those in Italic to footnotes.

INDEX OF PLACES

Modern spelling is used and the spelling in the MS added where there is uncertainty or where this could indicate a different pronunciation at the time. Place locations are identified by modern County. Only for Greater London are individual buildings and streets listed, identified by postal district or London Borough name, abbreviated as:

Barking & Dagenham	–	Bark. & Dag.
Bromley	–	Brom.
Enfield	–	Enf.
Greenwich	–	Greenw.
Hackney	–	Hack.
Hammersmith & Fulham	–	Hamm. & Ful.
Haringey	–	Har.
Havering	–	Haver.
Hounslow	–	Houns.
Islington	–	Isl.
Kensington & Chelsea	–	Ken. & Chel.
Kingston	–	Kingst.
Lambeth	–	Lamb.
Lewisham	–	Lew.
Newham	–	Newh.
Redbridge	–	Redbr.
Richmond upon Thames	–	Richm.
Southwark	–	Southw.
Tower Hamlets	–	Tow. Haml.
Wandsworth	–	Wandsw.

SELECT INDEX OF SUBJECTS